Y0-DTC-650

THE EARLIER RENAISSANCE

THE

EARLIER RENAISSANCE

BY

GEORGE SAINTSBURY

NEW YORK

Howard Fertig

1968

First published in 1901

HOWARD FERTIG, INC. EDITION 1968
Published by arrangement with the Executors of George Saintsbury

Library of Congress Catalog Card Number: 68-9660

PRINTED IN THE UNITED STATES OF AMERICA
BY NOBLE OFFSET PRINTERS, INC.

PREFACE.

Of the difficulties, as regards delimitation of frontiers, in the designing and editing of a *History of European Literature* by periods, none are more obvious beforehand, or more substantial in experience, than those connected with the all-important and interesting time of the Renaissance. To that word in general, and to the signification commonly and generally attached to it, no serious objection need be taken, when the possible error of supposing any death, or even suspended animation, in the rich and vigorous literature of the Middle Ages is once guarded against. The effect produced on literature by the revived study of the classics, direct from the originals, is a fact of which it is equally impossible to deny the reality or to contest the importance. But it is no less a fact, though a much more complicated one, that this influence was exerted at different times in different countries, and in different manners at different times in the same country. Thus, for instance, some, not without plausibility, have carried the Renaissance in Italy as far back as Petrarch, if not even as far back as Dante—authors dealt with, and necessarily dealt with, not even in the volume preceding this, but in the volume preceding that.[1]

Still, one of those exercises of the *communis sensus*, which are generally right, has regarded the Renaissance of Literature in Europe as not practically beginning till the fifteenth century was far advanced, nay, till the various but converging influences of the capture of Constantinople, the invention of printing, the discovery of America, and the final uprising against the ecclesiastical tyranny of Rome had been successively brought to bear. And without further argument on the point of right, we may say that for the purposes of this book "The Earlier Renaissance" means the closing years of the fifteenth century and the first half of the sixteenth—the time when, the study of Greek having previously come to support and correct that of Latin in Italy, the full classical culture was transmitted from Italy herself to France and England, and so helped to install, in forms which cannot even to this day be said to have been wholly antiquated, the two greatest literatures of Europe.

It is this process—the "Italianation," as the Elizabethans called it, of France and of England—which forms for History the central interest of the period,

[1] See *The Fourteenth Century*.

and therefore of the volume. As regards Italy herself the interest is somewhat less—great as are some of the names that have to be mentioned as Italian. Such minority is almost necessarily implied in the mere fact of such influence itself, which is, in accordance with a general law, never fully exerted abroad till the forces producing it have passed their first period of energy at home. Ariosto is great—his greatness has been, I think, of late years rather insufficiently acknowledged by critics. But it is only necessary to compare him, I do not say with Dante (for the First Three are not in comparison save as standards), but with such a far lower kind of genius as Boccaccio's, to see that the stationary state, if not exactly the age of decadence, has been reached. The poet of the *Orlando* is, indeed, as much greater in individual gift than Boccaccio as he is lesser than Dante; but he wants "the wild freshness of morning," the relish of the quest, the closeness to nature and life. His luxuriant imagination turns at times and in parts to the lower, the secondary kinds of literature, to burlesque and grotesque. Compare him again with Spenser, his debtor certainly, though hardly his imitator, and the difference of a falling and a rising tide of poetry will be easily seen.

Of the other literatures German presents a problem engagingly interesting in character and most conveniently limited in extent—the problem of discovering why the triple influence of Greek and Latin and

Italian failed to do for her what it did for English and for French; while the companion but different problem of Spanish has been already dealt with in Mr Hannay's volume.[1] The rest require only very slight treatment.

On the other hand, we have in this period, more than in most, the interest of certain general divisions, departments, or kinds of literature which are peculiar to none of the languages, but appear in all. The first of these is the New Drama; the second, the Revival of Criticism; the third, that of Latin writing, which is really literature. This last we have here almost for the last time, and in a more considerable degree than in any volume of our history save that dealing with the Dark Ages, when most of the vernaculars were unborn. It may be questioned whether any man of our time, except Ariosto and Rabelais, has the literary value—intrinsic as distinguished from influential and symptomatic—of Erasmus, and Erasmus is nothing if not a Latinist. The allotment of the first and the longest chapter in the volume to this phenomenon may therefore not seem excessive.

The bibliography of the subject is enormous—to give it in any detail would quite overload the notes. Almost every recent German writer seems *addictus jurare in verba* of L. Geiger, *Renaissance und Humanismus in Italien und Deutschland.* For Italy, the names of Gregorovius, Burckhardt, Villari, and

[1] See *The Later Renaissance.*

many others need no mentioning, save to those who are not likely to take an interest in them. For France, MM. Darmesteter and Hatzfeldt's *Seizième Siècle en France* (Paris, 1878), though it takes the unpretentious form of a collection of extracts for students, with introductions and notes, is one of the very best pieces of literary-historical work that have been produced for many a year and decade.

It so happens, however, that as regards great part of the subject we need not go beyond English for text-books of quite exceptional excellence both in information and original power. To Roscoe, who led the way some century ago with his still famous *Leo the Tenth* and *Lorenzo de' Medici*, there is doubtless due the credit not merely of having produced these capital works, but of having stimulated his countrymen to follow in his steps. A little later the name of Hallam is to be mentioned with the usual and thoroughly deserved praise for width and co-ordination of knowledge, and for the constant endeavour to maintain a judicial attitude; but also with the usual caution as to the defects of his qualities, shown in his absence of enthusiasm, his distrust of anything abnormal or extravagant, and as to his necessary ignorance of much that is now easily accessible.

Mr Symonds' well-known *Renaissance in Italy*, nearly half of which is devoted to our subject, is both peccant and virtuous in exactly opposite kinds: his fluency and exuberance of language contrasting with

Hallam's measured dignity as his *engouement* and excess contrast with Hallam's rigid justice. But I am bound to say that the more I know of the subject, the better, with some important allowances, do I think of *The Renaissance in Italy*. With regard to France, Mr Arthur Tilley's most promising introductory volume,[1] now sixteen years old, has unfortunately never been followed up; but as an Introduction it is excellent. As for German, Professor Herford's *Literary Relations of England and Germany* (Cambridge, 1886) is one of the most thorough of English literary monographs, and has a far wider bearing on the general subject than its title would necessarily indicate. Mr Froude's *Erasmus*, with the usual defects which infuriate pedants against its author, has, in measure hardly affected at all by age, that author's qualities of artistic-historic grasp, of vivid presentment, and of admirable style; while Mr Seebohm's earlier *Oxford Reformers* has stood the test of examination by more than a generation of specialists with almost unsurpassed success.

He who, not being a specialist all round, enters a province so infested with vigorous specimens of the kind, carries his literary life more than usually in his hands. I found, indeed, when I was arranging this series, that more than one actual specialist was too much afraid of the others, in the subdivisions of the period not specially his own, to venture upon it. So

[1] *The Literature of the Fnench Renaissance.* Cambridge, 1885.

it fell to the Editor to undertake the adventure; let him at least hope to emerge from it an *Eckius* not too much *dedolatus*.[1]

I should, in conclusion, like, now that the History of which this volume is the seventh has gone so far on its way, to point out, if it be not improper, that neither this volume nor any other of the series to which it belongs aims *primarily* at being what I have seen its predecessors sometimes called in reviews, a "text-book," a scholastic or academic manual. It is, as was fully explained in its general prospectus, and as should have been evident to any careful reader of any of its volumes, an attempt to do, with the enormous additional material which has accumulated during great part of a century, what Hallam did with the very much smaller resources at his disposal; and to do it by more hands than one, because no single hand could well suffice. It is, indeed, hoped that, in whole or in part, it may be of service, and very great service, to students of literature *in statu pupillari;* but that is not its sole nor even its main purpose. It is principally intended to perform for the educated and intelligent reader the same function which a historical atlas of the better kind performs for him in another department—to give a connected, a critical, and a comparative view of the Literature of Europe. And while its several volumes have been planned so as to be reasonably complete in

[1] *Vide infra*, p. 99.

themselves, they, like the several maps of such an atlas, are necessarily interdependent, and complementary of each other.

I must acknowledge very particularly the assistance I have received in this volume from Mr Gregory Smith, who read my proofs with the greatest profit to me.

EDINBURGH, *August* 1901.

CONTENTS.

CHAPTER I.

THE HARVEST-TIME OF HUMANISM.

CHAPTER II.

THE ZENITH OF THE CINQUECENTO.

CHAPTER III.

FROM RHETORIC TO PLEIAD.

CHAPTER IV.

THE SCHOOL OF ELIZABETHAN LITERATURE.

CHAPTER V.

THE GERMAN VERNACULAR.

CHAPTER VI.

THE CHANGES OF EUROPEAN DRAMA.

CHAPTER VII.

THE REVIVAL OF CRITICISM.

CHAPTER VIII.

THE MINOR LITERATURES—CONCLUSION.

THE EARLIER RENAISSANCE.

CHAPTER I.

THE HARVEST-TIME OF HUMANISM.

REASONS FOR BEGINNING WITH THIS SUBJECT, AND FOR THE SPACE DEVOTED TO IT — THE POSITION AND HISTORY OF HUMANISM IN 1500 — THE ACCOMPLISHMENT OF THE EARLIER HUMANISTS IN CLASSICS—THEIR RELATION TO THE VERNACULAR—WORK OF THE HUMANISTS OF THE LATE FIFTEENTH CENTURY IN BOTH—HUMANISM IN RELATION TO THE NORTHERN VERNACULARS — INSTANCES OF THE 'COLLOQUIES,' THE 'UTOPIA,' ETC. — DISTRIBUTION OF THE SUBJECT — LATIN VERSE IN ITALY—POLITIAN—PONTANUS—VIDA—FRACASTORO — SANNAZAR — BEMBO — SADOLETO — CASTIGLIONE — NAVAGERO — FLAMINIO — MOLZA AND OTHERS — THE 'QUINQUE POETÆ HETRUSCI' AND THE ANTHOLOGY OF UBALDINI — TRANSALPINE LATIN VERSE: FRANCE — JOHANNES SECUNDUS AND HIS IMITATORS—OTHER LATIN VERSE: GERMAN—ENGLISH—BUCHANAN —HIS PROSE — THE PSALMS AND THEIR DEDICATION — THE 'DE SPHÆRA'—THE MINOR POEMS—LATER LATIN POETRY—MACARONIC VERSE—FOLENGO—HIS LIFE—AND MINOR WORKS—THE 'ZANITONELLA'—THE 'BALDUS' OR THE 'MACARONEA' ITSELF—LATIN PROSE-WRITING—ERASMUS—THE 'COLLOQUIES'—THEIR RELATION TO THE

FUTURE NOVEL—THE 'ENCOMIUM MORIÆ'—MORE: THE 'UTOPIA' —THE 'EPISTOLÆ OBSCURORUM VIRORUM'—'ECKIUS DEDOLATUS' —THE 'FACETIÆ'—LETTERS.

Reasons for beginning with this subject, and for the space devoted to it.

In beginning this volume with a chapter on the Latin writings, prose and verse, of the period with which it deals, not without a certain glance before and after at other work of the same class, it is not necessary to prefix many general remarks. But it would be improper to prefix none. In no other of the volumes of this *History of European Literature,* except the second, has a special chapter been, or will one be, devoted to Latin writing. And here as there, though to a somewhat less degree, an apology is required for the comparative brevity of the treatment of the subject. Not merely a whole volume, but half-a-dozen volumes might very well be devoted to Latin literature from the fifth to the eighteenth century; for it was not till the latter was far advanced that literature, except of the technical kind or representing the mere pastime of scholars, ceased to be written in the universal language. And it is doubtful whether any one, except some accidental specialist, would now be competent to write them. In fact, Dr Johnson was probably the last great man of letters in any part of Europe who can be said to have been actually fitted for the task. On the other hand, such a book, when written, would, in regard to most of the periods, be very much of a work of supererogation, or at the best a history of curiosities; and it would certainly discuss, outside of philosophy and religion and a few other divisions of the literature of knowledge, very few books of really great merit. We have not omitted, and shall not omit, to notice the greater Latin work, whether in the literature of knowledge or in that of power, whensoever it presents itself. But the occasions requiring such notice have been and will be few.

At the junction of the fifteenth and sixteenth centuries, however, as at the junction of the twelfth and thirteenth, the case is altered. Here as there, though for different reasons and with different results, a much greater contingent of positive literary genius turned itself into the channel of Latin writing. In each case the original cause was no doubt the existence—partly explicable, partly not—of an unusual amount and force of this literary genius, which in the earlier period applied itself to hymn-verse, scholastic philosophy, the flower of Latin mediæval history, stories and miscellanies of all sorts, simply because the vernaculars were not ready to receive it fully. In our present period a similar "spate" of genius and of learning found its way into the Latin channel for reasons equally obvious but not quite so simple. The vernaculars (with the single exception of Italian, unless we add Spanish) were indeed still not quite fully ready, yet they undoubtedly might have been, and perhaps[1] ought to have been, made sufficiently available. But the New Learning had brought about a partly excusable contempt of these vernaculars; it had pro-

[1] I say perhaps, remembering that the practice of Humanists in Latin invariably did much to perfect the vernaculars that they despised.

vided men with tempting patterns, as they thought, for all the possible literary styles, and in reality for many of them. Besides this, there was the subtle and not dishonourable temptation to appeal, not to the limited audience of a single tongue and country in a fashion which the choicer spirits even of that country would sincerely or affectedly disdain, but to a European Areopagus in its own curial speech. Therefore in these two periods, and in that before us most of all, we must pay to modern Latin an attention which would elsewhere be superfluous.

Purists in the subject sometimes call attention to the fact (as it seems to them) that by the beginning of the Sixteenth century, if not by the end of the Fifteenth, the work of Humanism proper was nearly or quite done. The work of the labourer generally is done, as far as all but ingathering is concerned, when the harvest comes; and the caution, though it may be advantageous in some respects, is superfluous in others. Humanism in at least one sense may be taken to mean, on one side the attempt almost to limit literature to Greek and Latin in the past, on the other to employ Latin and even to some extent Greek, always with preference, and sometimes with scorn of anything else, as a vehicle for literary redaction in the present and for the future. And this Humanism had not, up to nearly the end of the Fifteenth century, produced any original literature of even the slightest importance in combined matter and form. Nobody, I suppose, considers Petrarch's *Africa* such a work: Boccaccio's *De Genealogia Deorum*, in its later part at anyrate a work of the highest interest in substance, might be in any language for any advantage that it derives from the language it actually uses. As for the Fifteenth century proper, its one great Latin book, the *Imitation*, is in thought and in form irreconcilably opposed to Humanism: the spirit of both can enter no house of the soul save by casting that of Humanism utterly out. On the other hand, the great books of revived classical Latin, or would-be classical Latin, on the Humanist side—the *Colloquies*, the *Epistolæ Obscurorum Virorum*, the *Utopia*—are all books of the Sixteenth century; and the first half of that century, our own more special period, probably produces more such Latin literature of the first and second class than all other periods from the Fifteenth century to the Nineteenth put together. The course, therefore, of giving Humanist literature a special place here, and even glancing backwards and forwards a little to make the survey of it complete, has almost every justification.

The position and history of Humanism in 1500.

That Italian Humanism, from which all other varieties were to spring more or less immediately, draws its fount and origin, as such things go, from Petrarch, is an accepted *datum* of literary history which need not be attacked or denied. It is, indeed, necessary here as elsewhere to repeat the warning (so constantly neglected by literary historians, yet so necessary for the literary historian to keep as a sign upon his hand and as a frontlet between his eyes) that such things never really come from an individual—that they are winds of the spirit blowing no man knows whence, dews of heaven sinking into the earth and reappearing as streams no man knows how. All that we can in such cases justly say is that one man seems to trim his sail before others to the breeze, to hold his pitcher before others to catch the stream. Petrarch certainly does appear to deserve this credit in the present instance. His Latin work has been considered in some detail in an earlier volume of this History,[1] and we need not repeat the consideration. Boccaccio's, a little later in date, is also rather different in kind. It is much less ambitious in form and much fuller of fact. But both agreed in that eager and almost ferocious quest for the actual writings of antiquity, as to which all sane critics are agreed that it was the work which Humanism had to do, and the work which it is chiefly to be thanked for doing. And putting the points in which they agreed together with the points in which they differed—that is to say, Plutarch's quest for Latin style and Boccaccio's for Latin and Greek knowledge—they may be said between them to have very nearly exhausted all that Humanism had of good in germ if not in fulness, with the exception of the purely critical side, which neither shows. To recover and make sure of the riches of antiquity; to understand them; to copy them as far as was possible—these were the aims of these two great men. Petrarch at least showed something of the coming folly of despising his mother tongue, or affecting to despise it; but it was not really possible for the author of the *Rime* to do

[1] *The Fourteenth Century*, p. 247 *sq.*

this seriously, and so long as he was the author of the *Rime* it did not much matter whether he was serious or not. He and Boccaccio between them gloriously continued the work of Dante in verse, while Boccaccio extended it in the direction of prose, so far as the vernacular was concerned. What they also did in reference to the learned languages was therefore pure gain in every respect.

Not so much can be said of their successors, the travelling scholars and lecturers who represent the first three-quarters of the Fifteenth century.[1]

Although it has been generally admitted that these Humanists of the main body did not, as a rule deserve very well of their mother tongue, yet their services in assuring, not merely to their own age but to all future time, the possession of the inestimable treasures of antiquity have been justly counted to them as more than counterbalancing righteousness. And they have also appealed to the natural appetite for picturesque contrast, and to other appetites not quite so respectable. The notion of these scholars—wandering first over Italy and then over Europe; rising by their own efforts from the position of penniless nobodies, destitute in many though not in all cases of birth, breeding, or wealth, to that of the familiar and honoured companions of princes and prelates; marrying beautiful, rich, and well-born damsels; allured from state to state and city to city by golden bribes; setting out in quest of the buried treasures of learning like knights

[1] For their relation to the vernacular see *The Transition Period*, p. 118 *sq.*

of adventure; helping to despatch generation after generation of neophytes, often from half-barbarous nations, to spread learning and the appreciation of beauty all over Europe; honoured in their deaths with stately monuments, and rewarded by posterity for no few generations not merely as good workers in their day and way, but as men of genius and public benefactors,—all this has excited interest neither unnatural nor ungenerous, though perhaps sometimes a little uncritical. Even their much more questionable virtues, and their quite unquestionable vices, have also made them interesting. The ludicrous vanity and the cat-like quarrelsomeness which distinguished most of them have not been disagreeable to that somewhat morbid taste for "curiosities of literature," "quarrels of authors," and the like, which undoubtedly does exist in many persons. It is to be feared that the licence, conventional or sincere, of their sentiments and language has not been without a certain attractive effect in some cases. And the devotees of free-thought have not failed to celebrate them as "champions of the modern spirit," as having "vindicated the rights of the human soul," and all the rest of the well-known cant of anti-cant.

We have here, fortunately, nothing to do with free-thought, or the rights of the spirit, or any other of the regalia and paraphernalia of this kind of craft or mystery. We have not much, but something (for it is a distinctly literary feature), to do with the peculiarities which make the lighter work of Beccadelli and Filelfo, of Politian and Pontanus, so exceedingly "curious," in the bibliographical sense of that adjective. With the position of the Humanists in literary history and the value of their work as literature, we have a very great deal to do.

It is admitted that till we come to the extreme end of the century, the intrinsic value of Humanist work, vernacular or Latin, is exceedingly small, while its critical attitude to literature shows no advance, and even some falling off, from that of the Middle Ages. In regard to the first head, the *Facetiæ* of Poggio and the *Euryalus and Lucretia* of Æneas Sylvius are not exactly great literature, yet it would be difficult to say what better things the early and middle divisions of the century produced. With regard to the second, Vittorino da Feltre, one of the best of the whole school, is admitted to have been the first, and was apparently for a long time almost the only, teacher who was himself alive, and who endeavoured to make his pupils alive, to the differences of style and kind in the writers of antiquity.

The accomplishment of the earlier Humanists in classics.

But, it is said, they gained the classics for us and made them known. If this were wholly, as it is partly true, and if it were the whole of the truth, there would be little or nothing more to say. But, in the first place, the actual recovery and publication of MSS. was a small part of the work of the Humanists of 1375-1475; in the second, a great deal more was previously known than is sometimes allowed; in the third, the credit is at least not less, perhaps more, due to the princes and merchant-princes who would have these things, than to the scholars, who were often little more than their commercial travellers or collectors; and in the fourth, considering the general trend of thought in all countries, the thing would pretty certainly have been done if these particular men had not done it. But let us grudge them no possible credit for what they did do in this way.

They cannot, it may be feared, be said to have done very much in others. Aided by, and aiding, the fashion, they were no doubt sometimes good, and always more or less useful, teachers; but there are good and useful teachers in all times, and the office, alas! is seldom more than that of the unprofitable servant, who does but what it is his duty to do. They were not, as a rule, good grammarians, and were scarcely ever good critics; and if it be said that it is ungenerous to blame them for this, let it be remembered that if they had spent on real study half the time that they wasted on vain jactation, and idle quarrelling, and the composition of indecent verses, they might have made themselves very good grammarians, and much better critics than they were.[1]

But the chief mistake and the greatest error of the

[1] I should like to except Laurentius Valla (1406(7)-1457) from most, not all, of the strictures in this context. Valla appears to have had not a few of the defects of character of his congeners, and he has benefited rather *plus æquo* by the tendency which Heterodoxy even more than Orthodoxy has to justify all her children. But his work on Thucydides cannot but receive high admiration, when the time and circumstances are considered; his conception of Latin style was far beyond his age, and, for the matter of that, beyond most ages; and altogether he was a critic and a scholar of no ordinary kind, though, perhaps, not a man of letters in the very best sense.

Their relation to the vernacular.

Humanists, when tried before the high court of serene historical criticism, is the enormous waste of their energies on Latin translation of Greek. It is true that it was the most paying work that they, as working men of letters, could undertake ; but this excuse, though valid up to a point, is not valid beyond that point. It is true also that though, in the reluctant epigram extorted from a defender of theirs, these translations "were done for the most part by Greeks who had an imperfect knowledge of Latin and by Italians who had not complete mastery of Greek," it would be really ungenerous to lay much stress on this. The important point, from the literary point of view, is that a translation from Greek into Latin could at most do good to the man who made it by improving his own knowledge of the two languages, was but too likely to hinder the study of Greek itself, and could hardly fail to produce the impression that the matter of Greek, and not its literary beauty, was its title to greatness.

This process of translation from Greek, not into the vernacular but into Latin, and the concomitant use of Latin itself for original or quasi-original composition, not only could do little or nothing for the progress of the actual vernacular, but were even antagonistic to that progress. The process resembled in no whit the effect produced on English most of all, and on French and German to some extent, by the age-long practice of translation from Latin, and from modern languages, into the actual living tongue. It is to this process that English in particular owes its extraordinary wealth of vocabulary, and the unrivalled splendour and variety which, even more than mere wealth, distinguish it. But Italian remained unenriched by any contributions of the kind. Nor could the additional familiarity with Latin itself fail to weaken as well as to refine Italian. For it was a kind of process of "breeding in and in," of pouring in more water where the water had already choked. The wonderful effect [1] of the blends of Latin and French, which were unceasingly poured into English between the eleventh and the sixteenth century, and which by the latter date had made it a not much more than recognisable descendant of the language of Caedmon and Cynewulf, is paralleled by nothing in Italian. On the contrary, the accomplished Italian of our present period is far thinner and weaker than Dante's own, though it may be more elegant; nor does the language seem ever to have fortified itself since. The Fifteenth century was the great time of this process of fortification in all other European tongues, and the missing of the opportunity was, at least partly, the fault of the Humanists.

Work of the Humanists of the late Fifteenth century in both.

It may, however, be urged, with some show of reason, that at the end of the period immediately preceding our own, no small atonement was made. Most assuredly the great Florentines and Neapolitans, whose vernacular work has been fully noticed in the preceding

[1] It is strange that the obstinate refusal to recognise this fact and its consequences should still continue. But some very recent English scholarship of the philological kind seems as hopelessly blind to it as was Guest himself.

volume,[1]—Æneas Sylvius, Sannazar, Pontanus, Alberti, Marsilio Ficino, Pico della Mirandula, and above all Politian,—whether they write entirely in Latin, or, like Sannazar and Politian, are masters of either instrument; they provide literature of an accomplished kind in both classes of writing; they advance, refine, reform the literary quality.

Once more we must not deny the truth of this; yet once more it will be difficult for even the greatest representatives of Humanism at this time to make good any very much higher claims than those secure and great ones, of having been the channels and the distributors of classical learning to countries and to individuals that could make better use of it than themselves.

For throughout—in the Utraquists as well as in the Monoglots, in Politian and Sannazar as in Piccolomini and Pontano — the fault and the mischief of the Humanist position are seen in the strange unrealities of many kinds, which mar their vernacular and their "regular" work alike. Everything is out of focus. The famous transference of the Pagan ecclesiastical dictionary to Christian use; the employment of Jupiter Optimus Maximus to designate the divinity whose worshippers, in the very towns where the words were written, had been cast to the lions for refusing to worship the said Jupiter; the fitting of the whole terminology of Latin ritual into the services of the Christian Church; the sincere horror, late in our own period, of an equally sincere Christian like Lilius

[1] *The Transition Period*, chaps. iv. and xii.

Giraldus at the person who, *si Deo placet!* wanted of Sannazar *dictionem Christianam id est barbaram;* other well-known and often-quoted things, which it is not necessary to quote again, merely give the results of this mischief in one particular direction. The evil was, in fact, all-pervading in literature. The Latin poets themselves had gone beyond measure, and certainly far beyond the Greeks, in appropriating stock imagery, stock characters, stock phrases, to different literary kinds; but the Humanists out-aped them twenty-fold. To the practice of this time, and to its criticism a little later (see chapter vii.) are due the "pastoral" frippery which revolted even such a sturdy Latinist and neo-classic as Dr Johnson, and which, to make it quite tolerable, requires the superhuman poetry of a Milton or a Shelley,—the tawdry and tumbled finery of the "heroic poem," with its cut-and-dried exordia and invocations, its cut-and-dried supernatural interferences, its cut-and-dried revolutions, its cut-and-dried everything. In those who did not write Italian the principle and its practice produced at best *pastiche;* in those who wrote Italian as well, they produced something which was not only *pastiche* but patchwork. Even the great Politian, the man who really might, without much absurdity, have echoed Filelfo's absurd boast that he could write as well in Greek as in Latin, and as well in Italian as in either, suffers (at least in some judgments) terribly from this mixture, and from the sense of unreality, of the school exercise, of the copy of verses. And all the others suffer much more.

The circumstances of the more northern nations in reference to the study and practice of the classical, especially the Latin, tongues were remarkably different. In the first place, no one of them had ready to hand a vernacular of anything like the advancement and polish of Tuscan Italian. Even French, which had not merely the most abundant but the most brilliant literature of all,—a literature with which Italian itself could only vie by restricting the competition to the greatest individuals and not admitting mass or variety of work,—was still very immature, and had, by the latter part of the fifteenth century, rather gone back than advanced. French prose in particular was behindhand, and simply did not yet exist in any form suited to the majority of modern purposes. The Germans, Low and High, had fallen off still more remarkably from the promise which Middle High German had given of poetic beauty and Middle Low of quaint originality; so that the vernacular German of our present period is, outside Luther, one of the most unliterary tongues in Europe. Indeed Latin of a kind played more of the part of "second vernacular" to Germans in the late Middle Ages than perhaps to any other people. As for English, it had had one poet (as even Italians —*e.g.*, Lilius Giraldus—knew) of quite the first order, but it could hardly be said to have a second. The prose was behind France, and had only recently gone beyond Germany: the poetry was in a pitiable state of eclipse and disorganisation, and the very language was still in process of formation. The isolated and

Humanism in relation to the Northern vernaculars.

peculiar offshoot of literary Scottish-English was itself a kind of *grammatica*, an artificial literary tongue, though with strong and racy dialect character. Provençal was practically dead for literature; and the remoter Scandinavian had also finished its long and glorious season of productiveness. The languages of the Peninsula stood, in the aspect now being considered, nearly in the position of Italian. Besides, their vernacular literature is dealt with fully elsewhere,[1] and they supplied few great Humanists.

For all the others Latin supplied in differing degrees, but really and to their utmost benefit, the aids which, in reference to Italian, were mistakenly and superfluously demanded of it. To all it gave a prose medium infinitely superior, for the miscellaneous purposes of prose, to their vernacular, and intelligible to all educated Europeans, as that vernacular could not possibly be. To all (though here the differing measure becomes very important) it supplied vehicles for those kinds of verse for which as yet their vernacular was not polished enough, or not supple enough, or insufficiently supplied with vocabulary. To all it provided models of style of admirable accomplishment and adaptability, which (even for French to some extent, for the others to a very much greater) had the advantage of being slightly different from the native idiom and construction, and therefore of crossing, blending, strengthening, and varying that idiom's powers. And to all it gave in abundance

[1] See *The Later Renaissance.*

that vocabulary of terms of art, of philosophy, of literature, of business, which they lacked.

And so it comes about that while the *average* fifteenth- and sixteenth-century Latin of the Northern nations is no doubt not at all better in substance, and much worse in form, than the average Humanist Latin of Italy, these countries were justified in using Latin, even for such average purposes, as Italy was not. They were rewarded by sometimes accomplishing in it work which they probably could not have accomplished at all in their own vernaculars, while its circulation would, in these, have been deplorably limited. Let us imagine, but for a moment, the horrible calamity that it would have been to European literature in the strictest sense, as well as to European culture in the widest, if Erasmus had written in Dutch!

Instances of the Colloquies, *the* Utopia, *&c.*

This example might be almost sufficient, because everybody can appreciate it. It would not have been quite such a misfortune if he had been a Frenchman and had written in French, just as it is an immense piece of good fortune that men like Rabelais and even Marot did write in French. But French itself would not have fully sufficed for his purposes, which required the language not of Rabelais, not of Calvin, not even of Montaigne, but of Pascal or Descartes at the very earliest—that is to say, a language not reached till a full century after his time. And he would have been worse parted still with English. It is (or rather it is not quite) needless to say that More never wrote a line of the *Utopia* in English. But it is not probable that, if he had so written it or had translated it from his own Latin, or if Ascham or any of his contemporaries had done this, it would be much better than it is in good Master Richard Robinson's translation, executed a few years after More's death. Yet those who have only read the English may be excused for sometimes wondering at the reputation of the book, though they may understand it when they read the Latin. In the latter case the instrument of expression is adequate to the thing to be expressed, and if not perfectly, yet sufficiently under the command of the artist. In the other it is not. Compare in a different sphere the *Pammachius* and its very close English analogue *Kyng Johan;* read the *Epistolæ Obscurorum Virorum*, and think of what they would have been in even Murner's German. In pure poetry, indeed, the argument fails; but then in pure poetry no intelligent critic would ever think of applying it. Pretty, sometimes almost exquisite, as the *Basia* are, they would have been prettier in Italian, prettier still (Marot has actually made similar things) in French. They would have been prettier in English, and it is just possible that if the author had used his own vernacular, they might, to persons who can taste that language, be prettier in Dutch. But then poetry stands by itself, and as it happens, no vernacular in Europe, except Italian, was very strong in pure poetry at this particular time, so there cannot have been much lost.

But the importance, the general character, and the errors, such as they were, of this Humanist literature being thus dealt with, there remains the difficulty of dealing adequately with itself. Its mass, even if we were to limit ourselves to our strict period, much more if we look before and after, is enormous. To give an example, one of our modern benefactors, who has collected and selected an invaluable sheaf (*v. infra*) of the Latin-German poets of the sixteenth century, observes that he thinks he has read about a thousand such. And the volume of miscellaneous prose must be almost incalculable. Although the newly invented press lent itself with almost too much complaisance to the dissemination of the matter, the chief authorities appear to be agreed that by far the larger part is still in MS. Even of that which was printed much has never been reprinted, and the original editions, except in public libraries, are made inaccessible to students of moderate means by the entirely unliterary craze for such things on the part of collectors. Yet again it may be pretty freely doubted whether any one but a pure literary hedonist, with a competent fortune and his time to himself, would be justified in devoting this time to the extent necessary for this particular subject. For of almost all divisions of literature, till we come to the mere "book-making" of purely modern days, it is probably that which, in its *average* development, has least to satisfy not merely the intellect but even the taste. The average Humanist style is confessedly but an imitation of certain few and definite models, and the average

Distribution of the subject.

Humanist matter is, as confessedly, quite subordinate to the style. With Cicero and Livy, Virgil and Ovid, actually in our possession, it is surely the tamest of amusements, and the most light-minded of lost labours, to examine whether Henricus Pimpernellus or Johannes Napsius Græculus Senior has come nearest to or farthest from Ovid or Virgil, Livy or Cicero. And of any story to tell, any solid thesis to prove, any knowledge to convey, even any individual and original fragment of thought to utter, Pimpernellus and Napsius are, as a rule, emulously destitute.

Fortunately there are exceptions who can be made representative, not in the sense that their constituents in any but the least degree resemble them, but in the sense that they show at the best what was actually done, and probably at the best or very nearly so what could have been done, what all these constituents would have done if they could. Some of these—Erasmus, More, the authors of the *Epistolæ Obscurorum*—are famous; others are at least known to students; others have the merit of being accessible with ease or with not much difficulty. It should be possible, by accounts of these varying with their importance, and carefully selected to cover as many departments of literature as possible, to give no inadequate idea of the whole. In two important departments, Criticism and the Drama,—to each of which, in consequence of their special eminence in this tract of country, a separate chapter is assigned,—it would be inconvenient to disjoin the Latin experts from the vernacular, but we shall endeavour to deal with the rest.

Latin verse in Italy.

To deal at all exhaustively with even the Italian verse which resulted from this fancy or fashion—not quite, as we have seen, so unreasonable in its origin as unprofitable in its results—would require a volume;[1] but within reasonable space it is possible to note some typical specimens of its producers and their productions.

[1] The very *Deliciæ Poetarum Italorum* (*s.l.*, 1608), which is the nearest approach to a Corpus of this poetry or poetastry, consists of two enormously thick volumes, one of 1400 the other of 1500 pp. Smaller collections and selections are extremely numerous; and the odd Italian habit (which Sir Thomas Browne ought to have noticed in the *Garden of Cyrus*) of arranging them in quincunxes, or at least quintets, may lead to a great deal of confusion. Not merely is the disreputable *Quinque Poetarum Lusus in Venerem* quite a different thing from the respectable *Quinque Poetarum Hetruscorum Carmina*, but the identically same title, *Carmina Quinque Illustrium Poetarum*, covers two quite different selections—that referred to by Mr Symonds (*Revival of Learning*, p. 337, new ed.), containing Politian, Bembo, Navagero, Castiglione, and Sadoleto; and an earlier one (Florence, 1552), in which the places of Politian and Sadoleto are taken by Cotta and Flaminio. Pope re-edited a collection (*Selecta Poemata Italorum*, 2 vols., London, 1740), giving most of Vida and Fracastoro, much of Politian, the curious *De Animorum Immortalitate* of Aonius Palearius, and plentiful examples of Sannazar and the minors. But perhaps the best book for a reader who does not want to do more than fairly "sample" the subject is the anonymous *Poemata Selecta Italorum* (Oxford, 1808), which contains the *Poetics* of Vida, the *Syphilis* of Fracastoro, the *Benacus* of Bembo, the *Laocoön* and *Curtius* (Oxford should have asked her nodding son, "Why *Quintus*, sir? why *Quintus*?") of Sadolet, with selections from Sannazar, Castiglione, Navagero, Flaminio, Molza, the two Amaltei, Bonfadio, Muretus, and a few minors. Unfortunately, being confined to the *sixteenth* century, it contains nothing from Politian or Pontanus.

The two most famous of the poets whom, though directly belonging to the last volume[1] we borrow for the purposes and under the conventions of this chapter, are Politian (1454-1494) and Pontanus (1426-1503); for it is unnecessary, as it would be unedifying, to do more than glance at the exercitations, more impudent than interesting, of Beccadelli in his *Hermaphroditus.* The others, especially Pontanus, may go near to rival him in this respect, but at any rate they have other claims. Politian, indeed, has probably been more fortunate than any writer mentioned in this chapter, except Erasmus, in saving something more than a mere vague general reputation from the devouring efforts of Time on material which was fondly thought proof against the "monster of ingratitudes." The *Nutricia*, the *Manto*, the *Ambra* have been praised with discretion and judgment by Mr Symonds in our own day, and it is rather curious that not long after their own they were praised with judgment and discretion by Lilius Giraldus, who, as we have just seen, does not always exercise these gifts impeccably. The qualities which helped to restrain the admiration of the sixteenth-century Humanist are not improbably the same which may serve to animate that of the nineteenth or twentieth century critic. Politian's subjects—even the most literary—are to him the subjects of a real enthusiasm; and his temperament and powers, which, as his vernacular work shows, were both essentially poetic, raise the blood, both of himself and his reader, far above the frigid

Politian.

[1] *Vide The Transition Period*, chap. iv.

level attained by Naugerius or Bembo. We can always excuse roughness when it is associated with power, and Politian can be both vigorous and sweet.

Signor del Lugo's edition[1] (Florence, 1867) containing some unpublished Italian prose and all the extant Latin and Greek verses, presents in more ways than one a striking picture of this typical man of the Italian Renaissance. The word picture is doubly applicable, for it has an actual frontispiece portrait, arresting enough with the wild eyes, the extravagant Roman nose—more of a promontory than even Southey's or Herrick's—and the head twisted half round on the wry neck as of one who sees spectres.[2] But the contents of the book speak the author quite as vividly. The sermons—actual sermons—full of fervour and unction; the virtuous pedagogic dictations to little Piero de' Medici; and the graceful courtier-like letters to the Ladies Clarice and Lucrezia (the Italian account of the conspiracy of the Pazzi appears to be a translation by another hand) act in the most startling manner as foils to the unmitigated filth and blind fury of the Latin invectives against "Mabilius"—the Greek scholar Marullus—Politian's successful rival with the beautiful Alessandra Scala. These invectives[3] show not only the worse side of Renaissance manners and morals, but also the worse side from the artistic, not the ethical, point of view, of its imitation of the classics. Politian forgets

[1] There is said to be no edition, at once exclusive and complete, of Politian's Latin verse. The fullest seems to be that quoted.

[2] Nose and neck did not escape lampooners at the time.

[3] Mr Symonds very generously allows them pungency. I fail to see it.

that even Martial, and still more Catullus, never thought it sufficient to fling at an enemy a mere handful of foul thoughts, swaddled in fouler words—that, with the rarest exceptions, they put in wit as well, and generally at least managed to connect, and not merely to combine, obscenity with point. Fortunately such things are but a small part of the poet's exercises in "regular" verse; and in many, if not most, of the others the poetic fire which he assuredly possessed breaks alike through the extraordinary metrical licences of the Greek (which sometimes seems to scan "politically," and not even by the technical accent) and the sometimes prim Virgilisings or Claudianisings of the Latin. One may probably be excused the confession of having read very little of the Latin *Iliad;* but the *Manto* and the *Ambra,* the *Rusticus* and the *Nutricia,* can only be missed by any one who can appreciate Latin poetry at all to his great fault and infinite loss, while some of the smaller poems are really nectareous.

Pontanus.

Pontanus, whose prose is noteworthy as well as his verse,[1] and who wrote constantly in the learned language, falls short of Politian in poetic quality, but is not destitute of it. The

[1] The standard of the verse is the Aldine of 1513. (There is an abundant selection in [Gruter's] *Deliciæ:* Pope gives only a few pieces.) I possess a copy of the Lyons edition of the prose a year later. The latter is not of a succulent character, consisting of two Dialogues, *Charon* and *Antonius,* both, and especially the latter, containing verse as well as prose, and of nearly half a score of moral or political treatises—*De Fortitudinc, De Principe, De Liberalitate,* &c. He also wrote History and much else.

error of his *Urania*, a long astronomical poem in five books, with extensive mythological and other digressions and episodes, is the error of the whole time and kind. It lasted, indeed, so long that there may even seem to some to be a certain impertinence and presumption in calling it an error at all. The errors of his lighter and shorter poems are in the first place the occasional corrupt following of the licence of the ancients—less, it would seem, as a matter of hot-blooded sympathy than as a matter of cold-blooded literary convention; and the less odious mistake of refusing to clothe genuine Italian thought, and celebrate characteristic Italian scenery, in native Italian verse. But in the Neapolitan, as in the Tuscan poet, there is a certain massiveness and race which we rarely find in their successors, though there is something of it in their younger contemporary Sannazar.[1] Notice of him, however, may be conveniently postponed in order to discuss first the most solid and characteristic of the Latin verse-writers of our own special time, the poet of the *Poetics* and the poet of—*Syphilis*.

Of the critical value of Vida's[2] celebrated poem we may speak in the chapter specially devoted to criticism.

[1] Not only Sannazar, but his rival in pastoral, "Mantuan," Battista Spagnuoli (1436-1516), belongs specially to the last volume, and both have been duly noticed there. The vogue of Mantuan's Latin verse in the sixteenth century was almost incredible. Much as men worshipped Virgil, they did not hesitate to put his modern compatriot by his side.

[2] Marco Girolamo Vida, 1480-1566, born at Cremona, died Bishop of Alba. The *Scacchia*, *Bombyx*, and *Ars Poetica* appeared, with some hymns, in 1527, the *Christiad* eight years later.

But in the case of so famous (if to modern readers, perhaps, rather dimly famous) a person[1] something must be said here about its poetical and literary value. Neither, it is to be feared, even with the amplest allowance which can be made on the general principles of this chapter, can be said to be great. The mere versification of the *Poetics* leaves a good deal to desire; the occasional spondaics are not well chosen or adjusted, and though the verses will run trippingly enough for a time, there is generally before long an awkward "pull-up," or a maladroit adjustment of pauses. The phraseology is in one respect a model of the kind, in another a caution against it. It is the very embodiment of the *gradus*: one seems to move in a sort of snowstorm of minute Virgilian, Ovidian, and other tags, sleeting, like the Lucretian atoms, through a void. For, in truth, Vida's general drift (we still reserve the critical point) is empty enough of really important sense. He invokes the Muses; he addresses Prince Francis at Madrid, is very unhappy that his patron should be in captivity, and suggests that these *Poetics* may while away the captive's time. There are many kinds of verse; choose which you like best, only remembering that everybody cannot do everything. The poetic child must be carefully educated, kept from bad language (in the critical sense), taught the poets, but not whipped too much. Emulation is good, but not

Vida.

[1] "Immortal Vida" (Pope) was edited and translated unceasingly in the seventeenth and eighteenth centuries. Some half-score French versions are quoted; the standard English one is Pitt's.

precocity. As he grows up let him try easy subjects first. These commonplaces and their likes fill the first book; for the contents of the second and third we may refer to a future page. But though there is sometimes common-sense in the meaning, there is never anything but commonplace in the expression.

To different tastes (or the same taste in different moods) the *Scacchia* and the *Bombyx* may seem less or more worthy displays of Vida's art, such as it was, than the *Poetica;* but this can hardly be the case with the *Christiad.* This last is an application of his own principles in artificial heroic narrative (see chap. vii.) to those rebellious subjects on which judges so different in most ways, but so alike in general neo-classic taste, as Boileau and Johnson, agree that the system was inapplicable and impracticable, and which perhaps went nearer to wrecking *Paradise Lost* itself than Miltonolaters are always ready to allow. The others are merely exercises in the verse *tour de force*—examples of what the Greek rhetoricians called *ecphrasis*, elaborate and formal description, according to the specifications made and provided for such things. The taste for them continued long, and inspired, among other things, Addison's *Machinæ Gesticulantes* and *Barometer.* If not taken too seriously, they are a civil game enough; and if they be of no great value in themselves, one can only grieve to think that the chief reason of their disuse is the fact that fewer and fewer persons every year go through the practice necessary to appreciate the play. The worst of them was that they promoted similar exercises, more or less serious, in the vernacular, which have, to speak frankly, no interest at all. The *Cyders* and the *Arts of Preserving Health* and the *Fleeces* try the catholic spirit in literature perhaps more than any other division of literary production.

Fracastoro.

The once if not now world-famous *Syphilis* of Fracastoro,[1] belongs partly to this class, but more to another which is also represented in the later developments just referred to — the class of pure didactic verse. This, though it is almost demonstrably a bad thing (except as sometimes showing that poetry can be poetical in spite of everything), has of course a mighty ancestry from Hesiod in the one great house and Lucretius in the other downwards, and may plead the almost singular claim of having commended itself equally to Antiquity, the Middle Age, the Renaissance, and the Augustan period of modernity. The kind of the *De Rerum Natura* cannot possibly be stigmatised as a necessarily bad kind; but it is certainly unlike Wisdom, in that it is justified of very few of its children. Fracastoro's poem, if not of the best, is anything but of the worst. What may seem to modern readers the inevitably unsavoury nature of the subject is all but entirely deodorised by the treatment. The disease presented itself to Fracas-

[1] Girolamo Fracastoro (1483-1553), Veronese physician and poet. He was a professor at Padua, and also wrote divers Latin treatises on medical and scientific subjects, as well as a remarkable critical Dialogue, *Naugerius*, a *Joseph* in hexameters, and other poems. My copy of his *Opera* is that in 2 vols., Lugduni, 1591.

toro's contemporaries very mainly, and the poet-physician has himself treated it almost entirely, as a terrible epidemic, if not totally disconnected from any invitation by individual misconduct, yet in at least many cases quite independent of this. He is thus able to treat it, and does treat it, almost exactly as if it were smallpox or scarlet fever; and his setting forth of diagnosis, progress, and treatment is not only purely scientific but void of offence even to non-scientific readers. His medium is a hexameter which has been accused of harshness, but which may seem to some to be rather strong than harsh, and his chief concession to convention is the final story of the shepherd Syphilis (said to be the actual origin of the name). This hero is struck with the disease by the Sun, whose deity he has blasphemed, and cured by the nymph Ammerice (America) with help of the tree Hyacus (Guaiacum). On the whole, the worst thing to be said against the piece is that it could have been done much better in prose.

Sannazar.

We may now pass to less serious things. Sannazar (1458-1530), who belongs not less, or even more, to the fifteenth century[1] than to the sixteenth, has received much praise for his Latin poetry. It is certain that he has something of the grace and force of Politian and Pontanus, with something also of the inspiration of the former, when we compare him with the neat prettinesses or the frigid conventions of our actual period. And he is even more "correct." Thus, though he allows himself the

[1] See *The Transition Period*, p. 146 *sq.*

lesser licence of the quadrisyllable at the close of a pentameter, he is seldom guilty of the trisyllable, in which some Italians unblushingly wallow; and his Sapphics are often very agreeable. The *Villa Mergellina*, in particular, is one of the most satisfactory pieces of occasional poetry of the particular class, and almost as much may be said of all the group of poems on the same place and its neighbourhood. For in such pieces, while we admire the grace and skill of the composition, and are not unpleasantly reminded of our own classical studies, there is neither the tedious length nor the disparate subject of Vida's and Fracastoro's poems to annoy us, nor are we (as in the case of the former's *Poetics*) likely to be provoked by the contents. In no case does the unreality, which is admittedly the curse of the whole style, strike us less, though it would be rash to say that it does not strike us at all. A fuller acquaintance with Sannazar[1] will not greatly increase admiration for his Latin poetry. The famous *De Partu Virginis* is, in spite or because of the enormous pains which he is said to have spent upon it, a frigid production; the almost equally famous *Piscatory Eclogues*, by a process which would be ingenious if intended, exhibit, in the very fact of the transposition of scenery and machinery, the defects of the whole style; and while the severer *Epigrams* are, even with such inviting subjects as the Borgias, singularly lacking in point,

[1] My copy is the useful modern edition opening a series of Mediæval and Modern Latin Poets, which might have been extended with great advantage (Augsburg, 1833).

few of those dealing with miscellaneous subjects come up to the Mergellina series.

Bembo

I do not think so much can be said of Bembo,[1] the most admired, perhaps, next to Politian, of all these Italian Latinists. His occasional obscenity, whether of the frank or the sniggering kind, need not now much concern us. Little need be said on that vice of the age and country at all here, and what has to be said will be better said in another place. His Latin verse stands accountant to a more strictly literary charge, and one which needs no squeamishness in the discussion of it. There are very many worse poems of the style than the much-admired *Benacus*, and perhaps not so very many better; but hardly any poem shows the weaknesses of the style itself more damningly. It is not very long: the hexameters are for the most part, if not always, fluent and sonorous, and the author shows a real pupilship to Virgil, and not merely the relation of thief to victim, in the skill with which he selects and adjusts the local names of tributary or derived stream and of neighbouring city. But neither the moderate compass, nor the abundant material, nor

[1] Pietro Bembo (1470-1547), a Venetian of family. He became the favourite of several popes, a cardinal, Bishop of Bergamo, librarian of St Mark, and historiographer of the State of Venice. His love for Lucrezia Borgia may have been Platonic; that for his mistress Morosina was certainly not. He was the very Coryphæus of Ciceronianism, but his Latin prose has faded terribly. He will recur importantly in the next chapter for his vernacular work; and not his least brilliant connection with literature is the glowing peroration of the *Cortegiano*, in the style of the *Phædrus*, which Castiglione puts in his mouth.

the tempting scenery, can induce him to describe the latter in a fresh and first-hand way, without dragging in the frippery of gradus and lexicon. It would be cruel and ungallant to object to the Nymphs, but here as elsewhere what do we want with Jupiter? And even if Jupiter is to be passed, why drag in Bactria, and Scythia, and Thule, and Atlas, and the Caucasus, and the poor Muses once more? And yet Bembo really loved his native North Italy, could really (as we perceive from his vernacular work) see nature and feel passion. But with him in practice, as with Vida in theory, a literary Monmouth Street is the highway to Parnassus, and nobody can be admitted to the Muses' Court without a Court-dress of old clothes. As one reads this and other poems, an old story comes to mind. There was a schoolboy once who wrote a prize poem on the prescribed subject of Superstition. The head-master—a scholar of the old school, now with God, and in his day one of the best of men and scholars—admitted that the piece was fair of its kind and duly "crowned" it, as the French would say; but he was not happy. "There's nothing in it about the sacrifice of Iphigenia," he said mournfully; "I had expected something about the sacrifice of Iphigenia." Similar desires were universally prevalent on the part of readers in the sixteenth century, and the writers of Latin verses, to do them justice, were never churlish in gratifying them. The extreme oddity of the Hymn to St Stephen makes it to us a little more piquant, though the contrasts are much the same, and Bembo's elegiacs are not seldom pretty.

With less elegance perhaps, and even with less of the poetical spirit which, as has been said, we can see in Bembo's Italian if not in his Latin, Sadolet,[1] so often mentioned with the priestly lover of Lucrezia, has a much greater sincerity and depth of tone. The "Laocoön" piece[2] seems to me to deserve rather higher praise than Mr Symonds gives it, and that on *Marcus* Curtius reinforces the impression given by its companion. Both show not merely a man who is able to think in spheres above those of the mere fribble, the mere voluptuary, or even the mere dilettante, but one who can clothe his thought in words which have a certain quiver and ring in them. That Latin has this *timbre* there is no question at all; and it is one of the justest charges to be brought against the Humanists, that, with their far greater command of the language, they so seldom brought out what the hymn-writers of the Middle Ages had not the slightest difficulty in producing.

Sadoleto.

The notable author of the *Courtier*[3] is another

[1] Jacopo Sadoleto of Modena (1477-1547) became secretary to Leo X. and Clement VII., Bishop of Carpentras, and cardinal. He wrote mainly, if not entirely, in Latin, and was one of the best of the Ciceronians, as well as one of the best *men* of the Italian Renaissance. His *Letters* are numerous and important.

[2] This, like the other shorter pieces in the preceding and following paragraphs, will be found in the *Poemata Selecta Italorum* noticed above.

[3] Baldassaro Castiglione, born at Casatico in 1478. He was a diplomatist of eminence in the papal service, and was much respected by Charles V.; but was long resident at the minor Court of Urbino, which he has made the scene of the *Courtier* (*v. infra*, p. 169 *sq.*) He died at Toledo in 1529.

Latinist in verse of whom we may perhaps think rather better than we have thought of some, and than some have thought of him. He, too, was very fond of subjects taken from or connected with Art—the "Cleopatra" so called, the "Cupid" of Praxiteles, the Death of Raphael; but his best known piece is an elegy on the youthful poet Alcon. This undoubtedly had great influence on succeeding pieces of the kind, including even *Lycidas;* but we may, perhaps, incline the parallel between Castiglione and Milton in a somewhat different direction from that which has sometimes been given to it. The weak part both of *Alcon* and *Lycidas* is the conventional machinery; but this weakness is not in the Latin poem, as in the English, carried off by the blast and the fire of the poetry. There is more sincerity of personal regret felt or simulated in the *Alcon*, but the phrasing is mere classical *crambe repetita;* and though the hexameters are above the level of the time, they are mere school-work beside

Castiglione.

"So sinks the day-star,"

or—

"Where the great Vision of the guarded mount."

Castiglione's prettiest thing seems to me the letter from his wife Hippolyta, which, though of course suggested by Ovid, still rings remarkably true among the dead scraps and orts of this verse. The following lines on the absent husband's picture live and breathe most pleasantly, despite that sad *arrideo*:—

"Sola tuos vultus referens, Raphaelis imago
  Picta manu curas allevat usque meas.
Huic ego delicias facio, arrideoque jocorque,
  Alloquor, et tanquam reddere verba queat,
Assensu nutuque mihi sæpe illa videtur
  Dicere velle aliquid, et tua verba loqui."[1]

Naugerius or Navagero[2] is perhaps best known for the saying, transferred by Dryden from Martial to Statius, that he burnt a copy of the Roman epigrammatist every year to Virgil's *manes.* If he did so, it only proved that he was a very silly fellow; for not only is Martial a model and captain in his own style, but that style is not in the least comparable to the style of epic, and neither the merits nor the drawbacks of any performances in the two could be arranged in competition or contrast. But the story is at least interesting as a contribution to the history of the Virgil-mania of the time. It is also fair to Navagero to say that, though he has nothing like Martial's point, his strength, or the irresistibly sly and sudden wit which not seldom deserves the more honourable name of humour, he has other qualities which at least distinguish him very favourably from the run of modern Latin poets. The *Lusus,* which open the collection of his Poems in the Florentine *Carmina Quinque Illustrium Poetarum* (1552), almost hide their artificiality by the extraordinary

Navagero.

[1] *Op. cit.,* p. 40.

[2] Andrea Navagero (1483-1529), born at Venice, which he represented diplomatically. He preceded Bembo in the librarianship of St Mark. Catullus, not Virgil, seems to have been his real idol.

grace which has been justly compared rather to the Greek than to the Latin Anthology. It is still all Pan and Faunus and Amyntas, and offerings of violets to Venus, and barkings of Hylax and the like; but for once the poet has "got the atmosphere," and we are not tormented by any sense of incongruity. The longer pieces in elegiacs and hexameters—*Acon*, *Daphnis*, *Iolas*—are able to carry their length; and though Navagero is not, I think, quite Sannazar's equal at sapphics, he is often very happy with the miscellaneous lyrical metres, especially in the choriambics of

"Jam cæli reserat fores,"

and in divers hendecasyllabic essays.

Flaminio.

Nearly two-thirds of the volume just referred to is filled with the work of Marcantonio Flaminio,[1] of whom a very much smaller but fairly representative selection will also be found in the Oxford Anthology above quoted. Flaminio's poems are chiefly, though not quite wholly, addresses to persons—probably the majority of the celebrated Italian men and women of the time figure in his list—and they are mainly, though again not wholly, couched in Horatian metres. He can hardly be said to possess in perfection any of the qualities which have been praised as at least occasionally existing in some of his contemporaries—the descriptive elegance

[1] Flaminio (1498-1550) was, unlike the writers just mentioned, merely a man of letters. He wrote a good deal on subjects both sacred and divine, and had a father and brother whose work in verse was published with his at Paris in 1743.

of Sannazar, the grave fire of Sadoleto, the veracity and nature of Castiglione, the antique grace of Navagero; but he is a fair adept in all these respects. His phrase is sometimes awkward; for instance

> "Nunc mulgere mea manu capellam
> Lacteoque liquore membra sicca
> *Irrigare* per æstum,"

doubtless means that he *drank* the milk. But it literally suggests the singular picture of a person watering his dry limbs with goat's milk as a shop-boy waters the pavement in front of his master's shop. Flaminio is seen at his best in the panegyrical epicede on Vittoria Colonna to Turrianus: nor, despite the unlucky suggestion in the passage just quoted, has Mr Symonds exaggerated his pleasant love of the country and the pictures which it induces him to draw for us. Nor is he unhappy at more trifling things, such as the felicitation of himself on his verses being sung by Marguerite of Valois—the second Marguerite, less gifted than her aunt and less beautiful than her niece of the same name, but, like them, a patroness of men of letters.

The somewhat effeminate and morbid, but luscious, muse of Molza[1] shows herself not much otherwise in

[1] Francesco Maria Molza of Modena (1489-1544), a man not free from vices which are reflected in his verse, but of a temper, it would seem, almost as sweet as that verse itself. He had a very learned and poetical granddaughter (1542-1617). The rest of the writers mentioned in this paragraph can be afforded no more biographical notice than their dates. The Amaltei belonged to a family specially prolific in men of letters, some half-dozen between 1460 and 1603 being noticed in even summary biographical dictionaries.

Latin than in Italian dress, though the more masculine language does not admit quite such a sleepy ripeness as its daughter. Its best example in the older tongue is undoubtedly the poem, "In His Sickness to His Friends," and this[1] would be better if it were shorter. The Alcaics of Arco (1479-1546) and Capilupo (1511-1580) display not ill the idiosyncrasy of that curious metre—which is very rarely achieved in the supremest manner, but in which the execution, unless it is quite detestable, always rewards the poet for the trouble he takes with it. Giovanni Cotta[2] is very much less successful with it, and is also a special sinner with the trisyllable at the end of a pentameter. But the *Vicus Gazanus* of Bonfadio (1501-1559), connected in subject, and no doubt composed to some extent in rivalry, with the *Benacus* of Bembo, is a better piece of description than its pattern, though not perhaps a better piece of metre. Nothing in the whole kind was much more popular during the neo-classic time than the *De Acone et Leonilla* of Girolamo Amalteo (1506-1574), which is therefore worth quoting, as it is only a quatrain:—

Molza and others.

"Lumine Acon dextro, capta est Leonilla sinistro;
Et potis est forma vincere uterque deos.
Blande puer, lumen, quod habes, concede sorori;
Sic tu cæcus Amor, sic erit illa Venus."

Nor could, perhaps, that prettiness, with a touch of triviality, which is the note of so much of this verse, be better shown. Girolamo's Alcaics would be better if

[1] *Vide Carmina V. Ill. Poet.* (Florence, 1552), p. 85.
[2] 1479-1510 (?).

he did not rather frequently stumble over that rock of offence the third line; but his brother, Giovanbattista (1525-1573), has left an *Iollas* in very flowing *senarii.* The facility of Muretus in the same metre has obtained access for him to anthologies, but he will be better treated in the dramatic chapter.

The abundance of Latin verse in Italy at this period may be illustrated from two volumes[1] which appeared in successive years just about the end of it, and which, ranging exactly together in print and size, and all but exactly in set of page, are sometimes found together in contemporary binding. The first is the second quincunx noted above, and contains work by Vintha, Segni, Berni, Accolti, and Varchi.[2] The other contains an anthology from no less than forty different poets, including a few of those already named, but for the most part drawn from fresh sources. No very long poems are admitted, nor is there any hard-and-fast scheme of subject, so that the nearly two hundred pages of the first volume and the nearly a hundred leaves of the second must probably contain a good thousand of pieces—eclogues and elegies and epigrams, odes and addresses and epistles, the entire *supellex* of the occasional poet. One of the longest and most ambitious of the contents

The Quinque Poetæ Hetrusci *and the* Anthology of Ubaldini.

[1] *Carmina V. Hetruscorum Poetarum* (Florentiæ apud Juntas, 1562) and *Carmina Poetarum Nobilium Jo. Pauli Ubaldini studio conquisita* (Mediolani ap. Ant. Antonianum, 1563).

[2] For Berni and Varchi see next chapter. *Fabio* Segni was the poet; the better known historian was Bernardo. *Cardinal* Accolti (the "Cardinalis" is in the book) lived under Julius II. Of Vintha I know little or nothing.

of the miscellany is Molza's elegant, and for the writer unusually vigorous, expostulation from Catharine of Arragon to Henry VIII. This has some two hundred lines; not a few of the epitaphs content themselves with the consecrated distich.

From such a range of authors, subjects, and styles it is possible to make a judgment of the whole class of composition not less accurate, and much more clearly cut, than when the judgment is distracted and the memory made blunt by turning over scores or hundreds of volumes, though the latter process is no doubt essential to the ratification of the verdict.

The perusal, however, may only strengthen the inevitable reflection on all this work, that itself does not possess the "inevitableness" assigned, sternly but not unjustly, to poetry in Wordsworth's saying. Much of it is more than passable; some of it is distinctly good. But the second quality is rare, and even the first not abundant, in the work of Francesco Vintha, who takes liberties with the order of words, abuses the trisyllabic ending disgracefully in his elegiacs, and achieves neither the pointedness of the Latin nor the unlaboured elegance of the Greek epigram. He shows, perhaps as badly as any one, the tendency of the poet of this class to become a mere copy-of-verses man, and not even to turn out his copies of verse in good condition. Fabio Segni, if not much better in matter, is far superior in form, and now and then is really elegant, especially in choriambic metres. It may seem likely to be much more interesting to pass from these respectable nonentities to a real poet like Berni, and see what he can do in Latin. But the hope will be disappointed. Neither the vigour of some of his Italian things (such especially as the famous onslaught on Aretino, which would have done very well in the tongue of Catullus) nor the grace of others appears here, and Berni is particularly unlucky in attempts to imitate the Catullian diminutives, and the habit which the great poet of Verona has of "turning the word" and playing on it in a fashion of quasi-refrain.[1] The few epigrams of Benedetto Accolti (1497-1549) are conventional to desperation—on Pan and the Nymphs, on Innocence and Sleep, on stock fancy personages, or rather names, like Lycoris and Lycon. Of the quintet the best appearance is made, as might perhaps have seemed likely, by the variously tried literary craftsmanship of Varchi, which approves itself here also very fairly; yet even here it is difficult to single out any one piece for special praise.

The more numerous and more selectly represented contents of Ubaldini's book promise better entertainment. The elegiacs of Annibale della Croce have some merit. But why should a man, if the whole style did not tempt to triviality, think it worth while to turn "Donec gratus eram" into a longer metre, changing the names and a few of the words, but keeping as much as possible?[2] Aonio Paleario, who is better

[1] See especially *De Glyce*, *Carm. V. Hetr. Poet.*, p. 127.

[2] See *Carm. Poet. Nobil.*, f. 6, *Horatiana Imitatio* (*Cruceii et Lyces Dialogus*). The metre is elegiac.

known for mystic strains, attempts[1] an epithalamium for Niccolò Marino and Luisa Mendoza, and hashes up the old *clichés* of the subject with the utmost coolness; indeed much of this and his other work is mere cento. There is a touch of poetry, though no great correctness, in Antonio Marino's[2] iambic dimeters to the Evening Star; but Tebaldeo of Ferrara (f. 25, *v.*) oversteps the bounds of the most indulgent Humanism in his echo-verses. Some of these may excite a momentary terror as one thinks what would have been the results, not so long ago, to the English schoolboy if he had ventured to send up such lines as—

> "Æstus non facit hoc spes moriens? Oriens,"

or—

> "Orem animo exanimi pestiferam? Æstiferam,"

which is near nonsense without the context, and not very much farther off with it. The "Acon and Leonilla" epigram quoted above is here given (f. 29, *v.*) to Basilio Zanoni of Bergamo. Molza's coaxing verses of consolation (f. 37) to the Spanish courtesan Beatrice on the loss of her hair are exceedingly pretty, though rather for their good-natured and affectionate tone than for any great neatness of execution. The fine poem to Henry VIII. above noticed, and the

[1] See *Carm. Poet. Nobil.*, f. 17. Antonio della Paglia or Aonius Palearius (—— ?-1570) was one of the school of Italian semi-Protestants, but escaped the fate of some of them. His chief work is also in our kind, the long Latin poem *De Immortalitate Animorum*, which appears in Pope's collection, and has been praised rather beyond its deserts.

[2] Ibid., f. 25 *v.* 24.

still finer *Ad Sodales,* also referred to, give him by far the best position in the whole volume. This last-mentioned piece, written in his last days, with its regrets at the absence from his death-bed of the wife whom he had himself deserted, and its resigned and modest hope of some memory, is really touching. The Odes of Capilupo "intend" rather more than they achieve, and the verses of Geronimo Salina to the luckless Juana of Aragon apply the "Spanish ampulla" with more freedom than success. The verses of La Casa, which hold with Molza's the chief place in the book, surpass them in elegance, though the enigmatic bishop does not, like Molza, show in his Latin verse the same qualities as in his Italian. But La Casa is here very inadequately represented.

Transalpine Latin verse—France.

From him, however, and from his countrymen we must pass northwards to take a glance, since we cannot give more, at the Latin versification of more inclement climes.[1] Two writers, born not merely beyond the Alps but on the shores of the Northern Sea, long divided, and one still deserves, the repute of surpassing any Italian of their own time in skill of this kind. France had no poets of the class as yet to pit against Buchanan (who was indeed almost a Frenchman by domicile) and Johannes Secundus; but she could not lack versifiers,

[1] The almost appalling industry of Gruter followed up the *Delic. Poet. Ital.* (*v. supra*) with 3 vols. of Gallic (1609), 6 of German (1612), and 4 of Belgic (1614) poets in Latin. One of the German vols. has 1700 pp.

and some of them were of note. The unlucky printer-lexicographer Etienne Dolet (1509-1546), whose excellent biographer, the late Mr Christie, has made him better known in England than, save by Mr Christie's own means, he would have been to his own country, wrote verse of some merit in his general *Carmina* (Lyons, 1538) and the *Genethliacum Claudii Fili* next year; Theodore Beza (1519-1605), a Burgundian by birth, if a Swiss by enforced residence, owes a somewhat parti-coloured fame to his *Juvenilia* (Paris, 1548); and Daurat (——?-1588), a star of the Pléiade itself, darted Latin rays rather more willingly and successfully than French, while the list might be very largely extended. But the seventeenth rather than the sixteenth century was the palmy day of French Latin verse.

Johannes Secundus and his imitators.

The most graceful beyond all question of Renaissance Latin writing is to be found in the famous and widely imitated *Basia*[1] of Johannes Nicolaus Secundus. These are thought to have been addressed to a Spanish beauty between 1534 and the author's death two years later, and they appeared in 1539. The learned pains which have been spent on tracing their strain afar off to the Greek Anthology and Catullus, and more immediately to

[1] The recent handy edition of the *Basia*, with a few of the immediate originals and imitations, by Herr Ellinger (Berlin, 1899), is a monument of German industry in its discussion of parallelisms, &c., but also a less admirable model of German abstinence from criticism proper, and even from an account, however succinct, of the author. The other work of Secundus, which will be found in the *Deliciæ Poetarum Belgicorum*, iv. 147 *sq.*, is mostly inferior to the *Basia*.

Beroaldus and others, might have been spared. The lips of Neæra were probably quite sufficient to inspire her lover. But he has put the universalities of the subject with such a combination of scholarship and fire that no doubt he was imitated. There has been an occasional tendency, especially of late years, to sneer at the *Basia* as frigid and vapid. They are really nothing of the sort. A Dutchman, writing in the ghost of a language, was not likely to attain to quite the vividness in different ways of his contemporary Marot's *En la baisant*, or of some of our own Elizabethan, Jacobean, and Caroline pieces in the next generation or the next century. But the verses of Secundus are not mere literary exercises; flesh and blood as well as ink and paper have taken part in their production. Though quite decent, as the author, for once violating decency, himself protests, they are not in the least dull; and the way in which these things should, contrasted with the way in which they should not, be written about may be seen very well by contrasting almost any one of the *Basia* with La Casa's *Capitolo del Bacio*, one of the least offensive of its class. The splendid conclusion of the Eighth—

"O vis superba formæ!"

is not quite equally led up to; indeed the Anacreontic in Latin is apt to take a kind of *staccato* touch. But the hendecasyllabics of the Fifth—

"Dum me mollibus hinc et hinc lacertis"—

are quite delightful, while they are remarkably free

from *clichés*, "lubricus vultus" being almost the only importunate reminiscence. The opening piece—

"Cum Venus Ascanium super alta Cythera tulisset,"

though very pretty and possessing that pictorial quality in which the better Latin poetry of the time often sets a good example to the rising vernaculars, has less individual quality; and the metre of the second, Horatian though it be, is not so well suited to the subject as some others; while the third, aiming at quasi-epigrammatic form, shows us the poet rather "stumbling in paths of alien art." But the Seventh—

"Centum Basia centies"—

again sets tune and words in perfect accordance, and its subject-conceit (the quarrel of the eyes and lips because the eyes cannot see what the lips are kissing) is carried out with the daintiest and most suitable ripple of rhythm and phrase. The Alcaic stanza of the Ninth is rather too stately for these delicate transports: the elegiacs of the following piece, and of others, are far more in harmony. But tempting though it be, one must not mention all, where almost all are good. It is, however, quite worth while to turn over the examples and imitations which Herr Ellinger has subjoined in order to see what a prince of his class was this poet whom the gods took ere Neæra's kisses were dry. The *Osculum Panthiæ* of Filippo Beroaldo (1453-1505), which some would have to be his original, is long, verbose, frigid, and stuffed with classical-dictionary matter. The

Ad Neæram of Petrus Crinitus, though better, has none of the liquid fire of Johannes, nor has Sannazar's *Nina*. Among the imitators Buchanan is simply not to be mentioned; and though Bonefonius deserves a little better of his Pancharis and Muretus of his Margaret, Secundus is left without another second.

For German-Latin verse of our period two recent volumes[1] will give us an excellent text. There was, as has been already hinted, no subject for which the new Latin was more used, nor was there any perhaps for which it was better suited, than for occasional poetry. The second of the volumes cited contains a selection of "poems of places," the chief devoted to Nuremberg and embellished with interesting "cuts" by or after Dürer; the first is a more varied selection from a much vaster body of amatory and miscellaneous lyric. Eobanus Hessus, who has sometimes been regarded as the best poet of this class, figures in both, and in the *Lyrics* appear Euricius Cordus and others of the "Erfurt poets," who had so much to do with the rally of German Humanism in the *Epistolæ Obscurorum*.

Other Latin verse—German.

But what of the results? That they are much easier and (in a sense) pleasanter to read than the rough German of the time is of course perfectly true; that men like Hessus and Cordus had infinitely more sense of literature, more criticism, more of other

[1] *Deutsche Lyriker des 16ten Jahrhunderts.* Ed. Ellinger (Berlin, 1893). *Eobani Hessi Noriberga Illustrata,* &c. Ed. Neff (Berlin, 1896).

things, than such a man as Hans Sachs, is almost a truism. And yet the whole has the not unpleasant but faint and pale scent and look of *pot-pourri* as compared, not exactly with a brier-rose, but at anyrate with ragged-robin and meadow-sweet. The hexameters of the *Noriberga* are capital things of their kind — nervous enough and smooth enough, their cadence varied with a good deal of skill, the description by no means lacking in vividness, and the diction by no means too full of the curse of modern Latin, gradus-epithets and "tags." Among the Lyrics the same author's admiring Elegiacs to and on Luther combine spirit and polish; the Eclogue of Cordus, *Silvius and Polypheme,* has a good flow; the *Dream* of Melanchthon, in which Ajax and Christ figure, is vigorous and effective; Mynsinger's Sapphic hymn on the Ascension is neat; and among the erotic and Anacreontic poems, though nothing comes up to Johannes Secundus, the *Quisquis tela Cupidinis* of Bruno Seidelius, the pieces to Rosina of Paulus Melissus, and the *Suspiria* of Tobias Scultetus, though these latter would not commend themselves to a severely Ovidian form-master, are thoroughly agreeable to read. Also Sebastian Schefferus is scandalous but amusing in his "Nine Skins of Women," and distinctly ingenious in the epigram which explains why sheepish boys look at the ground while lively girls look at young men. But always less or more, except in forms and tones for which the vernaculars were not yet sufficiently accomplished, there is the sense of bastardy, of sterility, of mere imitation and echo as regards the past, and of want of promise and germ for the future.

English.

The production of England in this branch during the Tudor time was abundant in quantity—the mere dedicatory and complimentary verses prefixed to books, English as well as Latin in text, would make a very large collection. At the very beginning the Latin verse of More (see note, *infra*, p. 87) at once attained European recognition. At the end the Epigrams of John Owen (1560-1622) had an even greater vogue on the Continent, and served, in England itself, as a sort of centre to a very large body of epigrammatic writing, in English and Latin, which extends from Heywood at the beginning of the sixteenth century to Tom Brown at the end of the seventeenth, and which would be well worth collection and study. Yet the laureate of Great Britain in these alien bays during this time was no Englishman but a Scot.

Buchanan.

Not the least notable or characteristic name in the present chapter is that of George Buchanan (1506-82),[1] who at one time earned for his native country of Scotland the credit of possessing the best Latinist living in Europe, a possession long considered as implying that of the foremost of European men of letters. This point of view is unlikely to be

[1] The standard edition of Buchanan's Latin works is the fine one of Ruddiman, 2 vols. folio, Edinburgh, 1715: of his English, that of Mr Hume Brown for the Scottish Text Society, Edinburgh, 1892. Another signal instance of Buchanan's fame is that Rapin, a century later, in spite of all national, political, and ecclesiastical grudges, allows him "Odes worthy of Antiquity."

recovered; but the fact that it was once taken by a man like Dr Johnson, to whom Buchanan's nationality was, to say the least, not a cause of attraction, and to whom both his principles and his character were in the strongest degree repulsive, would of itself give him a place here. Fortunately we can afford to dismiss those principles and that character, as well as the life which exhibited them, with the remark that the principles may commend themselves to those who agree with them, and that the character may seem excusable to those who hold the principles.

But the works are not so to be dismissed; and with the exception of the *Detectio Mariæ* it is easy, and even in that case not impossible, to a trained critical intelligence to examine them with due impartiality. It is fortunate, that while in the case of Erasmus, to whose place, though not to whose gifts in prose, Buchanan succeeded, and whom he actually surpassed by his skill in verse, we possess no vernacular compositions to assist us in our view of his Latin books, Buchanan has left us vernacular work of unmistakable power. The most famous and the best of it, the violent diatribe against Maitland of Lethington, known as the *Cameleon*, is perhaps intentionally as well as unintentionally embroiled and obscure in style. The weapon is neither rapier, nor broadsword, nor even club; but a sort of *morgenstern* or ghisarm, as complicated as it is clumsy. Yet the swashing-blow is of formidable sharpness as well as force.

For such elegance as Buchanan possessed we must look to his verse, which is also the only part of his

Latin work that possesses any interest, except for the historian. The *Detectio* itself, the *Res Scoticæ*, and the *De Jure Regni*, as well as the *Letters*, exhibit to the full the study and the practice of a diligent scholar and imitator of Cicero and of Livy. But they have no other literary interest, and this is itself but small. Even in Cicero himself the prevalence of the same forms of speech and phrase, the set rhetoric, the method as of *cloisonné* enamel, the carefully wrought and curiously selected diction, are found, by some readers at least, more curious than delightful, and more tedious than curious. In a Scotsman writing at the most burning, if not the most shining, crisis of Scottish history, the tagging of stale shreds and thrums becomes inexpressibly unreal and almost positively offensive, quite apart from the matter. And it contrasts curiously with the sentiment expressed years before by Ascham on the other side of the Border, that it was time to "write English matters in the English tongue for English men."

His Prose.

Let us turn, however, to the verses,[1] of which a Scotophobe, a Tory, a hater of Republicans, and a severe critic like Dr Johnson, said that their author was "the only man of genius his country ever produced," that he was not merely "a very fine poet," but "a great poetical genius." It was the dedication to Queen Mary, *Nympha Caledoniæ*, which (though he did not illustrate it therefrom) elicited from the dictator the observation that all the modern languages

[1] These are obtainable separately in more than one pocket form. My copy of this is the edition of Wetstein (Amsterdam, 1687).

could not furnish such melody as Latin verse—an observation which of course simply means that Johnson's ear, by nature or training, or both, could appreciate

> "Formosam resonare doces Amaryllida sylvas,"

and could not appreciate

> "But tricks his beams, and with new-spangled ore
> Flames in the forehead of the morning sky";

or—

> "Dolce color d'oriental zaffiro";

or—

> "Un doux nenni avec un doux sourire";

or—

> "So diu blomen uz dem grase dringent."

The Psalms and their Dedication.

The *Nympha Caledoniæ* is certainly a piece of very smooth elegiacs; and as everybody has not Buchanan in their hands nowadays, we may give it, leaving readers to find matter of piquancy, or matter of disgust, in the remembrance that the poet not long afterwards discovered this paragon of her sex, this honour to her ancestors, this pattern of virtue, this blessing to her country, to be a pest to her country, a reproach to her sex, an incarnation of all the vices, and a scandal to her race:—

> "Nympha Caledoniæ quæ nunc feliciter oræ
> Missa per innumeros sceptra tueris avos:
> Quæ sortem antevenis meritis, virtutibus annos,
> Sexum animis, morum nobilitate genus,
> Accipe (sed facilis) cultu donata Latino
> Carmina, fatidici nobile regis opus.

Illa quidem, Cirrha procul et Permesside lympha,
  Pœne sub Arctoi sidere nata poli :
Non tamen ausus eram male natum exponere fœtum,
  Ne mihi displiceant quæ placuere tibi.
Nam quod ab ingenio domini sperare nequibant,
  Debebunt genio forsitan illa tuo."

The verses are certainly of the neatest, and Ovid would, I think, have gladly signed the italicised pentameter. For the spirit and its sequel, we may remember that the pedant is generally by turns sycophant and lampooner, and that the same person is not seldom the recipient of his absolute impartiality in the discharge of these functions.

It is less easy to share the admiration, which was once, no doubt, sincere, was for a long time fashionable, at least with scholars, and is even now in a dim sort of way traditionally existent, in regard to the version of the Psalms to which these lines serve as Introduction. That they are sufficiently elegant Latin is quite true;[1] but then elegant Latin is about the last kind of medium suitable to Hebrew poetry. It is almost impossible to describe, but it is worth while to recommend actual experience of, the curious shock of the contrast which strikes one between the fragments of the Vulgate which, as usual, head the versions, and the first lines in the same, or nominally the same, language which follow. Nor is this the only shock of the kind. Johnson, whose liking for and acquaintance with modern Latin verse gave him probably a greater

[1] Porson, I think, is said to have found false quantities in Buchanan ; but they are certainly not numerous, and are probably, as a rule, rather false readings.

right to speak than any one now possesses, specially commended Buchanan for his freedom from mere *cento*-work. This freedom may be comparative, but is certainly not positive. For instance, the 4th Psalm (*Cum Invocarem*) begins—

> "O Pater, o hominum divumque æterna potestas."

It is impossible that this "hominum divumque potestas" should not have been suggested to Buchanan by, and that it should not in turn suggest to any tolerable Latinist, not merely the actual phrase in Virgil, but also a certain "hominum divumque *voluptas*"; equally impossible that the contrast should not strike one as damaging in respect of poetry, and slightly ludicrous in point of context and subject. For the longer and more descriptive psalms Buchanan has sometimes selected the continuous hexameter, which has no ill effect in its way; and he is also not sparing of the dimeter and trimeter couplet, which is also tolerable. But the more definitely lyric metres, especially the Alcaic and the various choriambic arrangements, are equally incongruous in sound and in association, while the skip of the Latin Sapphic, so different (at least as usually ordered) from the Greek, is still more out of keeping. David might have danced before the ark to that measure, but he certainly very seldom sings to it.

Perhaps the chief historic interest of Buchanan's Psalter is that its production and popularity not improbably helped that disastrous process of translating the great mediæval hymns which was carried on during the sixteenth and seventeenth centuries, and which ultimately deprived the metrical portions of the Breviary of a very great part, if not of all, of the ineffable music and charm of those wonderful compositions. Even if the work of a heretic cannot be supposed to have had much direct influence in this way, it is none the less significant as a symptom.

The tragedies, translated and original, will receive their best notice in the chapter on drama; the *De Sphæra* and the miscellaneous poems concern us here.

The De Sphæra.

Not much need be said of the *De Sphæra*, where the poet has endeavoured to treat a Lucretian subject in a Virgilian manner, and has at least succeeded in accomplishing, with extraordinary diligence and cleverness, an exercise which was not worth accomplishing at all by any one who had emerged from the *status pupillaris*. To have written such a description of the planets, for instance, as that in the Second Book (p. 129 of the folio, p. 429 duodec.) would not merely be creditable to any undergraduate and an extraordinary feat in any schoolboy, but it would argue in both the acquisition of faculties in literature which could almost certainly be turned to uses both of profit and delight, and of intellectual habits serviceable in every relation of life. As a pastime of maturer years it would be liberal and refreshing. But as forming part of a serious and adult performance in some thousands of lines, treating a subject which requires prose, and had best be done in vernacular prose, it is not much more than naught.

The long satire of the *Franciscanus* weakens its

satire on priestcraft and monkery by a profusion of detail which never once collects itself in one of the true Juvenalian onslaughts; while in the epigrams of the *Fratres Fraterrimi* we look equally in vain for the salt of Martial, though not in vain for his ribaldry. So that the results of a rather tedious reading are, first the conviction that most of the things are impossible to quote, and then the consolation that not one of them is worth quoting.

The *Elegies* are very much better. Of no metre was Buchanan such a master as of this, and the wide range of his Ovidian and Propertian models allowed him a certain apparent unconventionality even in his conventions. The woes of a Professor of Humanity at Paris, leaving his bed at five o'clock to wield the tawse in one hand and the *Virgil* in the other, correcting and flogging all day, open the series with no feigned note. And though the succeeding poems mostly display the artificiality and sometimes the licence of Latin, they are always pleasant to read for mastery of metre and phrase, not interfered with by too great length on the one hand, by brevity without point on the other, or by radical unsuitableness of subject on both. Even where he is both prolix and trivial (as he can be), the complete absence of effort and the easy flow of the verse produce a certain soothing effect. The *Sylvæ*, exclusively hexametrical, supply the (to us) bitter irony of the Epithalamium of King Francis and Queen Mary, and the more genial, though equally obvious, satire of the birthday poem for the British Solomon. For this kind of artificial

The minor poems.

work no language is so well suited as Latin, and none disguises the essential hollowness better. Some of the hendecasyllables addressed to Neæra are really pretty, and seem now and then to throb with something more like blood than the ink (or rather the neat gall) which usually runs in Buchanan's pedant veins. Those on the famous diamond heart which Mary sent to Elizabeth only just miss, and perhaps do not entirely miss, a great success. The conventional scurrility of most of the so-called *Iambics* is, as before, relieved with little wit; but the more varied subjects and greater bulk of the three books of *Epigrams* and the one of *Miscellanies* may seem almost certain to give better results.

They do, as a matter of fact, display Buchanan as an *artifex* to some advantage. Leonora and Neæra are still contrasted with an odd mixture of convention and sincerity; for though much of the abuse of Leonora is mere copy of Horace in his more vulgar moods, the continual iteration of the complaint that she admits the love of *coqui* seems to correspond to something actual. Indeed it is natural that the tutor should be jealous of the *chef.* But the complimentary addresses, sometimes to persons of real merit and interest such as Ascham and Jewel; the emblematic poems, and some of the epitaphs and other pieces, once more show us capitally the singular suitability of classical Latin for the "occasional" verse. There is, perhaps, not a happier instance anywhere of orthodox but not cut-and-dried expression of the pedagogic spirit than the Sapphics *Ad Juventutem Burdigalensem* (which *juventus*, by the way, included, among others,

Montaigne). On the whole, while we shall seek without finding that "great poetic genius" which Johnson's different interpretation of the words enabled him (perhaps on his own standard truly) to find in Buchanan, we shall be able to allow him in his Latin verse the praise, lesser but not small, of having accomplished that which he set himself to perform. But we shall scarcely find in him much cause for mitigation of the judgment which has to be pronounced on this whole class of work, and which may be thus summed up: The modern Latin poet, except in the cases when his own vernacular was at the time of writing too unaccomplished in itself or too limited in its diffusion, always sins by neglecting to adorn the Sparta to which he owes allegiance. Even then the things that he can do better in Latin are mostly things that need not be done. Taking Buchanan's prose and verse together, it may even be doubted whether he had very much literary faculty beyond vigour and the knack of copying the ancients. In other words, both the heaviest curses of the rhetorician are on him; for if he had some skill in making the worse appear the better reason, he was still more often occupied in giving an appearance of existence and even of beauty to what had no reason to exist, and no right to be beautiful.

Later Latin poetry.

In the later volumes of this History there will in all probability be little room for noticing books written in Latin, and especially little for the later fruits of Latin verse. We may therefore, without impropriety, take a foreshortened view of these. During the rest of the sixteenth century, and during the greater part of the seventeenth, the language of the Republic of Letters held its place, and something more than its place. Nor were the results of its exercise, as they have been called by a rather unworthy sneer, a *littérature de collége* only. Enough has been said already of the limitations and drawbacks to which this literature was inevitably exposed. But it had still a real, though always a diminishing, reason for existence. That this existence was partly due to delusion must indeed be acknowledged. The Baconian notion (derived or partly derived from Cheke, *v. infra*) that the modern languages would "play the bankrupt" with books had no solid foundation, and was founded in part on the unjust contempt with which the Renaissance regarded the inestimable vernacular products of the Middle Ages, in part on a hard-driven metaphor. And it has been punished as it sinned by the equally unjust neglect which for full a century past has come upon modern Latin literature itself. But the notion of a general European audience instead of a merely national one was not in itself ignoble; and to such an audience in the political and social circumstances of the time no vernacular —not even Italian—could hope to present itself.

At the same time a critic who could have raised himself to a kind of "Pisgah sight" of literature would even then have distrusted Latin as a literary medium. Almost before the end of the sixteenth century, and with increasing decision during the beginning of the seventeenth, it came to be best written in the smaller and less important nations—in those, too, which had dwindling or not yet adult vernaculars. The Scots, the Dutch, the Poles, the Germans, were great at Latin; the French, the English, the Spaniards, the very Italians themselves, grew less and less expert in it, though some of these latter translated their works into Latin in order to cater for the larger auditory.

For some fifty years after the stricter limits of the present volume have closed we still find Latin competing, both in verse and prose, as a general literary medium with every language on its own ground. But the books in it which have lived in general literary history are few, and among the bilingual writers the vernacular works, as in the case of Bruno (1549-1600), have always carried it over the "regular"; while of those who mainly or wholly wrote in Latin, such as Campanella (1569-1639) the memory has become dim and second-hand. In the first half of the seventeenth century two admirable Latin verse-writers, Arthur Johnstone (1587-1641)[1] and Casimir Sarbiewski (1595-1640), compel the admiration of scholars, if they are hardly known to the general reader; but the one represents a vernacular which, after a short but brilliant flourishing time, was about to drop into the state of a dialect, and the other one which had not yet attained to anything like majority among the languages of Europe. A

[1] Johnstone was part editor, and in much greater part author, of the *Deliciæ Poetarum Scotorum* (2 vols., Amsterdam, 1637).

group or succession of groups of brilliant French hymn-writers, of whom the brothers Santeuil (1630-1697; 1628-1674) are the chief, puts in some little excuse for the persevering efforts of the Roman curia to emasculate and "restore" the exquisite hymnaries of the Middle Ages. In England poets or men of letters of the greatest distinction in successive generations—Milton, Addison, Johnson—cling to the tradition of verse-writing, and Pope edits a collection of Humanist poetry. But even those who take most delight in Latin poetry will hardly admire with warmth the *Epitaphium Damonis* when they think of *Lycidas*, the *Epigrammata* and even the *Elegies* when they think of the *Sonnets*. If the *Barometri Descriptio*, and the *Sphæristerium*, and the *Machinæ Gesticulantes*, and *O qui canoro blandius Orpheo*, can be read with much less distraction, this is due, first, to the fact that Addison was not, in English, a great poet at all, that his poetical gifts were much more adequate to his actual occupation; and, secondly, to the fact that all these poems frankly range themselves under the class of the "copy-of-verses," the kind of poem which is not inevitable at all, and does not pretend to be so. And this is increasingly the case with the Latin poems of Johnson, with the version of the *Messiah*, the *Urbane nullis fesse laboribus*, and the pieces on Skye. If it is not so with some of his short religious epigrams and ejaculations, that is precisely because the form and the thought are here indissolubly married, and the memory of *Vexilla Regis* and *Dies Iræ* carries *Summe dator vitæ* and *Eterne rerum conditor* under the shadow of its wing.

The writer of these pages would be more chagrined than by any other possible misunderstanding if it were to be supposed that these remarks, or any that have been made in this chapter, rank him in the society of those who regard the practice of Latin and Greek verse as mischievous or superfluous in youth, and as trivial in age. Experience intrenches him impregnably in the belief that the disuse of composition in the classical tongues, and especially in their verse, is the greatest and most fatal mistake of recent educational reforms, and is more responsible than anything else for the decline, at once of elegance and of vigour, in vernacular English compositions during the last two or three decades. As for later exercises in either harmony, they possess the double character of all worthy pastimes, that of giving at once pleasure and exercise itself. But excellence as discipline and excellence as pastime are quite different things from the substantive excellence of literature. Whensoever a language has attained to such a position of importance, and to such a faculty of expression that it is adequate to the conveying of literary matter that is worth the conveyance, then for a man of genius, or even a man of talent, to write in another language, dead or foreign, for any other purpose than mere amusement and display of his versatility, is *μόχθος περισσὸς κουφόνους τ' εὐηθία.* This was not the case with Erasmus or even with the authors of the *Epistolæ*

Obscurorum Virorum, and they were accordingly justified, and their books have lived. It was dubiously the case with More. It was quite certainly *not* the case with Ariosto or with Molza, with La Casa, or later with Milton.

Yet when all is said, how venial (except in the case of the very greatest men, whose every word in their proper medium is priceless) are transgressions of this sort! How near to virtues they come when we compare them with the slovenly facilities of the vernacular, wherewith in ever-increasing measure we have been afflicted for these last three centuries! To these Latin works, even to the merest exercises among them, and the least successful of these, there went some knowledge, some pains, even some rudimentary exertion of judgment and taste, and some special selection of subject, language, form. He who seeks similar monuments in vernacular literature had need to be much more circumspect.

Macaronic verse.

Before passing to the Latin prose—in some cases so much more brilliant—which also distinguishes our time, I have thought it allowable, and perhaps on the whole most convenient, to notice the singular freaks in what is called "Macaronic." For these are closely connected both with the popularity of the Latin and the immaturity of the vernaculars, and they contribute to European literature work but a little below the best of the period in power.

There is no more curious figure (in the best sense of

the adjective) to be found during our period than that of Girolamo Folengo,[1] or Teofilo, or Merlinus Coccaius, or Limerno Pitocco, or Triperuno, of which abundant sheaf of aliases the first is his proper name and surname, the second Christian name that which he assumed in cloister life, and the third, fourth, and fifth the various appellations with which he subscribed different parts of his eccentric but far indeed from negligible work.

Folengo.

As has been suggested in the note, Folengo is very much "for thoughts" to those who are not happy unless they can connect literature with philosophy, sociology, religion, and the like outside things; but his purely literary interest is amply sufficient and in one sense unique. What celebrity he has enjoyed of late years has been very mainly due to the fact of his being to some extent a creditor of Rabelais, who

[1] Most conveniently accessible in Signor Attilio Portioli's edition of all but the late and (it is said) negligible divine poems (3 vols., Mantua, 1883-89). This contains not merely the *Baldus*, but the *Zanitonella*, the *Moscheis*, the Italian *Orlandino*, and the very remarkable, though more than enigmatic *Caos*. This last, of which even Mr Symonds, a warm admirer of Folengo, says nothing (probably because in its great rarity before this reprint he had not come across it), is a partly Italian, partly Macaronic medley of prose and verse, where figure three of Folengo's female relations — his mother Paola, his sister Corona, and his niece Livia — the poet himself under his various *noms de guerre*, and divers abstractions. It is in part an apology for his youthful errors, in part a philosophico-religious allegory of the kind not uncommon in Italy between the days of Francesco Colonna and those of Bruno. For that very puzzling history of Italian thought at the time, which, despite the pains and genius which have been spent on it, has never been fully cleared up, it has probably not a little importance. But it scarcely belongs, like its fellows, to the text as literature.

refers to him as Merlinus Coccaius, and who may not at all improbably have borrowed from him not merely something of Panurge (who is in parts very like the Coccaian Cingar), but even something of the whole notable Gargantuan and Pantagruelian Odyssey. He is, however, far indeed from being obliged to rely on the calling in of this lent splendour. In three respects — as the chief, without like or second, of Macaronic poetry, as a master of expression in Latin, Macaronic, and Italian, and as a satiric realist of remarkable force, with an amount of imagination to which the realist does not often attain—he deserves a place only below the very greatest of the period.

In a History of European Literature the first claim is not the least. The scorn with which Macaronics are frequently, if not always, spoken of is not the least unwise of scorns—which is saying a good deal. It is true that the word has several senses. In its widest it is applied to a deliberately mixed jargon of different languages — Greek and Latin, Latin and modern of various kinds—the words being used in each case according to their own grammar, and as they would have been used in continuous work of their own languages. Examples of this may be found (not to mention Cicero's constant introduction of Greek words into his letters) in Ausonius (especially in the *Epistle to Paulus*) and in many of the popular Latin poems of the Middle Ages. It not seldom produces an amusing effect in a short piece, but would be very tiresome in a long one. The stricter Macaronic dialect is formed by the admixture of pure Latin words with words in some modern language formed and inflected as if they were Latin. The Macaronic writer of this stricter school would never have been in any danger of offending Dr Johnson by making Carteret a dactyl, though he might have taken the liberty of scanning "Carteretus" "Carterētus," or "Carterĕtus," according as he was writing hendecasyllabics or hexameters.

Macaronics of this sort were written, during and after the Humanist period, in most European languages, the inducements being the familiarity of writers and educated readers with both tongues, and the amusing effect that most jargon has till it gets wearisome. But, for reasons the most obvious, no language offered such facilities for the practice as Italian. Not only did the words assume forms very similar to those which they probably, if not certainly, held during the obscure passage of Latin into Italian itself, but it is by no means certain that divers of the Italian terms now hatted and booted with Latin garb had not actually existed in the vernacular speech of Italy during classic times. It is not rash to say that some of Folengo's own Mantuan patois may very possibly have been familiar, in much the same form, to Virgil as a boy.

Accordingly an Italian, and specially North Italian, school of Macaronic poets had arisen long before Folengo.[1] By these, however, Macaronic had been

[1] On the chiefs of this, Tifi Odassi, Alione d'Asti, &c., see Symonds' *Italian Literature*, chap. xiv. But those who can should consult Delepierre's *Macaronéana* (Paris, 1852, published also at

chiefly used for burlesque *novelle*, comic scenes and characters of a detached kind, and sometimes for local or other satire. It was reserved for Folengo to use it as an engine of imitative attack on the two most popular and considerable forms of verse in the Italy of the early sixteenth century, the Epic and the Pastoral.

Folengo resembled his great follower in being for most of his life a self-unfrocked monk; but, unlike Rabelais, he was of noble birth. He was born at Cipada, the village which he has drawn so freely in *Baldus*, was a student at Bologna, a pupil of Pomponazzo, and seems to have been driven to take the cowl by the wildness of his conduct. He joined the Benedictines at Brescia, and took Teofilo for his "name of religion"; but after a few years, in 1515,

His life

Brighton; there is a second part, London, 1862, which I do not possess), and the Italian collection of *Cinque Poete* (the usual *five*) *Maccheronci* (Milan, 1864). The contents, however, require a rather strong stomach, and a brain agile in the interpretation of jargon, from the reader. They confirm the existence of a sort of gallimaufry of Romance, older and younger, connected with hybrid French-Italian romances of the Carlovingian cycle, and they show how a person of genius can raise the basest of styles and lingos to—or near—literature. Perhaps it may be well here to take notice of another jargon, which is sometimes called the *lingua pedantesca*, and opposed formally to Macaronic as substituting a Latinised Italian for an Italianated Latin. It is found to some extent in the *Hypnerotomachia* (see *The Transition Period*, p. 393), and still more eminently, it is said, in some smaller, rarer, and less noteworthy productions which I have not thought it necessary to hunt up. For it seems to me a mistake to isolate this "pedantesque." It is, as Mr Gregory Smith hints *in loc. cit.*, simply the Italian variety of that "aureate," *rhétoriqueur*, "ink-horn" jargon which overflowed all Europe in the fifteenth century, and for which Italian naturally offered peculiar facility.

when he was not five-and-twenty, fled from his convent with a certain Girolama Dieda, with whom he seems to have been passionately in love, and who long accompanied him, it is said, in the wanderings about Italy, then necessary to a man living by his wits. He was still quite young when the long *Baldus* or *Macaronea par excellence* appeared, and he seems to have remained eleven years a wanderer. But after the *Orlandino* he wrote the repentant *Caos* in 1527, was taken back with the ease which still governed ecclesiastical things (though it was on the point of being exchanged for the severity of the Roman Catholic Reaction), accomplished certain pious works, and died, still in middle age, in 1544. There is, however, a good deal of uncertainty about all these events. He is thought by some to have glanced severely at La Dieda in the *Baldus;* but the reference seems to me of the most doubtful character, and a passage in *Caos,* which contains her name in an unmistakable acrostic and is animated with equally unmistakable affection, is years later. That his verse is often extremely severe on love and on women is true; but he was a monk, and an Italian, and a satirist.

And minor works.

He was also something very like a man of genius; and savage as he can be now and then, coarse as he is too often, his work seldom or never leaves that "bad taste in the mouth" which is too frequently the consequence of reading Italian of this time when it is indecorously amusing, or that inclination to cover a yawn with a "bravo!" which comes on us when it is decorously rhetorical.

His talent shows better in the Macaronic pieces than in the vernacular *Orlandino*, and better in the *Baldus* and the *Zanitonella* than in the *Moscheis*. This last, though not unamusing, is only one of the numerous imitations of the *Batrachomyomachia*. The *Orlandino* may be open to the charge of linguistic and metrical shortcomings; my own Italian is not choice enough to make these teasing to me. But it is certainly open to one far more formidable from the literary point of view, the charge which was once put in the question: "X., what is the good of throwing your clumsy half-bricks, when Y. has just been shooting his beautiful silver arrows?" With Pulci or Politian (Folengo seems to have believed in Politian's authorship) long before, with the great *Orlando Furioso* itself just out, and with Berni's rehandling of the *Innamorato* coming, Italian hardly wanted a thing like the *Orlandino*, which is not only a fragment but a fragment of uncertain purpose, now burlesquing the romances, now violently attacking the monks, and now adding to this attack something like an open display of Lutheranism. It is, however, full of vigour: and there is little doubt that Rabelais knew it, as well as the *Macaronea*.

Before coming to this latter we must devote a little space to the *Zanitonella*, where Folengo is very clever and almost good-humoured. The absurdities of the conventional pastoral, and the crudities of the real, are displayed in a most suitable medium. The cruelty of Giovanina (Zanina in Lombardo-Venetian), the sufferings of Tonello, the

The Zanitonella.

good advice in vain of his friend Salvigno, and the final revolt of the injured swain, are all told in a series of Eclogues, *Sonolegie,* and *Strambottolegie,* in elegiacs or hexameters, where the quaint lingo suits itself to the purpose singularly well.

The Baldus *or* The *Baldus* tries a higher flight, and (though Folengo was, in fact, anticipating most of the critics) observes, with what looks like intentional irreverence, all the conditions which for two centuries were to exercise the mind of critical Europe about a "heroic poem":—the noble origin of the hero, his early struggles, his friends and enemies, the *deorum ministeria,* the visit to the infernal regions, and the rest. It is also in uniform hexameters, which sometimes observe fairly classical Latin for a batch of lines together and then break off, only the more amusingly, into the grotesque, but spirited and by no means always unmusical, jargon of Macaronic proper.

The Macaronea *itself.* From more than one feature in his work Folengo would seem to have been of those who, sometimes not in the least from poverty of imagination, like to repeat and re-work their motives. The earlier cantos of the *Macaronea* exhibit this feature, both in reference to the *Orlandino,* which, though published later, was we know written earlier, and to the *Zanitonella.* The birth and parentage of Baldus and Orlandino are extremely similar, and many points of the *Zanitonella* repeat themselves with a difference in the earlier *Macaronea.* It is only after the Tenth Canto, when the hero is freed from prison by the devices of Cingar, that the poem rises higher than village and domestic quarrels. Baldus, Cingar, the giant Fracassus, and the dog-man Falchettus set out on a series of adventurous travels, in which they are joined by others, from the Virgin Knight Leonardo (who is slain by bears because he will not yield to the blandishments of a sorceress) down to miscellaneous ne'er-do-wells.[1] They suffer a great tempest—wherein Cingar's terrors furnished the model to those of Panurge[2]—they visit the stars, they study the sciences, they have difficulties with pirates. But the later books settle down into a curious battle between Baldus and his "barons" on the one hand and the community of witches and warlocks on the other. They first encounter the above-mentioned sorceress, Muselina, and then the Queen of the Witches, Smyrna Culfora (Mr Symonds reads *G*ulfora), in her capital, which Fracassus destroys, while Baldus and the rest make a murder grim and great of the queen and her courtiers. Emboldened by this success, they visit the infernal regions themselves in the last three books; and the poem closes half abruptly, half properly, in the depths of an enormous gourd, the destined region of vain poets in Hell, where they lose teeth and grow them again perpetually in punishment for their lies.

[1] It is worth observing that at the outset of the voyage Folengo brings in, as an already known and settled thing, the hatred between peasants and soldiers, which, beginning no doubt still earlier, is so evident in the sixteenth and seventeenth centuries, and which serves as a motive as late as the *Simplicissimus* of Grimmelshausen, and perhaps later still.

[2] As the adventure of the sheep had previously done. Rabelais, however, improves on both most remarkably.

Now Merlinus Coccaius himself is a false poet: therefore he will be detained in the gourd: therefore he can go no farther. Nothing can be more logical.

The respectable folk who think that everything has an explanation, and are miserable till they have got this explanation into a condition satisfactory to themselves, have not meddled much with Folengo; indeed, for centuries past he has been very little read. But it is obvious that the Delilah of interpretative allegory would have not the slightest difficulty in spreading her snares for his readers; in fact, Mr Symonds all but falls into them, and wrenches himself out with a kind of effort. Those who are content to understand without explaining, and to appreciate without hypothesis, will have no great difficulty in untwining, if they care to do so, the various strands which at least may have made up the fantastic rope of Folengo's thought. It is one of the main glories of Romance that burlesques of it always end by glorifying and illustrating the charms of the Muse of Romance herself, and Folengo is no exception. *Baldus* is a burlesque romance of adventure, no doubt, but it is a romance of adventure all the same. The wayward ex-monk availed himself of what has been called the glorious Romantic freedom to hunt many subordinate hares, and bring a vast amount of miscellaneous oddities into his treasure-house. Lucian was a particularly popular author at this time, and the influence of *The True History* and perhaps other pieces is clear. The character-sense was being much developed, and Cingar is one of the earliest very ambitious and elaborate exercises of it in modern times.

In wit and a certain perenniality and universality he is not the equal of Panurge at his best; but he is a rather better fellow, more practically ingenious, and perhaps truer to the comic side of specially Latin nature. Baldus, like most heroes, is rather colourless; and his anger at finding that his wife Berta, whom he has practically deserted, has married somebody else, is more natural than reasonable; while Berta herself, though quite flesh and blood in her battles with her sister and her pranks on the amorous Tognazzo, disappears early, reappearing but dimly as a witch. The witchcraft episodes are certainly very curious in connection with the extraordinary outburst of fanaticism on that subject in the hundred or hundred and fifty years following. It is not at all improbable that the semi-Protestantism which is unmistakable in the *Orlandino*, and which may hide itself under the mystical circumlocutions of the *Caos*, counts for something in the *Macaronea* itself. And though Italy was never (her sons always having been well educated in a manner) bitten with the education-mania to the same extent as Germany, France, and England, this also appears. But on the whole Folengo exhibits, in a singularly suitable medium, the quaint waywardness of a soul *et vitiis et virtutibus impar*, not quite fortunate in its surroundings at any time, having lost its way in so far as any coherent scheme of life is concerned, but generous, instructed, aspiring. No Italian writer of his time is more affected by Dante, which is in itself a mighty quality. None speaks more generously of Ariosto, his own contemporary, and to some extent the subject of his ironic exercises. His swashing-blows in the combat of Lombard *v.* Tuscan are thoroughly good-humoured; and his Macaronic dialect itself is a sort of sneering concession to the general Italian refusal to recognise an Illustrious Vulgar, and to the endless naggings and nigglings of philological pedants. His hatreds—of the French, who were the curse of Italy throughout his life; of the monks, his sojourn with whom had proved so intolerable; of the landlords, with whom he had also had difficulties in his resourceless wanderings—are never bad-blooded, and always relieved by humour.[1] And as for his lingo, whosoever does not perceive the charm of *parlatus* in

> "Et sic parlatus subito discedit ab illis"

will never perceive it, and whoso does will perceive it at once.[2]

To pass from the artificial verse of the Renaissance,

[1] There are indeed ugly exceptions which remind us that we have, after all, to do with an Italian of the sixteenth century. The worst of these—under the rubric, it is true, of "Atroce supplicio," but related with perfect coolness and apparently no kind of disgust at the torturers—is the story of the horrible mutilations inflicted, without despatching him, but leaving him to be eaten alive by gadflies, on the wretched Podesta, not merely by Baldus, who thinks himself a peasant's son, and though a brave is a decidedly brutal champion throughout,—not merely by Cingar, who *is* a peasant, and of a ruthless and cowardly nature,—but by the stainless knight, Leonardo.

[2] Better still, perhaps, as a single line is the description of the third kind of wine furnished by the abominable hosts—

> "Et qui dum bibitur ventris penetralia *raspat*,"

where the sudden barbarism after the orderly Latin of the first six words gives the real comic surprise.

and from the less really than apparently unnatural Macaronic, to the Latin Prose-writing of the time, is not merely, in the old parallel, to step from a conservatory into a garden, but to pass from a museum of dried plants into the natural wealth of fields and woods. Here, though we may a little regret in some cases that the writers did not use the vernaculars, there is hardly any loss in their doing so. The language which they use was as easy to them as the vernacular itself, and in most cases much better suited to their purpose. Accordingly we have, in the literature to which we are coming, more than one or two of the really great books of the world on any fairly wide estimate of greatness. Yet, neglecting the charge of paradox, we may add that the prose needs less elaborate handling than the verse, for two reasons. First, because the much greater detail which will be given to the best examples of it carries a representative treatment of the rest; and secondly, because a very great deal of it—in fact by far the greatest part—is not really literature at all, but mere journey-work and business communication. The most unsuccessful writer of the most trivial or inelegant Latin verse was at anyrate trying to be a man of letters; in the majority of cases the user of Latin prose was using it merely as he might have used a plate or a spoon, a chair or a table, to carry on the ordinary occupations of life. But the *Colloquies*, the *Utopia*, the *Epistolæ Obscurorum Virorum*, these will give us texts of interest hardly distinguishable from that attaching to the greatest vernacular writings, the *Orlandos* and

Latin Prose-writing.

the *Pantagruels*, of our time. And we shall be able to notice a few minor books and some important classes, incidents, and aspects of literature generally.

Erasmus.

The pathetic story of the hapless and technically lawless loves of Gerard and Margaret—father and mother of Desiderius Erasmus—has been embellished and preserved by the genius of not the least of English novelists.[1] Erasmus was born at Rotterdam in 1467, and after a life even more wandering than that of the average Humanist, died at Basle in 1536. He was educated by the Brothers of the Common Life at Deventer, took (but only provisionally) Augustinian vows, was ordained priest, finished his studies at the sordid Collége de Montaigu at Paris, the butt of all Northern Humanists; spent much time in repeated visits to England, where he learnt Greek at Oxford and taught it at Cambridge; lived in Italy and in the Netherlands, but was in his later years constantly gravitating towards the place of his final sojourn and death. Basle was the home of the great printer Frobenius and the place of publication of Erasmus's own edition of the New Testament, 1516, to which, by common consent, all modern Scriptural study owes its new start. These later years were passed in the controversies, natural at a time of the most violent and revolutionary intellectual excitement, between a man too moderate in temper, too cool in judgment, and too wide-ranging in erudition to be a thorough partisan. Erasmus, though nobody of competence failed to regard him as the

[1] In *The Cloister and the Hearth.*

head of European letters, was the object of abuse from Luther and Hutten as being a Pelagian and not a Protestant; from the extreme and more pedantic defenders of the papacy as being an opponent of Scholastic philosophy, an innovator in Scriptural studies, and a leaner towards heresy; and from Scaliger and others as a satirist of the absurd Ciceronianism which marked the decadence of the Humanist epoch.

Besides the Greek Testament just noted, which requires no further comment here, Erasmus produced a very large amount of work[1] entirely in Latin, and almost entirely (as far as value is concerned, though he wrote verse like other people[2]) in prose. Besides his extensive *Correspondence*, part of which was published in 1529 and reprinted with additions by himself, and the *Colloquies* and *Encomium Moriæ*, which will be fully noticed in a moment, his chief productions are two large collections of *Adagia* (1508) and *Apophthegmata* (1532? 3?), which had immense influence in their own time, but are now chiefly curiosities. They

[1] The fullest edition is that of Leclerc, Lyons, 1703-1706, in ten volumes. Lives of him, down to that of Mr Froude, which has been noticed *supra* in the Preface, are very numerous, the material afforded by the *Letters* being tempting. The separate works are in most cases only obtainable in old editions. But the *Adagia* (especially in abridgments) and the *Apophthegmata* were very often reprinted. The *Colloquia* and the *Encomium Moriæ* occur consecutively in two volumes of the little Tauchnitz classical library, and will be found one of the best of pocket-book companions for a lifetime. Erasmus should never be read in any language but his own Latin, which is a perfectly living tongue and as easy as possible.

[2] There are some seventy pages of it in the *Deliciæ Poetarum Belgicorum*.

contain an enormous collection, constantly enlarged and revised by the author, of stories, sayings, maxims, proverbs, &c., of all times, but especially of ancient times, digested into a sort of moral and intellectual *vade mecum.* The *Adagia* in particular were epitomised in a still voluminous form,[1] and served as a Thesaurus of literary and general culture for some two centuries. So did the *Apophthegmata.*[1] These books show the point of view of the Renaissance admirably, but have not the living and intrinsic literary quality of the *Colloquies.* The *Ciceronianus,* above referred to, is later, and shows us Erasmus from another side, but always with the same innate and constantly maintained good sense, the same quiet but bright and dramatic humour, taking part against the abuse and caricature of that scholarship which, more sensibly used, was one of his own great titles to fame, and seemed to his contemporaries to be his greatest.

The Colloquies.

The *Colloquies* rank among the books which everybody is supposed to have read, though it might perhaps be interesting to test the reality of this supposition in any chance society of well-educated people. However this may be, the book is one of those which can sustain their reputation, and which, read over and over again for many years, at longer or shorter intervals, and in the most diverse conditions of age and knowledge and circumstance, must always please fit readers. It is, indeed, rather an odd book.

[1] Of the epitomised *Adagia* I use the Oxford ed. of 1666, which has more than 800 pp. of small and close print. Of the *Apophthegmata,* that of Ravenstein (Amsterdam, 1671).

One seldom finds the true key to anything in its *Ad Lectorem;* and the elaborate apology, *De Utilitate Colloquiorum,* which the author thought fit to append, though itself by no means devoid either of use or of interest, tells nothing like the whole story. To tell that story might have consisted with the modesty of Erasmus, which, though considerably greater than that of the average Renaissance scholar, was not his strongest quality; but he could hardly have gone far enough from his own work, or regarded it from a sufficient height, to appreciate its true character and excellence. For it is, as may have been said elsewhere, one of the best mirrors of the time, and with the *Utopia,* the *Epistolæ Obscurorum,* and *Gargantua and Pantagruel,* one of the four books of the Manual of the Renaissance out of Italy. In it, as in the others, with the exception of a gleam or two in Rabelais (too often missed by his readers, or at anyrate denied by his critics), we find, indeed, nothing of romance or of poetry—the busy eagerness of the time left little room for such things except in Italy itself, where circumstances infected both either with a sensual and erudite superficiality or with a touch of burlesque. But of the prose, the actual life and business of the time, even of its aspirations beyond mere business in some respects, we find an astonishingly faithful mirror in the *Colloquies.* Of philosophy there is again little; but then the time, out of Italy once more, was not one of abstract philosophising. But there is abundant religion, and of a very good kind. Erasmus has been too often spoken of in this respect, as though he were of the race of Facing-both-ways, if not even of that of By-ends. He must have been a most accomplished hypocrite if this be true, and if, nevertheless, he was the author of the *Pietas Puerilis* and the *Puerpera*, to name no others. For healthy and at the same time amiable morality we may open the book almost at random; while it yields, almost as universally, that cheerful and intelligent interest in humanity and things human which is the best side of the whole movement and period. One may well sigh—though knowing all the time that the Might-have-Been is simply the Might-not-have-Been—to think that this combination of qualities, at once delightful and estimable, should have had to give way to the coarse and earthy partisanship of Luther, to the sour fanaticism of Calvin, and to the reactionary Machiavelism of the Jesuits, in the contest for the position of ruling spirits of the time. And Englishmen—Anglicans at least—will be a little comforted by the thought that in no part of the Christian Church has so much of the spirit of Erasmus been preserved as in the Church of England. Indeed his only drawbacks here are a slight touch, not by any means a strong one, of Puritanism, in which the Church of England fortunately did not follow him, and an almost unreasoning though not unreasonable detestation of monachism, for which indeed there were many excuses, but which he, like Rabelais and others, carried much too far.

The *Colloquies*, intended as they are for popular reading, do not exhibit the excellent quality of his erudition to quite such an extent as some of his other work; yet we have it in the *Convivia*, in the *Synodus Grammaticorum* and others. In all these we see the enemy at once of the barbarous and of the exclusively Ciceronian, the wide reader, the patient yet not merely or meticulously philological scholar, and even now and then the seeker after a kind of critical appreciation which had been almost unknown in mediæval, and not too common in classical, times.

But all these things are still somewhat in the outskirts, in the applied departments of literature proper. As regards its most central and purest functions, the *Colloquies* make a great book still. Their admirable expression throughout — the gift which makes their Latin the most living and accomplished of its kind, at once neither slavishly classical nor barbarously modern —is a very great matter. That Erasmus comes third, and by no means a bad third, to Plato and Lucian in the use of the dialogue, is perhaps even a greater. Nor should he lack the highest praise for his adaptation of motive and material. The legend of St Thais, and perhaps Hroswitha's play of *Paphnutius*, founded on it,[1] left him, for instance, not much to do in regard to the *donnée* of the *Adolescens et Scortum*; yet how admirably has he presented the old matter!

Their relation to the future novel.

Perhaps, however, his very greatest merit is one which has not been very commonly allowed him. This lies in the immense strides which his *Colloquies*, universally popular as they were, made in the direction of the two great literary kinds wherein modern literature was to make progress as com-

[1] Conrad Celtes had printed Hroswitha in 1501.

pared with ancient—the drama and the novel. The first point needs no labouring: many passages of the less didactic *Colloquies*, and some of them even as wholes, are stage-play ready made, and of the modern much more than of the ancient kind. But the experiments and advances in the direction of the novel made by the *Colloquies* are even more remarkable. The story, especially the short story, had of course been one of the chief, though the most haphazard, triumphs of the Middle Ages; but in this, as well as elsewhere, the mediæval shortcomings in respect of Character, and the rudimentary, though distinct, conception of its dramatic faculty, had made themselves felt. Erasmus, though choosing to speak "by personages," writes what are really finished novel-scenes. Everybody ought to know the way in which the failing but still admirable art of Scott has turned, with the slightest possible alteration, the famous account of the German inns in the *Diversoria* into a vivid chapter of *Anne of Geierstein;* and very many people know how Charles Reade wrought this afresh, and many other passages of the *Colloquies* for the first time, into *The Cloister and the Hearth.* But it would require far less skill than that of the author of *Waverley*, or the author of *It is Never too Late to Mend*, to perform this process. Colloquy after colloquy, in whole or part, gives example to the fit artist how to manage original matter in the same way. A batch of four running, the *Procus et Puella*, the *Virgo Misogamos*, the *Virgo Pœnitens*, and the *Conjugium*, are simply novel-chapters; the clumsiest novelist could hardly spoil them in turning them into the narrative form, while any practitioner of spirit and gift could not but have been guided by them, if the novel-writing spirit had been at all abroad. The vividness of the *Naufragium* is admitted and incontestable: Defoe himself not improbably borrowed from it. The *Miles et Carthusianus* is rather satire or satirical drama than novel, but it would give a hint. And the *Convivium Poeticum*, with the stock but freshly adapted part of the grumbling *gouvernante* Margaret, is a "Scene of Literary Life" three hundred years older than the nineteenth century. As much may be said, in its different kind, of the *Colloquium Senile*, all the parts of which would bear expansion into Tales, and of the *Franciscani*, where, by the way, Erasmus is far less rabid against the friars than is usual with him and with his fellows. This cannot be said of the *Peregrinatio Religionis ergo*, one of the best known of the whole, and one of the most interesting to English readers. But its novel-quality, in the description both of place and performance at Walsingham and Canterbury, is simply unmistakable.

There are similar touches in the curious medley of the *Ichthyologia* and elsewhere; but the chief *loci* for the purpose of the novelist have been noted, and we must not allow this historical, or rather prophetic, interest of the book too much to obscure its intrinsic excellences—consummate felicity of expression, and an extraordinarily vivid presentation of the real ways, thoughts, wishes of men. The writer is not thinking of the rules; he is not thinking of copying anybody, except, perhaps, Lucian now and then; he is not aiming at stock allegory, or stock anything else. He is simply holding up the mirror to life as steadily and as adroitly as he can, and now and then preaching, with sincerity, geniality, and good sense not too constantly found in sermons.

The *Encomium Moriæ* (1511), which is usually printed with the *Colloquies*, though a rather famous book, is inferior to the best of them, but still not unamusing in parts. To carry off the ironic handling at this length a stronger, not to say a fiercer, satire than Erasmus could, or would, apply is necessary: we want Master Francis or the Dean, not the amiable Desiderius. Strength, indeed, is at no time this pleasant and invaluable writer's eminent quality. He is astonishingly fertile, erudite, deft, accomplished, even in a way original, but he somewhat lacks intensity. And this is why, no doubt, he was in a sense, and for a time, something of a failure, why he seems even something of a *fainéant* among the martial Martins and the swaggering Scaligers of his time. Violence was required just then, both to take, and to save from storm, the kingdom of heaven; and Erasmus could never be violent.

The Encomium Moriæ.

Of the scholar, however, he is an admirable type, one hardly less admirable of the man of letters, and one not to be despised of man simply as man. Some vanity, some disposition, half-arrogant, half-cringing, to be a pensioner on great men's bounty rather than an independent, or nearly independent, professional person, and a certain vagabondage connected with this, were ingrained in the average Humanist; and Erasmus displays them all, though not malignantly. But the comparison of him to Voltaire, though no doubt meant as a compliment, and with some colour from the merely literary side, is grossly unfair to Erasmus in more ways than one. Of Voltaire's spite, of his sniggering and semi-virile indecency, of his cheap cynicism and free-thought, of his smattering erudition, there is no trace in Erasmus: on the contrary, the opposite of each of these things is among his honourable distinctions. If it be true (as a critic, himself a scholar, M. Nisard, put it) that he is now "only a great writer for the learned," this is only a proof of the degeneration of European culture. Except in very few cases where a glossary may be required, Erasmus is perfectly intelligible to any decently educated schoolboy of fourteen: he wrote in the language which he himself no doubt spoke almost exclusively for ordinary purposes; and to this day the absence of "deadness" about it is one of its most remarkable characteristics. On the other hand, it had, as has been so often insisted, the quality of suppleness and adaptation to the special literary purpose which no vernacular, not even Italian, possessed, or was to possess for some years to come. Had he written in his native language he would now be really "dead," the plaything and privilege of the few persons who give themselves the trouble to learn a secondary modern tongue. And it would not be the least cogent of a thousand arguments against the disuse of classical education that it would make Erasmus as inaccessible as if he had actually written in Dutch.[1]

More: the Utopia.

As a man of letters, More, who will be noticed again in the English chapter, is a much lesser man than Erasmus, and the *Utopia* is a much lesser book than the *Colloquies*. The place which it has sometimes enjoyed in English literature is absurd, for, as pointed out above, it is really not English at all except as a translation, while it cannot as such pretend to any such place as is enjoyed, for the mere merit of the English, by the *Froissart* of Berners or the *Montaigne* of Florio, the *Æneid* of Dryden or the *Iliad* of Pope. To us, however, who are considering European literature, it belongs most properly, and even by a double title. It is in the first place a capital example of the cosmopolitan use of Latin, which at this time reached its zenith, and henceforward began, though not at first rapidly, to descend. In the second it exhibits the Renaissance tendency to a curious hybrid perfectibilism — half Pagan, half Christian on the one side, half Science,

[1] A note may be the best place for a capital example of a class of literature now ostensibly defunct—Melanchthon's *Declamations* (reprinted in parts, ed. Hartfelder, Berlin, 1891-94). There are not, to my knowledge, any better examples extant of those "promotion" or graduation addresses, which were once universal (and which are still retained in the Scottish universities, though in the English they are chiefly confined to the honorary graduates) than Melanchthon's orations *De Gradibus* and *De Ordine Dicendi*, while those *De Restituendis Scholis*, *De Studiis Linguæ Græcæ*, are discourses of the first importance on two of the most important subjects of the time. Nor are those *De Artibus Liberalibus* and *De Miseriis Pædagogorum* less than very neat harpings on very old tunes.

half Romance on the other—and the Renaissance enthusiasm for education. Not merely written in a foreign language, but published abroad, it was addressed very much more to Europe than to England, and it was from men like Erasmus that More hoped for his chief welcome and acceptance. Indeed, save some slight adaptation to the special economic and historical circumstances of our island, there is nothing specially English about it. The effects of the discovery of America, the new Platonic imaginings, even that kind of desire for moderate reformation in religion which commended itself to Erasmus himself, and which perhaps might have been carried out if there had been no Luther, no Calvin, and (best of all) no Human Nature—all appear.

The *Utopia*[1] appears to have been written in the

[1] It must be repeated that the book ought to be read in Latin: though for those who cannot or will not do this, Mr Arber's well-known edition in his *Reprints* is very useful. My copy is the Basle edition of 1563, with other Latin works of the author, *Progymnasmata* (not in the rhetorical meaning of the word, but emulative translations of classical verse by More and Lilly), *Epigrams*, Lucianic translations, exercises, and *Letters*. The *Letters* will be noticed with their kind. The verses (for "Epigrams" is even according to the widest interpretation of that word too narrow) are of some considerable extent, and even where they show no great poetical power, sometimes though not always exhibit already in prosodic respects that superiority to Continental versification in Latin on which English scholarship has since justly prided itself. The *In Anglum Gallicæ linguæ affectatorem* (the *bête noire* of all good English students at this time, from More to Ascham), the fine thoughtful *In Hujus Vitæ Vanitatem*—

"Damnati et morituri in terræ claudimur omnes Carcere"—

the *Ad se gestientem Lætitia* in the same sense, and the pleasant pieces to his old love and to his children,—show More at his best here, and deserve no mean place in the general Anthology, which has yet worthily to be made, of this Renaissance verse in Latin.

winter and spring of 1515-16, and being first printed at Louvain in this latter year, went rapidly through three other editions, with revision by the author and his friends. These, like the first, were Continental—at Paris in the spring of 1518, at Basle in November of the same year, and at Vienna in 1519. It was also translated into foreign vernaculars long before it appeared in English, and it gave both its author and his country a very high standing with foreign Humanists.

Perhaps on the whole the deserved reputation of More for character, his hapless fate, and the various traits in him which represent the Englishman of all but the very best type, have conciliated an undue amount of admiration to the book. More's humour shows excellently. The grave banter of the Introduction—on the different reports of travellers respecting the breadth of the river Anyder, the localisation of Utopia, and the attempts of some to make a "key" to the book and identify its characters with individuals—is not unworthy of a country which had already Chaucer to its credit, and was to produce Shakespeare before so very long, not to mention Swift and Fielding, Peacock and Thackeray later. And this tone is kept up in the beginning of the book itself—the presentment of Master Raphael Hythlodæus or Hythlodaye, and the conversation at Cardinal Morton's table. Nor are counsels wise and witty on divers points of politics and manners to seek throughout the text. But on the whole a political student may be justly doubtful about the mixture of the arbitrary and the unpractical in the scheme of Utopian economy: while the purely literary critic, admitting it to be a good book, will hardly, from the literary point of view, admit it to be a masterly one. It is probably the case that all invented polities neglect human nature, unless (as Swift had the wit to see) their builders make them purely negative and satirical. But Plato can enchant us as critics even while we shake our heads as politicians: More hardly does as much.

All this, however, does not affect the fact that the book is a highly representative book. The dissatisfaction of the Renaissance with things existing, its harking back to old models, and its hankering after an elaborate, more or less socialist, system of state-education, state-interference, and state-management of everything—its tendency, in short, to despotism, whether of the monarchic, the aristocratic, or the democratic kind, appears eminently. Nothing—it is no news to students—can be a greater mistake than to present the spirit of the Renaissance as a spirit of liberty; it was only a spirit of violent resistance to authority, which was used to make it do or believe what it did not like, and which prevented it from enforcing what it liked upon other people. And this, though religious toleration nominally exists in Utopia, is really the motto of Amaurot and its dependencies.

The Epistolæ Obscurorum Virorum.

The spirit of Erasmus, reinforced with a stronger if less delicate humour and a more definite partisanship, appears in a famous book where he himself figures not unfrequently by reference, and at least once as an actual interlocutor. I believe that superior persons, for the last generation or two, have made up their minds that the *Epistolæ Obscurorum Virorum*[1] are not really very amusing; and it is pretty certain that (as is the case with other less notable books of the period) they have dropped out of the reading of the average educated man. He cannot too soon return to them. The whole book is the result of many additions and afterthoughts. The *Defensio Joannis Pepericorni*, with its endless testimonials from universities, and the so-called *Lamentationes Obscurorum Virorum*, need only be read by those who wish to consider the thing from more than a merely literary point of view, though one or two things in the *Lamentations* are amusing. Nor has the third volume of the *Epistles* proper the pith and grace of its predecessors. These and the *Dialogus Mire Festivus*, in which Erasmus himself, Reuchlin, and Faber Stapulensis (Le Fèvre d'Etaples) are brought face to face with three protagonists of the Obscuri, contain the root of the matter.

The book took its origin, as is not uncommonly the case with such things, from a long and rather vague quarrel, brought to a head by a particular incident. The Humanists in Germany, during the later part of the fifteenth century, had gained a considerable hold of the universities, and were known by the honourable if not honourably bestowed nickname of "poets," from their new-fangled attention to metrical rules instead of to the old Latin rhythmed doggerel, and their enthusiasm for Virgil and others. They had

[1] I use the Teubner ed., 2 vols. sextodecimo, Leipsic, 1869. Böcking's *Hutten* (*v. infra*) gives the best commentary.

raised among the monastic Orders and the older sort of University Masters, who had been brought up on logic and mediæval manuals, a spirit of opposition both bitter and dogged. This grew, both in bitterness and in doggedness, by the identification of the Reforming element in its earlier stages with the studies of the Poets, and was further envenomed by resentment at the Humanist enormity not merely of reforming the study of Latin, not merely of adding thereto the troublesome novelty of Greek, but of actually proposing to pile Hebrew also on the hapless shoulders of the average *magisternoster*. About the year 1510, a converted Jew named Pfefferkorn, with the usual real or feigned *trop de zèle* of the neophyte, distinguished himself by declaring all Hebrew writings, except the Bible itself, to be anti-Christian and fit only for the flames. The great scholar Reuchlin (1455-1522) entered the lists against him, and the matter became a sort of duel between the Faculty of Theology at Cologne, which was ultra-conservative, and Reuchlin, to whose assistance came a group of young scholars from the younger University of Erfurt. Ulrich von Hutten, the best known of these (see chap. v.), does not seem to have contributed any of the best of the *Epistolæ* (first issued 1515) which were mainly written by Crotus Rubianus (said to be the chief spirit), by the much-extolled Latin versifier Eobanus Hessus, and by a Canon of Gotha, Conrad Mutianus, who was a sort of minor Mæcenas to the crew. They pitched upon a certain Ortuinus Gratius of Deventer, long a favourite theological teacher at Cologne, making him a friend (for reasons none too honourable) of Pfefferkorn and Pfefferkorn's wife, a mortal enemy of Reuchlin, and a holder towards the minor Obscurantists ot the whole of Germany of much the same position which Mutianus actually occupied towards the Erfurt "poets." These "Obscuri Viri" accordingly address to Ortuin letters, sometimes definitely and almost always indirectly touching on the Reuchlin-Pfefferkorn dispute, scarcely ever missing a fling at Humanism, Biblical study, and the rest of the New Learning, but incidentally, and at great length, revealing their own ignorance, immorality, and general slovenliness of life and thought. The most obvious source of the fun (one which has seldom been neglected even by the greatest humourists) is the fantastic nomenclature of the Obscuri—a nomenclature judiciously varied by quite ordinary designations, such as Conrad of Zwickau and Johannes Arnold, but constantly diverging into the grotesque, from the moderate and probable appellations of Thomas Langschneyderius and Bernhardus Plumilegus, to the more farcical fancies of Cornelius Fenestrifex and Paulus Daubengiggle. The next lowest, but still moderately used and ingeniously controlled, is the reliance on sheer coarseness of situation and language. In this the Erfurt men do not come near the common indulgence of the fifteenth century in most countries, or the recrudescence of the same thing in the mouths of the Reformers; but they are sometimes pretty free. Very much more respectable and more literary, is the delectable dog-Latin — a little but not much further *caninised* from the later mediæval pseudo-vernacular—in which the *Obscuri* write, and which, in the *Dialogus Mire Festivus*, is contrasted with the fairly Ciceronian and Terentian style of Erasmus and Reuchlin. But above and beyond all these things are the genuine humour, the command of character, the mastery of that crowning satiric gift—the gift of making the enemy make himself ridiculous, the range of subject and circumstance, the access (as obvious as in the *Colloquies* themselves) to the as yet all but undiscovered and very rarely utilised stores of the matter and means of novel and drama.

These latter good things are absent from very few pages either of the original *Epistles* or of the *Epistolæ Novæ* (1517). Sometimes, as in the very opening letter of the first batch and the thirteenth of the second, we have mock-solemn accounts of scholastic discussions of a certain kind: Whether you ought to say *Nostermagistrandus* or *magisternostrandus*, Whether it is possible, seeing that one member cannot belong to more than one body, for a man to be a member of more than one university. This last *aporia*, put by Thomas Klorbius, a humble doctor of theology (" Parcatis mihi," he dares to say to the great Ortuinus, " sed vos estis incongruus "), is perhaps one of the very best and most characteristic of the whole. Elsewhere[1] there is the parlous case of a short-sighted scholar who has mistaken the black garments of a Jew for academical dress and has made obeisance to the Hebrew: of another[2] who has got into difficulties by drinking too many

[1] Ep. 2. [2] Ep. 3.

canthari of *cerevisia* and then using the *cantharus* itself for purposes military and not civil. Bachelor Nic. Caprimulgius excuses himself[1] for the practice (convenient, no doubt) of writing "lady's Greek without the accents," by the example of the great Ortuinus, and others match Latin doggerel against the pedantic "metres" of the "poets" or quote impossible books, the twentieth *Æneid*, the fifteenth of the *Ethics*. Our reverend Master Conrad of Zwickau, with a sort of innocent impudence, admits[2] that he himself has not the gift of continence, but tenderly remonstrates with Ortuinus for unkind conduct to his fair friend—nay, more, he is mildly contumacious when Ortuin announces his own repentance. Here[3] we have the wicked deeds of an intruder who lectured on Pliny and other poets, and scoffed at those who knew nothing but Peter the Spaniard and the *Parva Logicalia*; who, in fact, was such a fifth wheel to the coach, or rather such a thorn in the side of his university, that the rector had him sent down for ten years. There[4] the inestimable Conrad of Zwickau intimates his latest flame for a certain Dorothea, who plays him evil tricks; but for whom, to beat the poets at their own weapons, he composes a beautiful copy of elegiacs after this fashion—

> "O pulchra Dorothea quam ego elegi amicam
> Fac mihi etiam sic qualiter ego tibi."

Most affecting is the tale[5] of the affection of Mammotrectus Buntemantellus, Master in the Seven Arts, for

[1] Ep. 6. [2] Ep. 9. [3] Ep. 17. [4] Ep. 21. [5] Ep. 33.

the bellringer's daughter, Margaret; most agreeable the argument[1] of a certain Antonius, doctor in medicine, who dared to maintain to the great Erasmus his face that Cæsar could not have written the *Commentaries*, because so busy a man could have had no time to learn Latin. And, indeed, we have seen authors deprived of their books in these very days on not much better grounds. The long account[2] by Magister Wilhelmus Lamp of his journey to Rome, with a comrade whose conduct was far from becoming, is a most admirable piece of narrative, worthy, *mutatis mutandis*, of Defoe. And the same good person's subsequent[3] discussion on points of prosody with an important member of the Roman Curia is worthy of it, though perhaps not quite so pleasing as another letter[4] from Rome about the wonderful ways and sad death of the Pope's elephant, the beast that Emmanuel of Portugal gave to Leo the Tenth.

Among the most masterly touches is the picture[5] drawn by Henricus Schluntz of the mighty Ortuinus in his library. He is sending his master a book, but fears it may be ill taken.

Sed possetis dicere, Quare talis mihi mittit talem librum? Credit quod non met habeo libros satis? Respondeo quod non facio propterea. Et quando putatis quod misi vobis talem librum propterea, tunc facilis mihi injuriam quia feci cum bona opinione. Et non debetis credere quod parvipendo vos quod habetis paucos libros; quia scio quod habetis multos libros. Quia vidi bene quando fui in stuffa

---

[1] Ep. 42. [2] Ep. Nov. 12. [3] Ep. Nov. 35.
[4] Ep. Nov. 48. [5] Ep. Nov. 52.

vestra Coloniæ, quod habuistis multos libros in magna et in parva forma. Et aliqui fuerunt ligati in asseribus, aliqui in bergamenibus. Et aliqui fuerunt per totum cum corio rubeo et viridi et nigro, aliqui pro dimidio supertracti. Et vos sedistis habens flabellum in manu ad purgandum pulveres abinde.

And it further seems that Ortuinus told his pupil that you might always know whether a man is learned or not by the care he takes of his books—a sentiment not discreditable to the *coryphæus* of the Obscuri, despite the disgraceful insinuation that *his* books might have been in danger of gathering dust for all the reading he gave them.

The etymological line is taken up elsewhere,[1] the most ingenious example being the explanation of *latus clavus* as *nomen dignitatis,* derived from the practice of military tribunes throwing a metal *clava* or mace into the ranks of the enemy, the recovery of which was valiantly sought by the soldiers. Magister Abraham Isaac de stirpe Aminadab (evidently an analogue of Pfefferkorn) declares,[2] with as evident sincerity, that he would rather have a living of a hundred florins and a simple damsel of twelve years old, at Deventer in his dear native land, than one of thirty florins and a cunning *gouvernante* of sixty in the High Germany. Marcolf Sculteti inquires[3] of John Bimperlenbumpum (who doubtless gave his name to a certain "powder of Pimperlimpimp") what on earth is the meaning of this "Gabala" that they talk about, and which appears neither in the *Catholicon* nor in the *Gemma*

[1] Ep. Nov. 56. [2] Ep. Nov. 66. [3] Ep. Nov. 69.

Gemmarum. And for a final touch[1]: "Ars dicitur a Græco *artos*, id est panis: quia omnes qui sciunt artem aliquem possunt acquirere panem et potum et amictum." We learn, too, that the University of Erfurt, like all our universities in all our times, "meo tempore fuit in flore," and then had nothing to do with fantastic "poesy," but consisted of sound Aristotelians and good Realists, with a famous notion of getting the better of Nominalism in argument.

I have given this flying sketch of some, but only a very small part, of the more amusing matter of the *Epistolæ,* in order to throw some light on their most remarkable literary character. It will, I think, almost by itself (though all persons who love humour are most earnestly exhorted to have recourse to the original) show how well that original deserves the name in reference to modern literature, not merely by the impetus administered to the elaboration of the great new kinds of drama and novel, but by the display of a variety of comedy which is itself essentially modern. In this last respect the *Epistolæ* are a good deal in advance even of the *Colloquia ;* and it is not a little remarkable, and shows no small genius in the person concerned (whoever he was, Crotus Rubianus or another), that this spirit should be shown first in Germany. For the humour of Germany has always tended—and at this particular time tended more, perhaps, than at any one other — towards violent horseplay, extravagant coarseness, the "humour of the stick." That of the *Obscuri Viri,* on the other hand, is partly Lucianic

[1] See the Commentum Mag. Nost. Schluntz, ed. cit., p. 409.

and so not original. But it acquires originality by a considerable admixture of the fun of mere nonsense, to which, except in the Old Comedy, ancient wit, even in its most consummate exhibitions, was unluckily and unwisely averse. The differentia of modern from ancient literature is also well seen in the peculiar glancing or lambent divagation of the fun. The Epistolers are almost always coursing several hares at once, yet there is no real confusion. The Reuchlin-Pfefferkorn quarrel is never left long alone; but it is dropped constantly, for the moment, in order to attack monkery, or the older and more obscurantist fashions of University life, or the mere and sheer degradation of scholarship by sensuality and sluttishness, or other things suited by their vivacity and reality to enliven the general picture. If we compare the book with such representatives of almost contemporary French and Italian humour as *Gargantua and Pantagruel* and *Merlinus Coccaius,* we can but be surprised to find that by far the most uncouth nation has turned out by far the most refined fun, relying the least on mere extravaganza and burlesque, and, if more limited than either, more academic than either likewise. Nothing could, perhaps, better show the enormous harm done (whether with or without compensation does not at the moment matter) by the controversies of the Reformation in general, and in particular by the temper of the chief Reformed controversialists.

Sometimes, however, even Reformation pamphlets in Latin show something better than black gall and choler. There can be few livelier followings in the footsteps of the *Epistolæ* than the dialogue, or almost drama, entitled *Eckius Dedolatus*,[1] and published about 1530 (the first edition has no date), as a song of triumph on the Protestant side over the champion of Rome who had been, as the Protestants thought, so thoroughly unhorsed by Luther. It takes, as has been said, the dialogic-dramatic not the epistolary form, and nothing shows more forcibly that influence of Lucian which has been mentioned. The action is much livelier than that of any of the *Colloquies;* and the author, whoever he was, allows himself not only considerable licences of language but a good deal of fancy in his incident. In fact the thing shows more concentrated literary talent than any work of the time on the same side except Kirchmayer's (*v. infra*, chap. vi.), while its Rabelaisian and uproarious humour contrasts remarkably with the grim intensity of the *Pammachius*. The story is that Eck, writhing under his defeat, and finding that copious libations (which are supplied by his Boy with asides of comic abuse) do him no good, sends for his friends, and, at their advice, to Leipsic for help. The messenger is the witch Canidia, who travels on her speediest he-goat, and by the same vehicle brings back Rubeus and a surgeon in woful plight. The surgeon declares that only the most heroic remedies, and the actual knife, can save Eckius, and that he had better "make his soul" before the operation; but the confessional scene is more curious

Eckius Dedolatus.

[1] Ed. Szamatolski, Berlin, 1891. The ascription of the authorship to Pirkheimer seems not proven.

than edifying. Then the unfortunate patient is strapped down, purged, blistered, bled, and subjected to more alarming operations still, in order to clear him of his evil humours and corruptions of all kinds—the mildest remedy being a severe thrashing (*dedolatio*) and the severest one requiring delicate and distant allusion. The effect however is good, the naughtiness being effectually taken out of the papal champion, and the piece ends with one of the odd fasciculi of scraps—epigrams, orations, &c., common at the time. It is full of classical, even Greek, quotation, and obviously written by a scholar for scholars: but the authorship seems entirely a matter of guess.

The Facetiæ.

It so happens, too, that though the much earlier *Facetiæ* of Poggio deserve the praise, such as it is, of putting these things to the credit of Humanism, the chief examples of sixteenth-century *Facetiæ*[1] that we possess are German. German stories had already taken, in such vernacular work as *Tyll Eulenspiegel* and the *Kalendberger*,[2] a

[1] The commentatory literature of the great story-collections, Latin and vernacular, is enormous, and in regard to the earlier ones it is barely necessary to name Wright, Loiseleur Deslongchamps, Oesterley, Comparetti, one scholar from each of the great literary countries. On this present subject special assistance will be found, by those who desire it, in that excellent book of Professor Herford's, which I have to mention always with honour, often with indebtedness, *The Literary Relations of England and Germany in the Sixteenth Century.* There is a neat little collection of the *Facetiæ* of Bebel and Frischlin, with additions from others, starting with Poggio himself (Amsterdam, 1660). It may be observed here that the *Grobianus* literature is reserved for the chapter on German Vernacular.

[2] See *The Transition Period*, pp. 401-403.

tincture of sheer nastiness which surpasses even that of the French *Fabliaux* themselves. Edification, therefore, is much more to seek than to find in the work of Bebel, of Frischlin, and of others in Latin, not to mention *Schimpf und Ernst* and other things in German. The pieces are indeed sometimes of some importance as preserving and handing on useful literary subjects and motives. In face, however, of the great development of the vernacular *novella* and *conte* in Italy from the *Decameron* to the *Hecatommithi*, and in France from the *Cent Nouvelles Nouvelles* to the *Heptameron*, the importance of these Latin stories is considerably lessened; nor has their more or less classical style the interest of the barbarous but piquant Latinity of their predecessors. For all the *gros sel* that he allows himself, it is curious to contrast the comparative stolidity of Bebel with the piquancy constantly given by Erasmus to much less automatically laugh-provoking subjects.

Letters.

It would be improper to close this long chapter (which should, however, have been longer still in order to do justice to the subject) without a slight further reference to the Latin correspondence which forms so important a part of the literature of the time. In the case of many of the great men mentioned or to be mentioned —Erasmus, More, Bembo, Sadolet, and others—in the case, indeed, of almost every man of importance in our special period, letters written in Latin form a more or less important part of his literary work, besides supplying data almost more important for his own biography and the history of the time. A considerable part of these letters, indeed, consists of barren formalisms and compliments, couched in an artificial would-be Ciceronian style, and of no more pith or substance than the declamations of the School Rhetoric. But a great part also is as vivid and as interesting as any one can reasonably desire, particularly in the case of Erasmus. Yet even in this department the handwriting on the wall appears, as where, for instance, we find Ascham beginning his career as a letter-writer in Latin, even when he is writing to ladies, and ending it in English, even when he is writing on public business. Such a fact speaks for itself, and what it says is *Mene, Tekel.* It may still suit Barclay, nearly a hundred years later, to write even the *Argenis,* the first of "novels with a purpose," in Latin. It may, after another century and a half, still seem more proper and even easier to Johnson to state in Latin to his doctor the particulars of the paralytic stroke from which he has hardly rallied. But these are survivals. The kingdom of Latin is passing and to pass to the despised vernaculars.

CHAPTER II.

THE ZENITH OF THE CINQUECENTO.

ITALIAN LITERATURE, C. 1500—THE ITALIAN LITERARY TEMPER—ARIOSTO —HIS LIFE—HIS WORK: THE MINOR POEMS—THE 'ORLANDO'— ITS QUALITIES AS ROMANCE—DESULTORINESS—ITS SARCASM AND LICENCE—BRILLIANCY OF STYLE AND VERSE—STORY-CHARACTER— OF ITALIAN ROMANCE GENERALLY—ITALIAN HUMOUR—BOTH AS IN ARIOSTO—SCENES, PERSONS, AND PASSAGES—ARIOSTO'S RANK AS POET, AND AS MIRROR OF HIS TIME—ARIOSTO AND RABELAIS— OTHER EPIC-ROMANCES—LYRICS: SONNETS, LA CASA—MADRIGALS AND CANZONI—ARIOSTO—MICHELANGELO—MOLZA—VITTORIA COLONNA—GUIDICCIONI—ITALIAN DIDACTIC AND BLANK VERSE—THE 'CAPITOLI,' ETC.—PROSE-WRITERS—MACHIAVELLI AND GUICCIARDINI—MINOR HISTORIANS—THE "NOVELLIERI"—BANDELLO— CINTHIO—FIRENZUOLA AND GRAZZINI—STRAPAROLA—MISCELLANEOUS PROSE: LETTERS, DIALOGUES—ARETINO—MISCELLANIES OF GELLI, FIRENZUOLA, BEMBO, VARCHI, CARO—CASTIGLIONE AND 'THE COURTIER.'

Italian literature, c. 1500.

IT is perhaps barely necessary to repeat the caution of the Preface that, as regards the subject of the present chapter, though of that only, the title of the present volume is a frank and self-confessed misnomer. The first half of the sixteenth century, with in some cases, perhaps, a very few years at the end of the fifteenth, undoubtedly constitutes the period of the Early Renaissance in general European Literature. But that period in Italian Literature hardly even falls within the limits of the volume which has preceded this. For Italy, as luck or ill-luck would have it, has always, and necessarily, stood in a dislocated position in regard to general European culture. One is sometimes almost tempted to say that Italy has no mediæval period. The precinct of the ancient capital of the world, the patrimony of the modern Church, passed almost without a gap of twilight from Darkness to Renaissance. The latest of all European countries to achieve a real literature in the vernacular, Italy was by far the earliest to revive the study of the ancient tongues; and this revival, notwithstanding that it brought about a more unintelligent and pedantic undervaluation of the vernacular itself than anywhere else, ripened this vernacular at the very same time. When France and Germany already had a brilliant national literature, Italy had only a cluster of dialects, with little more than folk-song to serve them for record; yet within a century at most she had far outstripped the rivals that had had so great a start of her. In the middle of the thirteenth century the rich and varied literature of France, the exquisite lyrics and wild or polished epics of Germany, were confronted, south of the Alps, by a beggarly array of formal poetry imitated from Provençal, of non-formal poetry that was mere folk-song. By the middle of the fourteenth, Italy, besides not a few minors, had three writers, one of whom was of the greatest of all time, while the three together had brought Italian, in prose and verse, to a pitch of accomplishment which no other European language could rival for at least two hundred years to come.

It is, perhaps, not wholly philosophical to put down the comparative falling off at the end of the fourteenth and the beginning of the fifteenth century, as has often been done, to the encroachments of humanist pedantry. This, no doubt, had something to do with the matter; but not all, nor even very much. The burst of the Trecento, in fact, did for Italy in two or three generations what was done for the rest of Europe in two or three centuries, and the falling off after it was simply the phenomenon corresponding to the comparative decadence and sterility of all Europe during the same fifteenth century. But the Italian dead season lasted for a shorter time, and broke once more into spring and summer with a brighter though briefer luxuriance, for reasons connected partly with the character of the earlier flourishing itself, partly with the occupation of the interval. The period from Dante to Boccaccio had been too short to exhaust the literary faculty of the nation; and the attention bestowed upon the classics by the Humanists had inevitably if unwillingly reacted upon the equipment of the vernacular. When there began that wonderful after-bloom of seventy or eighty years, the later period of which falls to our lot here, the Italians settled once more to the production of literature, with advantages in all but one respect far superior to those possessed by any other nation whatsoever. To take

Politian or Pulci in the earlier, Ariosto or Machiavelli in the later half, and compare them with Rabelais or Ronsard, with Surrey or even with Spenser, far later than the latest whom we notice, is almost like comparing a modern astronomer with the possessor of an astrolabe. The Italians had a language somewhat lacking indeed in strength, but already tuned and tempered to the utmost possible pitch of melody and music. All important metrical problems were conquered for them; their grammar, if not formally, was practically fixed; their vocabulary was as wide as they wanted. Prose, which was struggling into being in England, and still much unformed in France, had with them already reached comparative perfection. They were rather behindhand in drama, but in every other kind they were ahead, and in tale-telling very much ahead, of all other peoples. Lastly, they had been acquainted for a hundred years and more with a very large portion, and for a considerable time with practically the whole, of the Classics, whence they could derive at once instruction and example. Meanwhile the Frenchman to some extent, the Englishman to a much greater, had to struggle with something like a complete change of language, with prosody never fully formed, and rendered almost useless by the change of language itself, with an unconstructed grammar, with a vocabulary which still wanted feeding up to the utmost in every department of thought and matter. Before we can, as has been so often and for the most part so unsatisfactorily done, attempt to compare Ariosto and Spenser, we must remember that while the Italian is not more original than the Englishman in point of matter, his inherited advantages in point of form are to us almost inconceivable. He has everything ready to his hand—language, metre, grammar, fashions of handling. Spenser has to do almost everything for himself—to forge the very tools that he uses, to cut down the very trees with which he builds.

The Italian literary temper.

It is possible that in his admirable *Italian Literature* Mr Symonds, perhaps from less acquaintance with the other parts of the subject, has not quite fully allowed for the enormous advantages possessed by the Italians of this time. But he has not allowed one whit too much for the literary character of the Italian temper, its sense of beauty, its eye for proportion and harmony, its wide range and acute power of selection, its inherited justness of conception and expression. These qualities are so striking, so unmistakable, that one cannot be surprised at the rank which, not at one time or in one country only, has been allowed to the Italian Literature of the Cinquecento. Yet of its defects there cannot now be much denial. That the eighteenth century, and even to some extent the earlier nineteenth, regarded Italy as the home of Romance, came of course only from the fact that, not entirely by their own fault, the men of those times did not know what Romance was. Of the three great elements of that great thing—Variety, Mystery, Passion—the Italians indeed possessed the first in amplest measure; and if they were a little deficient in the third, they made by no means a bad substitute for it out of that sublimated sensuality which is really a sort of naughty twin-sister of Passion herself, an Anteros not wholly opposed to the better Cupid. But of Mystery they knew nothing, though they were quite aware, and very fond, of its caricature, Marvel. The Romans themselves had had very little sense of the mysterious; even the Greeks can hardly be said to show it strongly; and the whole course of Italian civilisation, especially the fatal familiarity of the Italians with a debased official Christianity, had served as a preventive to the importation of the most precious of gifts from the North. Even in Dante it can hardly be said to be present in any other sense than this—that as the greatest poetry is universal, it penetrates this region also. The dread countries of his voyage are all countries of mystery, of dream, yet the commonest of criticisms is, that though he never makes them prosaic he always makes them practical, real, objective. The very Beatific Vision is hardly vague, the descent on the wings of Geryon has the precision of a lift. He can do this without ever even approaching prose; but others cannot, even in his time, much more two hundred years afterwards. If there is a touch of mystery anywhere in the Italian Renaissance, it is in the *Hypnerotomachia*, which is but a survival of mediæval allegory. The Italian poet of all times, more or less, of this time particularly, can sing exquisitely, say consummately, see unerringly; but he cannot dream.

"On a work so well known, and so universally read, as the *Orlando Furioso* any observations would now be superfluous." So wrote Roscoe a century ago, and if he was right then, they might seem likely to be *plusquam* superfluous now. But Roscoe was not writing an ostensibly literary history; he was merely citing such aspects of Italian literature as he thought likely to illustrate the story of his actual subject, Leo the Tenth, and likely also to require expounding to his readers. Moreover, there are very good grounds for doubting whether the *Orlando* at the present moment is exactly "well known" and "universally read." That every educated person knows *of* it may be assumed, and some at least of its famous episodes—the island of Alcina, the journey of Astolfo to the moon, and a few more, are no doubt vaguely known to everybody. Yet a person of very good education, not ignorant of Italian, has been known to confuse Alcina and Armida; and I should rather like to try an intellectual company after dinner with such questions as, "What was the second heap of rubbish which Astolfo found?" "What dress had Alcina on when she came to visit Ruggiero?" not to mention such minuter and more recondite ones as, "What were the different fates of the sons of Marganorre?" or "What was Rodomonte's reply to the *novella* of Giocondo?" However this may be, the propriety of "making observations on the *Orlando*" here will hardly be contested, and if they seem voluminous in proportion to the size of the book or the chapter, there is, as in the case of Rabelais, a very complete answer ready. Not only are these two writers the greatest writers of their time from the point of view of world-literature,

Ariosto.

but their books happen to be quite extraordinarily representative of that time, and, moreover, to supplement each other in the most extraordinary degree. There is hardly more than one important feature of the Renaissance, the singular combination of voluptuousness and melancholy, that they miss. All the rest—its seriousness and its irony, its hopes and its cynical conviction of their folly, its freethinking and its enthusiasm for humanity, its reaction against asceticism, and its passionate love of visible, audible, degustable, odorous, tangible beauty,—all are in these two.

His life.

Lodovico Ariosto, a Ferrarese by extraction and education, and member of a more than respectable family, was actually born at Reggio, of which his father was governor, in 1474. He was intended for the law, but, like many others, left it for literature, a desertion which seemed likely to have awkward consequences when, at the age of six-and-twenty, he found himself left with a rather small independence and a family of nine brothers and sisters to provide for. He discharged this duty most creditably, however. Everybody who was anybody in the small states of Italy in those days expected some State provision, and received it to an extent which is still rather puzzling when one remembers that Italy has never been a rich country. Ariosto's first endowment, the Captainship of Canossa, was more interesting from its associations than on quarter-day; and when he was nearly thirty he became a confidential officer of Cardinal Ippolito of Este, brother of the Duke of

Ferrara. It seems that he might have had good benefices if he would have taken orders beyond the lower degrees. Ippolito has had the usual ill-luck of the great when they happen to be served by the greater—that of being extravagantly flattered by his servant and extravagantly abused by posterity. He seems to have been a very typical Italian prince of the time, with no morals, quite ready to put his brother's eyes out because a lady thought them handsomer than his own, and exceedingly unlikely to think of anybody else's interests unless it was quite convenient to himself. In two agreeable qualities, bravery and good looks, he also resembled his class; in a third, which they not uncommonly possessed, he seems to have been rather deficient. But we cannot all be good critics, and it is on the whole desirable that if a man does not like a thing he should say so. At any rate, whether Ippolito uttered the famous query [1] about the *Orlando* or not, he probably got the copyright secured to the author, and even, as Mr Symonds says pleasantly, bought a copy himself for one whole *lira marchesana*.

After being in the service of the Cardinal for some fifteen years, Ariosto transferred himself to that of Ippolito's brother, Duke Alfonso. He had to travel

[1] "*Dove diavolo, messer Ludovico, avete trovato* [or *pigliato*] *tante—*" and then what? The sentence is traditionally completed in three different forms, all expressing "rubbish," "rot," but ranging in coarseness from *coglionerie* through *minchionerie* to *cabellerie.* Roscoe, with the robustness of his generation, gives the usual (I can hardly say the consecrated) form; Mr Symonds drops *diavolo,* and takes in one place one, in another the other, of the milder substantives.

now and then, but for the most part resided at Ferrara, with a good salary and handsome allowances. In 1522 he was made governor of the Garfagnana, an out-of-the-way and brigand-infested district, which office he held, to his great discomfort, for three years. Then he returned to Ferrara, married (somewhere about 1525) a widow, Alessandra Strozzi, whom he had long loved, revised the *Orlando* unceasingly, and died of consumption, June 6, 1533. Personally he seems to have been extremely amiable and agreeable, and was (by his own and his natural son Virginio's testimony) fond of turnips.

His work.—The minor poems.

Ariosto's work[1] falls into three well-marked divisions: the minor poems, epistles, satires, *capitoli*, &c.; the plays; and the *Orlando*. The plays will be dealt with in the general chapter on the European Drama of the period. The minor poems have been extolled as extremely important for Ariosto's biography and private character. One would, of course, rather that he had not in them grumbled at the patron whom in full dress he went out of his way to load with fulsome praise; but this is unluckily very natural and very usual. Elsewhere the tone of these poems, though as amusing as we should expect, seems to me, I confess, to be rather conventional. From Horace and Persius downward there have been two satiric manners:—one that of

[1] Editions very numerous. I use of the *Orlando*, which was first printed at Ferrara in 1516, a 4to containing likewise Dante, Petrarch, and Tasso, dedicated to Goethe at Leipsic in 1826; of the *Opere Minori*, Lemonnier's, Florence, 2 vols., 1894.

the easy well-bred or would-be well-bred man of the world who suspends everything on the adunc nose and occasionally scratches with still more adunc claws; the other that of the indignant moralist reproving the corruptions of the time. Both have produced good work, and Ariosto has contributed not a little of it, mainly in the former key, but once or twice in the latter. But there is something, as usual, of the histrionic in either manner. The best passage is also the best known, that in which the poet describes his interview with Leo X. after the Pope's elevation to the Holy See. They had, it seems, been intimate friends and almost brothers before the Wheel of Fortune had carried Leo to the very top. Nor did the Pope, like some bad men, forget his friend. On the contrary, when Ariosto went to see him at home, he kissed him on both cheeks, pressed his hand, granted his request for securing his copyright, let him off *half* the fees (but some say this was for some small benifice, and we are usually told that Ippolito had got him the printing rights earlier), and—permitted him to walk down in the rain to his inn and eat his supper there. This is quite admirably told, and the excuses which the poet makes for the Pope are consummate morsels; but it is a pity that he allows the passage to tail off into the stock copy-book reflections that honours and riches do not bring tranquillity of mind. To be esteemed an honest man is true honour. Most trite if most true. And from Messer Ludovico, of all people, we do not expect ignoring of the fact that it is not absolutely impossible to possess honours and riches with tranquillity of mind; that you certainly do not secure this by *not* possessing them; and that it is quite as easy for an honest man to enjoy his honesty *plus* dryness and a good supper at the Pope's table as to wrap it in a wet cloak and feed it with the food of inns at his own expense. His vexation, or the conventional obligation of the form, has here and elsewhere made him succumb to an evil influence from which he is generally free enough—the influence of Cant.

The Orlando.

In his great work, whatever other objections may be made to it, this malign goddess is most conspicuously absent, while nobody pretends that the minor poems, satirical or other, display a tithe of the poetical power which reigns in the great romance. To it, therefore, let us turn. It may, despite what has been said above, be assumed without much rashness that readers are aware of the fact that it is a continuation of the great and long strangely undervalued poem of Boiardo on the same subject. And as Boiardo himself has been fully treated in the last volume, there is no need to do more than repeat that the *Orlando Innamorato,* though nothing like so accomplished a poem as the *Furioso,* displays a truer spirit of Romance. On the other hand, in adjusting the story rather to "an *arioso* key" our poet has avoided the extreme burlesque of Pulci (*v.* also as above). Although he sometimes shaves the burlesque very close, he never actually touches it, and of the enormous body of verse which Italy has composed on the ultimate base of the French Carlovingian epos, with a strong draft upon the Arthurian legend and the miscellaneous adventure-pieces, his essay transcends all others.

Its qualities as Romance.

Critics of that ancient school, still too numerously attended, which regards it as the first of critical duties to construct elaborate classifications, to copy their subdivisions upon labels, to stick the labels on, and to exhibit the result to the world as criticism, have decided that there are, in Italian at least, five kinds of epic, romance, or narrative poetry, to wit: Romantic proper, Epic or Heroic proper, Burlesque, Heroi-Comic, and Satiric. And they gravely tag to the *Orlando* the epithet Romantic, without, it may be allowed, the slightest danger of contradiction, but also, it must be regretfully added, with the least possible illustrative or informative result. Of course the *Orlando* is a Romance in any and every form and sense of that scarcely univocal word, though in some senses more than others. But what we may legitimately and advantageously investigate is the further question, What kind of a Romance is it, not by label, but in quality?

Desultoriness.

The unprejudiced but not unintelligent reader who has a fair acquaintance with Romances already will probably, before he has got far in his reading of the *Orlando*, begin to make up his mind that, whatever else it is, it is an exceedingly *desultory* one, and he will, at least possibly, not change his opinion when he gets to the end. But here again he will be taken up by some at least of the critics, who will assure him that for all its apparent vagaries the *Orlando* has really one main plot never lost sight of, in the bringing together of Ruggiero and Bradamante as fabulous ancestors of the House of Este; that additional plots or, as Chaucer would say, "knots" (they confess that they are less pervading) are provided by the Siege of Paris at Paynim hands and (now and then) by the title-incident; and that violently as the action appears to waver and see-saw between different adventures in East and West, the transitions are really managed with consummate skill. It is possible that on these points some such readers may remain unconvinced. They will say that the ancestor-legend, though a recognised commonplace of "regular" epic poetry subsequent to Virgil, is a poor thing at best, and that it here is nothing more than a sort of extended Dedication by which the obligatory flattery of patrons, instead of being concentrated in one place, is spread over the whole work; and that though Bradamante certainly does displace Angelica as heroine (so far as there is a heroine), Ruggiero, till close before the end, can only be called a hero because he is rather oftener on the stage than any one else. Of the Siege of Paris they will say that it is a mere occasion for striking episodes—the best of them the famous single-handed incursion of Rodomonte—and that the poet cannot, and evidently does not, expect us to take interest in it as much more than a background. The Madness of Orlando they will not merely pronounce episodic, but deny it much interest, except at the beginning (where the effect of the ever-new discoveries of the name of his rival, coupled with Angelica's, is very finely and powerfully imagined and described) and at the end in the rescue-operations of Astolfo. But most of all, perhaps, they will demur to the praise bestowed upon the transitions. Nay, without blaming Ariosto in the least for adopting the method which he chose to adopt, and which has given a charming result, they may refuse the name of transition altogether to what is in reality a mere sandwiching (generally without so much as butter and mustard to make a kind of cement to the parts of the sandwich) of Levantine and Ponentine adventures. They may even contrast the way in which Spenser effects his intertwinings of the different strands of his story, to the very great advantage of the English poet.

And those who take this line need not despair of Ariosto's own approbation, for he himself never seems to take the subject seriously. However this may be, it is certain that some at least of those who enjoy the *Orlando* most keenly, and not least critically, do not care one jot whether Ruggiero marries Bradamante or not, and are only interested in the Siege of Paris, on the sportsmanlike principle of backing your own side. And the attraction, to them, can be quite critically accounted for. If Ariosto took only a business-like and courtier-like interest in his general story, he took the keenest, the most craftsmanlike, the most masterly interest in the particular stories which he grafted upon it. In such a case, and with such a person, one can never be entirely sure how far the poem as it exists is the result of any definite plan. When Ariosto took up the unfinished story of *Orlando* from Boiardo's hands, we are not necessarily to suppose him actuated by any cut-and-dried scheme. These things shape themselves in the hands of men of genius even more than they are shaped by them.

Its sarcasm

But it may be said, "How about the sarcastic intention of the *Orlando?*" To which, perhaps, the best answer is, that we shall do well to consider the sarcastic expression rather than the sarcastic intention. The common fallacy of supposing that a man who sees the ludicrous side of a thing or person necessarily despises and probably dislikes that person or thing, has worked ill in this instance also. That Angelica, at once the cynosure and the prize of the world, after being doted on by, and playing with, the most peerless of peers, should throw herself into the arms of a good-looking nobody, is hardly even severe "criticism of life." The thing *is* life: the only thing to be said about it is that the poet has been exceedingly kind to his coquette, and that few Angelicas are lucky enough to find such unobjectionable Medoros. That Orlando's prowess should lead to nothing but jealousy and madness, only not commonplace because they are in excess, and that he should be brought to his senses, or rather his senses to him, with the aid of physical punishment and subjection, is not bitter satire. It is simply acknowledgment of quite usual fact, consistent with the highest conception of the romantic.

That Ariosto himself had this highest conception

need not be contended—would, indeed, be absurd to contend. As an Italian of the later though not latest Renaissance, he could hardly have had it. Tyranny and profligacy in the upper classes of the State, servility and profligacy in the lower, corruption and unbelief in the Church, hardly made an atmosphere genial for a quest of the Sangreal or even for a Court of Gloriana. But his view is not by any means such a low view as it is sometimes taken to be. Even his much-talked-of immorality may seem (though it is always dangerous to take up the cudgels for a defendant on this score) to have been not a little exaggerated. Let it be remembered that even Spenser himself shocks the pudibund nowadays, though Spenser's morality and his religious fervour are absolutely beyond question or suspicion. Of course Ariosto goes beyond Spenser, who would certainly not have given admission to *novelle* like that of Giocondo, and would have considered the young person a little more, if not in the history of Alcina and Ruggiero, at any rate in that of Ricciardetto and Fiordispina. But it may be strongly contended that the Ariosto of the great poem has here found but an ill friend in the Ariosto of the clever comedies. That they are tainted with an always disagreeable and sometimes disgusting moral or immoral tone, need not be denied for one moment. But the *Orlando* itself seldom goes beyond the mildly naughty, and not often beyond the simply voluptuous. In particular it must be again strongly urged that the most offensive characteristics of Italian licence, the positive nastiness and the admixture of

and licence.

cruelty with lust, are all but entirely absent from the *Orlando*. Its Venus may be of the earth earthy, but she is never of the mud or of the Devil; although she may have too much of Pandemos, she has nothing of Pandemonium. Lastly (for one may justly love to get objections over), the charge of flattery may be at once admitted, deplored, and dismissed to come up for judgment when called on. It is very disgusting that great poets should flatter Augustus or Alfonso, Ippolito or Cromwell, and they are the worse men for doing it. But they are by no means necessarily the worse poets, and it is as a poet that we are dealing with the author of the matters in *-erie*, which so did surprise Ippolito himself.

Brilliancy of style and verse.

To pass to the merits. In the very first place has to be put the extraordinary attraction of Ariosto's style and versification. Of his mere language it is no doubt best left to Italians to speak. They have been (not, of course, without right, considering their history) among the most punctilious of European nations on this head, and while it would hardly become any foreigner to enter the lists with them on such questions, it is an important fact that in regard to none of their great writers has there been such an agreement as in regard to Ariosto. There have been times when even Dante, even Boccaccio, did not meet the severe requirements of Italian Academic prudery: Petrarch has, in native taste to some extent, and still more in foreign, escaped criticism chiefly on the dangerous ground of "faultlessness"; with Tasso we are to some extent already in the presence of decadence. But Ariosto, Ferrarese as he was, has very nearly united all suffrages at home, and practically all abroad. Moreover, strictures on Patavinity are almost proverbially barren.

With style proper, and still more with versification, we come to more interesting and safer ground, for here the *orbis terrarum* is the secure judge. When purists in England tell us that Chaucer might have selected a better dialect than he did, that Shakespeare's English is not quite correct, that Dryden wants a stricter and purer grammar, we say, if we are wise, "Perhaps," and pass on. The style of all these admits no question, nor does Ariosto's. Its excellence must be apparent to any one who can appreciate style at all, as soon as he has acquired Italian enough to understand, even not yet in *minutiæ*, the mere words of the poem. Not Virgil, not Racine, not Addison, produces the effect of complete and easy mastery more thoroughly: and there is something in Ariosto which does not appear in any of the three. To say that he is never prosaic, would indeed only be true from a special point of view, but no other limitation is possible even *prima facie*. The ease, the variety, the interesting quality of his narrative manner have probably never been surpassed.

But to some tastes at anyrate it is the excellence of his versification, that *articulus stantis aut cadentis poeseos*, which is his greatest charm. The Italian hendecasyllable has many merits; but some at least of these are derived from a quality which hovers constantly on the border of defect. Even in its strict form with the feminine rhyme, and still more when that rhyme is extended to the *sdrucciolo* variety, it is just a little too skipping—it has a constant tendency to reduce itself from a five- to a four-footed line by sinking intermediate syllables, or if it takes the five accents, not to charge them with quite sufficient gravity. And this is specially the case when it is arranged in stanzas that terminate with a couplet. Among the almost innumerable evidences, major and minor, of Dante's poetical supremacy is his adoption (his invention possibly, but it really does not matter) of the *terza rima*, from this special point of view. The rhymes recur as the whole nature of the language demands that they should; but the constant break in their recurrence arrests the skip and pirouette—the slight "tumble" even—which is natural to them, and at least assists the poet to achieve his unsurpassed and seldom matched gravity, resonance, and echo. So the sonnet and the sestine, to take Petrarch's most successful forms, arrest the "tumble" by a still greater intricacy of recurrence. And though in the *canzone* the rhyme in pairs is strongly present, yet it is not single as in the *ottava*—its effect is largely conditioned by the varying length of the lines, and the much greater length of the stanza. Yet it may be doubted, with infinite submission to Dante's expressed judgment, whether the peculiarity on which we are commenting is not a slight blot on the supremacy of the *canzone* itself.[1]

[1] It was probably some unconscious consciousness of this defect of the hendecasyllabic couplet which made the Italians prefer the form of sonnet which does *not* end with it. As no similar defect attends

However this may be, the *ottava* of hendecasyllables, with all its merits, undoubtedly does fall short, in sincerity and gravity, of the forms most natural to compare with it — the English Rhyme Royal and Spenserian. This last, as has been shown not merely by its inventor but by poets so different as Thomson, Shelley, and Tennyson, is probably the greatest stanza in the world for serious poetry, though it also may have the opposite defects of its opposite qualities. Rhyme Royal is inferior to both in compass, and very greatly inferior to the Spenserian in power; but it has its own merits, and in what has been called "plangency" has no superior.

Ariosto, however, was almost bound by custom to use the *ottava*, was, like Dryden and some other very great poets, not a man to take the trouble of inventing when a good thing was ready to his hand, and, moreover, was by nature thoroughly disposed to the lighter touch and motion which this stanza invites. Yet it never tempts him (as it had tempted Pulci, and has tempted Pulci's English and French imitators), to give a merely burlesque touch to his verse. The undulating movement of the lines, whether in individual verses or in the octaves, is so exactly suited to his purposes, that there is hardly any tone, among those that he

the English decasyllabic couplet, the objection which applies to Italian does not apply to English. Had this consideration been present to the minds of those critics who, one after another, depreciate the Shakespearian form to exalt the Petrarchian, and even go to the preposterous length of refusing to the former the name of sonnet at all, they might have been saved from an absurdity which has found only too docile following.

wants to give, that he cannot give to it. He never does want to rise to Dante's highest or even to his higher levels, yet such passages as the immortal

"Vattene in pace alma beata e bella,"

the *epiphonema* to the chaste spirit of the self-martyred Isabel, show that, with a different purpose and a very little more effort, he might have come much nearer to Dante himself. While as to his management of verse in the lighter keys there are practically no deniers. In ordinary [1] description, in mere narrative, in gravely sly innuendo, he is admittedly supreme.

As regards the individual line we have the advantage of being able to compare all the four greatest poets of Italy; as regards the octave, a comparison of Ariosto with Tasso will suffice. As compared with Dante we shall find that Ariosto's line is very much more "enjambed," so that, while it loses gravity, it attains swiftness. It may be said that it is not fair to compare the inscription on Hell-gate to anything in such a poem as the *Orlando*, yet the passage quoted above on Isabella's death is not so entirely out of keeping with it as to be incomparable. Of the nine lines of the Inscription [2] not one really runs on, three end with full stops, five with lesser stops but with full completion of sense, and the ninth (l. 7) with no stop, but in-

[1] One must add "ordinary." Spenser beats him easily in his greatest efforts here, and many who have never read or perhaps heard of Lessing's quarrel with the portrait of Alcina, must have anticipated the German critic.

[2] See Dr Moore's ed., Oxford, 1897. Variations in others are trifling.

cluding a proposition in itself complete. In the eight lines of the apostrophe to Isabella's soul, the second, third, and fifth are "enjambed," and only three end with a real break. Nor, I think, would the contrast fail, however often it were applied; while it applies almost equally to the central pauses. The contrast with Petrarch is something of the same kind, though Petrarch is more prodigal of "enjambed" lines than Dante. It is, moreover, complicated by a fresh feature, resulting partly no doubt from the difference in subject, for it appears much less in the *Trionfo* than in the *Rime*. This is Petrarch's occasional—nay, frequent—addiction to an antithetical arrangement of verse, in which the second half balances the first or returns upon it,[1] instead of the resistless and unbroken march of Dante's line, or the undulating progress of Ariosto's. But the contrast of the versification of the *Orlando* and that of the *Gerusalemme* is specially interesting, because it is double, in stanza and in line, because the subjects of the poems are so similar, and because there is no great, if there be any appreciable, difference in the age and stamp of the language. These things should make for a great resemblance, and do actually make for some. But the differences are almost as remarkable, if not quite so staring, as the resemblance. To say that Tasso's verse drags, would be not only uncomplimentary but false. I have amused myself by opening the two poems alternately at a venture in divers pairs of places, and comparing the first lines of successive

[1] How great the effect of this was on Elizabethan poetry all students of that poetry should know.

batches of stanzas. Over and over again you will find in Ariosto stanza after stanza in which the first line runs straight and pauseless from beginning to end, very likely with not even a stop at the end itself. This may be sometimes found of course in Tasso also, but far less frequently; and even when it does occur, the lines move slower than Ariosto's. And this is all the more remarkable, that Tasso avails himself more frequently than his great predecessor of the licence of running one stanza into another; so that it is clearly not intentional.

The characteristics thus indicated, and others—interesting but too long to trace—result in a poetic medium which for its special purpose simply cannot be surpassed. Ariosto does not attempt to hobble or check the skip, even the pirouette above referred to, nor does he try to disguise it by running the stanzas on. But by keeping it well in hand he gives to both line and stanza the freest action, an agile grace of movement which is inexpressibly pleasing. With him, as with all the greatest poetic masters, however much one may enjoy the meaning, it is a constant delight from time to time to let the meaning take care of itself, and to listen to the music of the verse as one listens to running water or rustling trees, allowing the cadences to shape rather our own dreams than anything that they have to tell us.

But for those who do not feel this charm, as well as for those who do, he has story enough to tell. Those who, even more unreasonable than Mrs Martha Buskbody at the end of *Old Mortality*, are uncomfortable unless they know not merely what happens to the Guse Gibbies of a tale after its end, but what happened to them from the date of their appearance in this world up to the beginning of the fable, may indeed require to be referred to the *Innamorato* or to some analysis of it; others need not be so particular. It will be sufficient for them to know certain general outlines—if even those—and then to abandon themselves to the poet's guidance.

Story-character.

Great pains have been spent on the origin of what we can hardly call the Italian cycle of Romance—it is too late, too unoriginal, and too irregularly furnished for that—but may call the transformation or travesty of the Charlemagne story, on which so many great Italian wits exercised themselves. In Dante's time the far greater Arthurian Legend seems still to have had the chief attention in Italy, if indeed it was not Dante's own unerring wit and poetical enthusiasm which made him write, not merely the Francesca and Paolo passage in the *Inferno,* but the less generally known reference in the *De Vulgari Eloquio.* But Arthurian matters were rather too high for the Italians; and it is certain that at a very early date poems of the Carlovingian cycle had not merely been known in Italy, but had actually (*v. supra,* p. 67) assumed a sort of Macaronic form between French and Italian. The controversy, if there ever was one, between the two "matters" of France and of Britain had been settled by the date of the *Reali di Francia* (*v. The Transition Period,* pp. 388-390). Thenceforward the Italians half borrowed, half shaped for themselves a new "matter," in which the various stories of invasion of Spain and Italy by the Emperor *à la barbe florie* and his Paladins, together with the not particularly dutiful behaviour of those Paladins to Charlemagne himself, the treason of the house of Mayence, and the almost independent position of that of Montglane in resistance to the Saracens, were combined with elements borrowed from the *Romans d'Aventure*[1] rather than from the *Chansons de Gestes* or the Arthurian stories.

Of Italian Romance generally.

Further, in this new, rather sophisticated, and even bastard, but ingenious development, there appeared two new features, one perhaps suggested, the other certainly original. The first of these was that multiplication of mere wonders which is noticeable in the *Amadis* cycle,[2] and which was not impossibly suggested to the Spaniards and Portuguese by their Eastern intercourse. The popular connection of giants, witches, dragons, enchantments, and the like with romance is due to the fact that, from the sixteenth century onwards, the true old romances became mainly unknown, and for some three centuries in France and England the Italian *rococo* substitute was held to be the standard. In the *chansons de geste* the miraculous element is purely religious, and in the Arthurian story it is always more or less connected with the Legend of the Graal. There is hardly a trace of the

[1] See *The Flourishing of Romance*, chaps. iii., iv., vii., and *The Fourteenth Century*, chap. i.

[2] See *The Later Renaissance*, p. 127 *sq.*

kind of conjurer's supernatural, the Jack-the-Giant-Killer wonders, which are rife in the *Amadis* and the Italians, and which, from them and from other late fifteenth-century work, affected Spenser to some extent.

The new element, which is found nowhere previously, is the peculiar and rather *bourgeois* comedy, the Voltairian touch, as we may call it proleptically, which is flagrant in Pulci, present even to some extent in Boiardo (though less in him than in any one), incessant, though quietly managed in Ariosto himself, and pushed to various degrees of avowed burlesque and grotesque in writers like Berni, Folengo, and Fortiguerra. This, we say, is quite new. There is much more comedy in the *Chansons de Geste* than those who have not read them suspect; but it is of the hard Teutonic order. The "japes" of Sir Dinadan and others in the Arthurian story are not frequent, and are always of the simple, almost childish, mediæval kind; while *Amadis* and *Palmerin* are guiltless of humour. The Italians, on the other hand, thrust in their own peculiar variety of the humorous at almost every moment.

Italian humour.

Appreciation of this quality may vary. It may well seem, for instance, to some even of those who can thoroughly and pretty equally appreciate Aristophanes and Lucian, Erasmus and the *Obscuri*, Rabelais and Molière, Swift and Fielding and Thackeray, that the much-vaunted Margutte passages of Pulci are a little rudimentary in conception and a little exaggerated in execution;

and that while work like Folengo's is of course only to be judged according to its own rules, it can never receive a very high place. But in Ariosto we have this *narquois* tone adjusted as nearly to good taste as it ever can be, and never pushed to a mere sneer, much less to a mere guffaw. That Messer Ludovico definitely intended to satirise Romance, that he had even as much anti-romantic intention as Cervantes (who had not very much), is more than doubtful. His position, allowing for difference of time, nationality, and the like, resembles that of Chaucer in *Sir Thopas*, but is one of more complexity and refinement. In so far as he is a satirist at all in the *Orlando*, he is satirising much rather those generous but also half-witless and impossible impulses of human nature, of which the Romance is a delightful expression, than that expression itself. The universally known opening distich is perfectly valid: he does sing, and sing without any perfidious intention, ladies, and knights, and arms, and loves, and courtesies, and deeds of bold emprise—only, as he sings, the seamy side of it somehow occurs to him, and he lets us know that it does, and how it does, by certain masterly side-touches.

Both as in Ariosto.

Universally known as they may be, however, it may be doubted whether sufficient attention has really been paid to these two lines. For they indicate, and indicate justly, the desultory character of the work itself. It has been pointed out above that there is very little evidence of really sustained purpose: it is much if the poet's great art can hide the pillar-to-post character of his story. But, as we have seen, it does hide that character, and that is quite sufficient.

Scenes,

In perusing the book the reader will derive very little assistance from the so-called *argomenti*. These inscriptions are much longer than Spenser's much-ridiculed doggerel quatrains, and not nearly so quaint; but they are considerably less informing—a fact, no doubt, partly due to the much greater length of the Ariostian canto. There is, however, perhaps, some intention in the way in which, in the first two cantos, the attention of the reader is skilfully shifted from Angelica, the practically dethroned heroine of the *Innamorato,* to her successor, Bradamante. The flight of the former from Rinaldo and her adventures in the forest are mere ordinary *roman-d'aventures* work; the defeat of Pinabel, his treason to Bradamante, and her consequent introduction to the wonders of the tomb of Merlin and to the future of her own race, are real business, promising at least some connected thread of story. And it is worth observing that Ariosto handles his frequent introductions of contemporary personages and history with a skill which distinguishes him from almost all other poets. The second-rate part which Orlando plays is largely redeemed by the vigour and splendour of the passages where he does appear. Mr Symonds has rightly dwelt on the singular skill with which the two different battles with the Orc are managed, though one may doubt about going with him to the full extent of admiring Ariosto's elaborate similes. These things always have the drawback of suggesting a deliberate following of Homer, and, as a rule, this is the only way in which they do suggest Homer. But the simile is the superstition of the critic, who wishes sometimes, if not always, to remember the ancients.

Persons,

Again, in regard to Ruggiero, the poet has surmounted, with that usual and curious felicity of his, the natural tendency of intelligent mankind to hate a successful hero. Ruggiero is, indeed, not the most interesting of the knights on either side,—of that more presently,—but we never dislike him. His entanglement with Alcina, his designs on Angelica, excite in us none of the feelings of contemptuous loathing which the dealings of Æneas with Dido excite in every generous breast; and if Marfisa had not turned out to be his sister, we could, in spite of Bradamante, have tolerated his philanderings with her. On the other side, Rodomonte is perhaps less sympathetic than Turnus, as he is infinitely less grand than Milton's Satan. But he clearly did not mean (if he had known what he was about) to cut off Isabella's head, and there is something refreshingly sensible as well as just in his rally against the commonplace slander of the *Host's Tale.* It is more effective, though less genial, than the anonymous English excuse—

"Some be lewd, and some be shrewd,
Yet all they be not so."

And this brings us to the enshrined *novelle,* which

are such noteworthy features of the poem. They have too often shocked the grave and the precise: they are too often incapable of adaptation as furniture of books for the young. But they are sometimes very amusing, sometimes really pathetic, and almost always quite admirably told. Whether introduced as episodes or frankly thrown in as mere told tales, the passages which are suggested by the names of Giocondo, Fiordispina, Genevra, Lidia, Marganorre, and many others, display the author's powers of narrative verse at their very highest. One is, indeed, almost tempted to say that they, even more than the rest of the poem, put him at the very head of all poets as a mere *raconteur*. No doubt a poet ought to be much more than this; no doubt Ariosto might with advantage be much more than this oftener than he is. But this he is, and without losing sight of poetry—a thing that can be said of few.

and passages.

It is difficult, where there is so much to charm, to fix upon the most charming passages, but many of them have already been indicated in passing. I do not think that Ariosto shows at his very best in fights: it seems to be generally acknowledged, even by his greatest admirers, that he has nothing in this way equal to the great duel of Orlando and Agricane in Boiardo. Nor, unless we give it very great odds for its originality, will the island of Alcina obtain advantage, or even bear the comparison, when contrasted with Tasso's garden of Armida or Spenser's Palace of Acrasia. In the former case the poet's heart does not seem to have been enough in the matter, for Ariosto was never a practical soldier, while in the latter he is not quite dreamy enough. Now the dream-element is of the very first importance in such descriptions, both in saving the ornamental from the touch of the tawdry, and in saving the voluptuous from the smirch of the indecent. Morpheus is unabashedly sensual; but he has some strange charm against the obscene. On the other hand, in the *general* description of enchanted palaces and castles, hippogriff-rides and the like, Ariosto is quite infallible. His irony, while it is never tedious and teeth-on-edge-setting, entirely saves situations of this kind from mere childishness in the first place, from the too businesslike and so dull detail of the Amadis cycle, and from the third danger of "overdoing it," into which his great follower, Spenser, has been often led, partly by his devotion to Allegory and partly by a following of such originals as *Arthur of Little Britain.*

Ariosto's rank as poet,

On the whole, however, we may probably return to the Thirty-fourth Canto, with the matter belonging to it at the end of the Thirty-third, as the finest, though not the most beautiful passage of the poem; to the loves of Angelica and Medoro as the most beautiful, or, at least, the most exquisitely pretty; to the epitaph on Isabella as the noblest and least tainted with either worldliness or cant; and to Rodomonte in Paris as the most ambitious on stock lines; reserving the Giocondo story as the farce of the pentalogy, and claiming for it the excuses and licences of that position. And, for some at least, the first named may be pointed out as probably the greatest of all. It has character—Astolfo is much more of a person than most of the knights—sufficient but not excessive purpose, criticism of life in quantity and force enough to satisfy the veriest devotee of that test of poetry, a magnificent and quintessential power of adapting style and verse to subject, and, last of all, that peculiar blend of laughter, seriousness, and something as nearly approaching tears as an Italian of the Renaissance could feel, which constitutes Humour. Now, humorous poetry, if equal stress be honestly laid on the substantive and on the adjective, is one of the very rarest of kinds, and when it is found in quintessence there is perhaps no reason for refusing it rank among the greatest. As, then, Ariosto has at least in this supremacy; as he is very nearly if not quite supreme in more than one other respect; as it may almost be said that he never fails, and that this freedom from failure is not due to tame faultlessness or a cowardly abstinence from the most difficult attempts,—it will go hard but we must rank him, at lowest, just below the very greatest of all.

and as mirror of his time.

Such a place is, I believe, his right, even on the calculus of those who refuse the historic estimate, or at least admit it with grudging; but for history he has even more claims and interests. It has been said that with Rabelais he represents the greatest literature of his time, penetrated most fully by the extra-literary as well as the literary characteristics of that time; and it may be added not merely that few times have been so thoroughly represented, but that few have ever so thoroughly lent themselves to representation. The Renaissance is of those periods which are not at all simple and which are also not exactly genuine, resembling in this respect rather the society of the Roman Empire or that of the present day than that of Greece or of the Middle Ages. Its typical man was distracted by many preoccupations. His so-called paganism and his still real though sometimes rebellious submission to Christianity; his enthusiasm for classical literature and philosophy and his scorn for things mediæval; his vague sense of the wonderful gains that science and discovery and commerce might bring; his religious and political restlessness; his educational fury—all these things pulled him this way and that way, and left him no definite or single course. But they were all derived, to a great extent, from literature, taken "from a printed book," and therefore the printed book could reproduce them.

Ariosto and Rabelais.

Rabelais naturally does the reproduction under different conditions from those which act upon Ariosto: he is fresher, more unsophisticated, less troubled about the beautiful, and more about the good, an enthusiastic believer in humanity, and (in a way which for very good reasons he is careful not to define too closely) a believer in God. Ariosto has upon him the polish and the pressure of a much older civilisation, and especially of a much older culture, while the miserable conditions in Church and State which had so long affected Italy could not fail to affect him: yet though he displays little or no enthusiasm except for things lovely to see, and soft to touch, and sweet to taste and hearing and smell, this most genuine passion of the Renaissance makes him at least no pessimist. He laughs at humanity, but he quite tolerates it; some readers can see no active or aggressive free-thought in him. His motto is, "Enjoy"; and he does not seem to doubt that there is ample enjoyment for everybody, at least everybody about whom an educated gentleman need trouble himself, in sight and in sound, in book and in picture,[1] in wine and in meat, in the beauty of woman, the amusement of adventure, the good things generally of the universe. He will even heighten the possibilities of amusement with Orcs to fight and Hippogriffs to ride, with magic rings and horns and lances to give variety and range, just as he added "vinegar and wine sauce"[2] to his beloved turnips.

For the expression of the less aspiring but more elaborately enjoying mood of the period in such verse as he has given us we may be most profoundly thankful—even the grave and precise may surely say *Vattene in pace* to his soul. He has not, like Rabelais, mixed with his expression elements which puzzle or revolt the ordinary reader; even his much-talked-of immorality needs, as has been said, a Pecksniff or a Podsnap to make very much fuss about it. He is eminently uncontroversial: save on the moral ground just mentioned, a man must be suffering from litigious

[1] Let it be remembered that he definitely mentions both the writers and the painters of his time in elaborate passages.

[2] This may seem an odd mixture: it was probably a sort of sauce *au bleu.* Those with whom turnips do not disagree should try it and if it makes them write more *Orlandos* so much the better.

monomania[1] who picks a quarrel with Ariosto about anything. And so it happens, with a pleasant poetical justice, that he whose creed was this, "Enjoy," has actually provided, for reading posterity to all time, perhaps the maximum of unmixed enjoyment that any poet has ever succeeded in offering.

Other epic-romances.

This examination of by far the greatest of the Italian chivalrous romances or—neither to urge the word controversially nor to omit it with a suspicion of purpose—epics, when taken in connection with those given of the fifteenth-century poems in *The Transition Period* and of Tasso in *The Later Renaissance*, may probably dispense us from minute criticism of any other. The second place in our special period is undoubtedly occupied by the *Orlando Innamorato* of Berni, a rifacimento (and not the only one) of Boiardo's poem, which long usurped the place of the original. Francesco Berni, who was born at the classic spot of Lamporecchio in 1490 and died in circumstances of some mystery in 1536, will appear more than once in this chapter. The characteristic which gave his name to a special style of burlesque is sufficiently obvious in the poem; but the ignobility of the travesty hangs about it, and it is by no means certain that we have not received it in a garbled condition. Bernardo Tasso of Bergamo (1493-1569) should have had the privilege

[1] It must, however, be sorrowfully admitted that this disease seems to be rather common, when one sees even the late Mr Symonds drawing a face of nineteenth-century horror at Ariosto for allowing his armed and charmed heroes to butcher so many peasants and Saracens.

(so common in poems of our kind) of seeing his posterity in a magic glass. He might then have thought it wiser to rely on his son for his place in poetical history. He was a gentleman and a man of worth in every way, with a talent for versification which he used only too freely. But his enormous *Amadigi*, in which, for the space of some 60,000 lines, he turned into verse the *Amadis* story, rather as it appears in Herberay's French form (indeed he wrote it at Paris) than in the original, and added some sprouts of his own brain, is but with the *Africas* and the *Pucelles.* Gian-Giorgio Trissino (1478-1550) cannot be said to have added much of an additional hold on literature to his *Sophonisba* (*v.* chap. vi.), his critical work (*v.* chap. vii.), and his publication in the vernacular of the *De Vulgari Eloquio,* by his ambitious *Italia Liberata da' Goti,* blank in verse and blank in interest. The Florentine Luigi Alamanni (1495-1556), who also will recur, was a better poet than Bernardo Tasso or than the author of the *Sophonisba;* but his *Il Giron Cortese* and *Avarchide*, the first of which versifies one of the best, but far from the best known, of the later incrustations on the Arthurian cycle, are not more original and much heavier than the *Coltivazione* (*v. infra*, p. 148 *sq.*). The names, forgotten in this connection at any rate, of Brusantini, Pescatore, and others too many to mention,[1] are connected with the expression of different incidents in the accepted *Orlando* series, or the appending of

[1] For some of them see Dr Garnett's *Italian Literature* (London, 1898), p. 153.

continuations, or the prefixing of introductions to it, in measure probably as abundant as the innumerable jointings of the original *gestes* themselves. Even the *Ricciardetto* of the already mentioned Fortiguerra or Forteguerri (1674-1735), nearly two hundred years after our time, may possibly not close the endless series in which, if any hero or heroine of Boiardo or Ariosto has missed any possible development of his or her career, he or she may justly complain of unjust neglect.

Lyrics. Sonnets, La Casa.

It is both natural and interesting to turn from Epic to Lyric, and there is, as it happens, an excellently representative collection[1] of the so-called lyrical work of twelve famous poets of the sixteenth century, including such names of the first class as Ariosto, Michelangelo, and Tasso; of the second, as Bembo, Molza, Vittoria Colonna, La Casa, Guarini; and of some others, ranging from Annibal Caro downwards. There is here a very large proportion of exquisitely accomplished work, and not a very small one of work that may be called exquisite, without any dubious addition. Of the Sonnets, of which it is very largely composed, it is of course difficult to speak too highly. Those of Michelangelo are now well known in England; those of Giovanni della Casa (1503-1556) less so, in spite of the high and perfectly well-deserved praise which Mr Symonds has given them. If the

[1] *Lirici del Secolo xvi.* Milan: Sonzogno, 1879. For thoroughness, the selections must of course be supplemented by the complete works of the writers, but these are easily accessible. No country has cheaper editions of her classics than Italy.

student of literature were not from his very freshmanship broken to the eternal contrasts of humanity, it might seem incredible that the author of the niggling and sniggering obscenity of the *Capitolo del Forno* could also be the author of the great Sleep Sonnet—

"O Sonno, o della queta, umida, ombrosa"—

which was probably the direct ancestor of the divers beautiful things on the same theme that our own Elizabethan sonneteers composed; of that beginning

"Mentre fra valle paludose ed ime";

and of, perhaps, the best of all, as it is the best known—

"O dolce selva solitaria, amica"—

to which not a few others out of no great total might be added. Of the *furor arduus* of Michelangelo's compositions in this kind there is no need to speak; but throughout, these poets are well at the height of this, their own and their greatest poetical invention as a form. Even merely pretty talents like that of Caro can extract the ultimate prettiness from it, as others almost the ultimate grandeur; and even the rather scholastic and rhetorical elegance of Bembo acquires some touch of nature as it celebrates that *crin d'oro crespo* of Lucrezia, a tress of which is said still to be in existence irradiating Bembo's manuscripts.

But Sonnets, as the strictest critics have always contended, and as all but the loosest must admit, are dubiously and by allowance lyrics, if they are lyrics at all. And when we turn from them to the more strictly lyrical constituents of the volume, the Madrigals and the Canzoni, it is here that we find something wanting. Outside of Michelangelo (who here, as elsewhere, "sways as he thinks fit The universal monarchy of wit") the burden, if not exactly the curse, of the artificial is over all. The Italian Canzone, with all its merits, is, like all very elaborate and largely planned lyrical forms, especially liable to this, and few of the authors now under consideration escape it, though they may show it in different ways. The elaborate art of Bembo, that first Tuscan outside Tuscany, reveals to us, through its veil of rather thin perfection of form, the excessive Atticism which the story alleges to have been detected in the non-Attic Theophrastus, the quality in the Latin of Livy which is thought to have constituted its Patavinity in the eyes of Pollio.

Madrigals and Canzoni.

Ariosto was a much greater poet than Bembo, but the very quality of his greatness might prepare us to expect some disappointment in his lyric work. He could not but be smooth, and in his madrigals is often not merely smooth but light. These are good qualities in lyric, but they are not the highest: they make the butterflies, not the eagles and the birds of Paradise of the lyric tribe. Still less do his sonnets attain to perfection. The chief thing noticeable in them is the *anadiplosis,* the repetition of the same word or words in successive lines or at more or less regular intervals, which was eagerly caught up by our Italianising Elizabethans, and which indeed

Ariosto.

seems something of a genuine Italian device, inasmuch as it is found in Lucilius two thousand years ago.

Michelangelo.

Michelangelo has been mentioned more than once, and it is now pretty fully and pretty generally recognised that he escapes the faults of his contemporaries. That even those contemporaries should have seen the real greatness of his "uncouth" verses (as, surely with some exaggeration of "correctness," they have been called) is perhaps even more an honour to those contemporaries than to himself. But one may be permitted to doubt whether the state of those foreigners who hardly perceive the uncouthness, but do perceive the poetry, is not more gracious. This nearest approach to a universal master of the Higher Fine Arts (for Rossetti did not add sculpture or architecture to painting and poetry) has as a poet that quality of poetical sound which forces itself upon the appreciation almost independently of the meaning, but in increasing measure as the meaning is felt. A hasty retort may be made: "Is not that simply because of the natural music in Italian?" but this would entirely miss the point. Nearly all Italian poetry is smooth and musical, but the *poetical* music which has just been referred to is of quite a different kind, and, in particular, is quite independent of mere smoothness; nor is it by any means common even in the greater Italian poets. Dante has it, of course, pre-eminently, and, to descend a very long way from Dante, it is present in those sonnets of La Casa which have been referred to. In the lighter keys Ariosto has it pretty constantly, in the graver very seldom, and it is by no means universal in Petrarch or in Tasso. Probably the Madrigal—

> "Come puo esser ch'io non sia piu mio?"[1]

would be ranked among the uncouthnesses by the purists, yet this very first line, rough as it is, gives the poetic password at once. Such things transform the commonplaces of erotic into the uncommonplaces of poetry, as here—

> "Quella pietosa aïta
> Che teco adduci con gli sguardi insieme,
> Perle mie parti estreme
> Sparge dal cuor gli spirti della vita."

The thing is not new; it has been said a thousand times before and since, but here it is said consummately.

The *Sonnets*, which are more generally known, exhibit the same quality. One of the secrets of this form is the mysterious opportunity it gives to the practitioner of striking as it were in the very first line a key-note which rings all through the piece. No other language has ever caught this so well as English. Our great sixteenth-century practitioners of the sonnet mastered it almost at once; it is even present to some extent in the experiments of Surrey

[1] This phrase is a favourite one with the poet. It recurs in another ardent piece of the kind, that beginning—

> "Un nume in una donna, anzi uno Dio.

and Wyatt, unmistakable in Sidney and Spenser, and carried to its very highest possibilities by Shakespeare. Michelangelo at his best has it excellently in

"Non so figura alcuna immaginarmi."

The last word explodes, with a sort of double effect of sound and light, all over the sonnet-scene.

Not much of this will be found in the far less masculine luxuriance of Molza (1489-1544), the laureate of the *Ninfe Tiberine*—courtesans of Rome; but his sonnets have at least sufficient sweetness and a prettiness which is perhaps the most intense and peculiar to be found in the class. Generally the sonnet is either something much more than pretty or something a good deal less; but the "sugar-candy" effect which is sometimes (more irreverently than untruly) ascribed to Italian can suffer this transformation also. And there are few prettier sonnets with a touch of that real pathos, which almost makes one repent of using the word "pretty," than Molza's on his dead mistress—

Molza.

"La mia Fenice ha già spiegate l' ali."

The pathos and the prettiness are not absent from his *canzoni*, but these more ambitious and elaborate compositions require (as Dante, their great eulogist and almost creator, had seen and said) something more than these amiable qualities.

In the collection of Lyric poets which for convenience sake we have taken as text, only two of the very numerous poetesses of the time, Vittoria

Colonna and Gaspara Stampa, find admission; but a third, Veronica Gambara, with a more copious representation of the two just named, appears in another volume of the same collection, the *Rime di Tre Gentildonne.*[1] Even the amiable "weight for sex," which all critics who are not curmudgeons concede, has not given Gaspara (who died for love), or Veronica, any very prominent or permanent place in poetry. But Vittoria Colonna (1490-1549), partly by borrowed, but also by authentic, light must always shine. Her beauty, her rank, her touching fidelity to an idol which was certainly not quite worthy of her worship, the adoration with which she was regarded by some of the greatest of men, her character, acknowledged to be without stain, not merely in one of the most profligate, but in one of the most libellous ages of the world—all these things have swelled, and justly swelled, her fame. But it would not be small if it rested on her poetry alone. If not entirely religious, it is very mainly so, or else devoted to the memory of her husband, always invoked under some metaphor or synonym of "light" (*lume, Sol, fiamma*), and so of a religious turn. The fitness of the sonnet for this purpose is unquestioned, and Vittoria's sonnets are perhaps superior to those of any other poetess except Miss Christina Rossetti.

Vittoria Colonna.

The rather abundant work of Giovanni Guidiccioni (1500-1541), a correspondent of Molza and of most men of letters of the time, does not rise much above

[1] Milan, Sonzogno, 1882.

the average; but he is sometimes happy in the fantastic treatment of commonplaces, which this style permits with advantage. This little madrigal, for instance, is certainly what all have thought, but what not many have expressed so tersely and so lightly:—

Guidiccioni.

> "Veramente in amore
> Si prova ogni dolore.
> Ma tutti gli altri avanza,
> Goder solo una volta, e perder poi
> Tutti i diletti suoi,
> E viver sempre mai fuor de speranza."

Economy and completeness of phrase, joined to a certain accompaniment of rueful-playful music, could not be achieved much better. But his sonnets are too full of *clichés:* in hardly any instance, I think, does he achieve that opening detonation of plangent or splendid promise which has been noted; and he is irritatingly prone to that "stopped beginning," as we may call it, which Milton himself adopted rather too freely, and which some of our modern sonneteers abuse still more. The qualities which have been praised in La Casa's Sonnets are not absent in his Canzoni. In one the always difficult subject of senile, or at least not youthful, love is treated with singular force, and in almost all there is blood in the heart, and not merely wind in the pipe. The accusations of unreality and artificiality brought against the "Petrarchists" of the sixteenth century cannot be wholly put out of court; but there are large and splendid exceptions to be made.

Italian Didactic and Blank Verse.

A little collection of the Italian didactic poets of this and the next age,[1] containing the *Coltivazione* of Alamanni,[2] the *Api* of Rucellai,[3] the *Podere* of Tansillo,[4] and the *Orto* of Baldi,[5] will give us a good text both for noticing this class of poetry as it shows itself at this time and in this country, and also for saying a few words on Blank Verse in Italian—all the poems mentioned, except Tansillo's (which is in *terza rima*), being in *versi sciolti.* We cannot, on reading the *Coltivazione* and its fellows, be very grateful to their composers. That such pieces should be written was an inevitable result both of the general style and trend of Italian critical thought, and of the ever-increasing idolatry of Virgil. For had not the ancients in general, from their admittedly second - oldest poet downwards, allowed and practised the style? And had not Virgil written the *Georgics?* Therefore it is very

[1] Venice, 1786, with extremely pretty engravings in the French style.

[2] Alamanni, besides the epics noted above, and some dramatic work, performed, like almost all the Italian writers of this time, poetical exercises of the usual miscellaneous kind, from sonnet to elegy and from epitaph to hymn.

[3] Giovanni Rucellai (latinised as Oricellarius) was born at Florence in 1475 and died fifty years later. He will reappear in the dramatic chapter.

[4] Luigi Tansillo, 1510-1568, was a Neapolitan. He began at an early age with a "poetic licence," the *Vendemmiatore*, and ended, according to etiquette, with a *Lagrime di San Pietro.* He was a dramatist of some merit, and wandered in didactic poetry not merely to the farm but to the nursery (in *La Balia*).

[5] Bernardino Baldi, a little later than the rest (1553-1617), was an *abbate*, a linguist of some merit, and a hardened didactic poet, original and translating.

probable that even if the Italians had been backward, the other literary nations would, all the same, have engaged themselves in the path which leads to poems on the *Sugar-cane* and "Come, Muse, let's sing of rats." One may therefore turn over these Georgics with a certain languid interest, and can allow a livelier feeling at the skill with which Alamanni in particular (who takes his subject most seriously and allows himself most room) emulates, and sometimes approaches, the ornamental digressions of his pattern. The style adds a distinct feature to the literary presentment of the time. It is also valuable as exhibiting what no incompetent hands (for Alamanni and Tansillo at least were among the most accomplished verse-smiths of their day, and Rucellai must have had a touch of originality in him to enable him to launch the long series of "Rosmunda" tragedies) could do in Italian with a form of verse capable of accomplishing such magnificent results in other languages.

It will probably, however, not take long before even a cautious critic will be tempted to ejaculate, "This will not do!" In the first place, the mind forebodes, and the ear soon confirms the foreboding, that the iambic-trochaic hendecasyllable is not suited for rhymeless verse. It is true that the Latin hendecasyllable is a very delightful thing; but then the cadence of Latin is not the cadence of Italian any more than the cadence of Anglo-Saxon is the cadence of English, and the central dactyl of the Latin verse gives it a spring and throb where the sameness of the Italian feet can only lollop or crawl. In the second place, and more damagingly still (for the genius of the right poet might cure this defect), another and an almost insuperable one occurs in the shape of that uniformity of termination which makes Italian rhyme at once peculiarly easy and peculiarly necessary.[1] Whether the effect is the same to the native as it is to the foreign ear one would not attempt to say or judge. But to the latter this effect is that not merely of a teasing tangle of incomplete and accidental rhymes, but (which is much worse) of a positive *débris* of rhyme that is attempted. Every now and then (as an example taken haphazard from Book II. of the *Coltivazione,* p. 49 of the edition cited, will show) it is that of a completed tercet, with first and third rhyming all right, but with second left "in the air" with nothing in the succeeding to answer to it:—

> "Che l' soverchio aspettar soverchio offende:
> Parte di mille augei diventa *preda:*
> Parte a l' estivo sol s' astringe e' ancende;
> E' l già troppo maturo in terra *cade.*"

Indeed, turning leaves hastily from the *versi sciolti* of the *Api* to the continuously printed *terza rima* of the *Podere,* a careless reader might for a moment fail to perceive the change.

But neither of these things would be quite fatal, if one special peculiarity of the hendecasyllable did not marry itself to another peculiarity of at least a large

[1] And it is unnecessary to say that this same ending in English blank verse has to be managed, if not with the greatest parsimony, at any rate with the greatest economy, in order to prevent a slovenly and down-at-heel effect.

portion of Italian verse. The secret of complete success in blank verse, which was hidden even from Marlowe, but which Shakespeare discovered and taught to Milton, is that combination of variety in the pauses and the cardinal syllables by which the paragraph- or blank-verse stanza is sculptured, or rather built. Now great variety of pause is, as has been pointed out already, not an Italian characteristic at any time. And the termination practically bars the most important syllable in the whole line from serving as a hinge or springboard at all. With rhyme the music of the rhymes itself leads from one verse to another, and can be used by the poet as a link; without rhyme the hendecasyllables slip off, one after another, into the inane.[1] In other words, and to put it briefly, the secret of blank verse is symphonic effect; and the continuous feminine termination without rhyme is fatal to symphony.

The Capitoli, *&c.*

Mr Carlyle suggested, in a well-known passage, that any person who, for just professional purposes, was forced to read a certain book, should forthwith apply the Mosaic rites and times of purification to himself. The advice would apply better still to the *Opere Burlesche*, which Grazzini (or "Il Lasca") issued in its revised form at Florence in 1548, which has been repeatedly printed since,[2] and which, by no means to the credit of Italian

[1] It is worth observing that even the decasyllabic verse-paragraphs of Beaumont and Fletcher, though often full of poetical beauty, are not seldom spoilt by the predominance of redundant syllables.

[2] My copy is in three vols., Usecht al Reno, 1760.

literature, occupies, as no other book of the kind does in any other, the position of a classic. That the *Capitoli* and other pieces in which Berni, first of all and chief of all, disports himself with, as rivals or followers, La Casa, Caro, Firenzuola,[1] Bronzino the painter, Molza, and others, down to Aretino, are in many cases (not quite in all) deliberately obscene, is not the real head and front of their offending. It is the peculiar nature of this obscenity which makes them a disgrace to their writers and almost to the country which not only produced but admired them. Many writers, from Aristophanes to Rabelais, and some later than Master Francis, have said things not as they ought and as they ought not. But the worse side of the Bernesque licence, a side which unfortunately has never been entirely unrepresented since in literature, is almost new. To illustrate an awkward subject with the least offence, and to make comparisons with the utmost justice possible, we may take, to compare with Berni and La Casa, not the Titanic excess of Aristophanes or Rabelais themselves, not the musical and many-coloured sensualities of the Greek Anthology, but the much less admirable and more questionable licence of Martial. The epigrammatist is, no doubt, peccant —very foully peccant—in this kind. But he may

[1] Agnolo Firenzuola (1493-1546) has received high praise in some histories of Italian literature, but it is not easy to point to any single work of his that justifies it. He will recur as a dramatist and novelist, but it "doth something speak him" that his chief Italian reputation is founded upon a paraphrase or rehandling of Apuleius, which is regarded as a word-book of pure Tuscan.

plead, not merely literary skill and grace, a lightning wit, and a brevity which prevents his offence from being rank and stale as well as foul in itself, but also a certain virility and gusto. In this crew of Italian academics there is no virility, and the gusto, such as it is, is utterly morbid.

Perhaps the most fatal thing that can be said against them is that the Aretinesque foulness in their own midst is positively less offensive than the deliquescent and sniggering suggestiveness, the long-drawn-out equivoques and suggestions, of the usual *capitolo.* In fact, though Berni undoubtedly had great literary gifts, he may almost be said to have introduced the snigger into literature, and directly or indirectly to have taught it to Voltaire and Sterne. Even his most famous pupils north of the Alps had the grace (if such a word may be used in such a connection) for the most part to make their touches of this kind rapid and momentary. The Italians dwell on their nasty ideas, roll them with relish over their tongue and mind, chase them through the involutions of hundreds of lines in *terza rima* or other form, decline them as if they were precious irregular verbs, through scores of variations of innuendo. Except for the brilliancy of the versification and style in Berni himself and a few others, there is nothing vivid or vigorous in the whole composition, nowhere a flash of passion, hardly anywhere a touch even of hearty laughter. It is simply Rhetoric gone wrong; the always pedantic, and often positively dull, application of trope and figure and technical elaboration to a very limited selection of indecent ideas and images. Except to sworn students of literature and history, the reading of these things can be recommended to no mortal; but to these they are certainly valuable, as indicating the kind of putrefaction which it is not entirely easy to understand, but which had settled upon the Italian intellect. And they may perhaps be positively useful to create a violent appetite for purely moral and virtuous literature—for tracts, sermons, goody-goody stories, hymns, or anything which, while it cannot possibly be duller than they very often are, shall, at any rate, and at all costs, be *clean.*

Prose-writers.

The qualities of the Italian prose of the period are curiously, and we may almost say affectedly, contrasted with those of the verse. Too much of the latter seems deliberately to caricature the critical doctrine (which, as we shall see, was by no means that of most critics of the time) of the importance of form in poetry, and to read it as if it enjoined attention to nothing but form—as if matter did not matter at all. The prose—in at least two great departments, History and short Tale-telling—sometimes offers no particular attractions in style, but ranks among the most important divisions of the prose literature of the world for its substance, and for the qualities of composition which lie outside of style proper. Niccolò Machiavelli (1469-1527) yields to no prose-writer of the world in combination of literary and historic importance; Guicciardini (1483-1540) is in a very sound sense the first of modern historians, no longer, like Comines, half historian and half chronicler. Bandello, Cinthio, Il Lasca, Straparola set at work half the dramatists of Europe, at once, and half its *novelle*-writers before long, and gave a mighty impulse to the tendency of all countries towards the completed novel. Even in more nondescript kinds the *Cortegiano* of Castiglione is but one of a group of books remarkable in all but the very first degree. Yet, as invariably happens, the characteristics of the verse reproduce themselves to a very great extent in the prose, and prose work seldom requires that detailed comment which is at least sometimes imperatively necessary in regard to verse. It will therefore have the smaller half of this chapter, but most certainly not as an indication of any contempt for it.

Machiavelli and Guicciardini.

The names of Machiavelli and Guicciardini are inseparably and in manifold ways connected, as contemporaries, as friends, as joint revivers of that accomplishment of Italian prose which Boccaccio had splendidly originated, but which his successors had let slip, as historians or historical students of the strongly philosophical kind, as political philosophers even more remarkable still, and, lastly, as representatives, by no means wholly for ill, but certainly not wholly for good, of the very heart and soul of the Italian Renaissance.[1] Both

[1] I use for Machiavelli the handy if somewhat too tightly packed two-volume edition of the *Opere Complete* (Naples, 1878), together with Mr Burd's well-known and most remarkable edition of the *Principe* (Oxford, 1891). Lord Acton's introduction to this, and the abundance of editorial apparatus, make it almost a Machiavellian encyclopædia in little; but it is needless to say that the literature of the subject is enormous. Prof. Villari's *Life and Times of Machiavelli* is the

were men of action as well as of the study. Guicciardini was at different times ambassador to great Powers, governor for the Pope of important places, member of the Council of Twelve, &c., while Machiavelli had even greater diplomatic experience. But there is a wide difference in the range of their literary faculties. Guicciardini is known only as a prose-writer, and his prose does not go beyond history and its precincts of reflection, letter-writing, and the like. Machiavelli does almost everything, and does everything that he does do well. His very poems are not contemptible; his plays (*v.* chap. vi.) deserve almost the highest place in the first flight of Italian comedy. His *Discorsi sopra Tito Livio* and his *Arte della Guerra* have suffered, the first very little from the limitation of its ostensible subject, and the second not so very much more from the lapse of time and change of circumstance. And if his *Istorie Fiorentine* are stigmatised

standard biography, and extends far beyond the person of the hero, dealing especially with Guicciardini as well. In regard to the latter writer I must own that I have "preferred the galleys," and can speak of but a small part of him at first hand. This preference has become even more natural since the addition, during the present generation, of ten volumes of Miscellanies (Florence, 1857-1867), to the four old quartos of the *Istoria d'Italia*, though the *Storia Fiorentina* (written about 1509) has its admirers. It should be said that the most notable work of both writers is open to English readers in two volumes, translated by Mr Ninian Hill Thomson, the *Prince* of Machiavelli (London, 1883), and *The Counsels and Reflections* (*Ricordi*) of Guicciardini (London, 1890). Macaulay's essay on Machiavelli has found favour enough in Italian eyes to be translated bodily in the edition of the *Opere* noted above. Macaulay was certainly a far better judge of Italian than of French or of German; but he shows his favourite habit of zebra- or magpie-painting too often here.

as too rhetorical, he can write a crowd of minor things —dialogues, tales, letters, nondescripts like the life of Castruccio Castracani, almost anything, with vigour and brilliancy. The prolixity of which Guicciardini stands accused rarely damages his friend's work, and it certainly is not chargeable on the questionable and almost endlessly questioned tractate which has given him his high though sinister fame, the *Opuscolo de Principatibus* as the author calls it in private, though he also himself refers to it by the title always used since, *Il Principe.*

It is fortunately no part of our business here to discuss, or to do any more than allude to, the numerous and sometimes extremely fantastic speculations on the exact drift of this treatise or the genuine opinions and principles of its author. But few people who know anything at all about the men and the books of the Renaissance, whether in Italy or in France, in Germany or in England, in Scotland or in Spain, will find anything out of the way in Machiavelli's apparently scientific consideration, and on the whole approval, of the methods of Cæsar Borgia, or in his equally scientific constitution of a non-moral *virtue.* In fact, it is hard to see how this difficulty can survive the reading of the Reflections of Guicciardini, which, *mutatis mutandis*, preach exactly the same doctrine and tell exactly the same story. Nay, pass over the best part of a century and come to Bacon, and no very different gospel appears, allowing for the fact that Bacon is an Englishman and a man of the last stage of the Renaissance, Machiavelli and Guicciardini Italians at its very centre.

But the literary qualities of the *Prince* and its companions are almost of the highest, and those of the *Istoria d'Italia* are far from low. Guicciardini admittedly has purity of language and accomplishment of style, though his pages may be too many and his presentation of action not vivid enough for a modern taste. There is a restless undercurrent of fire in Machiavelli, calm and cool and even cold-blooded as he may seem, which saves him entirely from this fault. He may have been possessed by the personage to whom, according to Butler, he even gave a name; but as Voltaire observed to Mlle. Clairon, "C'est le diable au corps qu'il faut avoir," to achieve success in any art. A little more of the same possession would not have done any harm to Guicciardini himself.

Minor historians.

No small band of historical followers attend these captains, the chief being perhaps Paolo Giovio (much better known as Paulus Jovius) 1483-1552, a dexterous and successful time-server who wrote chiefly in Latin; Segni, *not* the poet (*v. supra*, p. 39), whose *Storie Fiorentine* gave him no small repute for style; and the versatile *littérateur* Varchi (1503-1565), already mentioned, and to reappear, who has less independence and force if not less technical elegance. With these and others—perhaps less their inferiors than they were the inferiors of Guicciardini, or than he was below Machiavelli—Italy started the great vernacular schools of modern history as she had started not a few others. But her own work in the department has hardly contributed, to the epoch-making books of the world, anything save *The Prince.*

The great tradition of the Italian *novella* was maintained during our period. The total number of examples composed during the time must be enormous, and many are accessible with difficulty.

The Novellieri.

But characteristic examples have been made better known than any other literature of the period, except such triumphs as the *Orlando* and the *Prince*, by the combination of intrinsic and accidental attractions in countries other than Italy as well as in Italy itself. For reasons good and bad these novels have always pleased the mere reader, and having been early translated, they exercised upon the literature of other countries, and especially of England, an influence unparalleled by any other except that of the still earlier French romances and *fabliaux*, from which they were themselves partly derived. The famous *Palace of Pleasure* of Painter is in very large part a thesaurus of Italian novels, and in a large part a thesaurus of the Italian novelists of this time; nor had France, rich as she was in this kind of literature on her own account, failed to take ample toll from them as they passed over the Alps northward.

The most famous *novellieri* [1] of our time are Bandello, Cinthio, Firenzuola, Grazzini (Il Lasca), and Straparola. The collection of the first is the most extensive; of the second the most artistic and influential on other literature; those of the third and fourth the best written;

[1] There is a large collection of these in many vols. (Milan, 1813 *sq.*), and the more celebrated are accessible separately in modern editions. Translations will be noted below.

and those of the fifth by very far the most interesting and the best in all qualities of literature except pure style.

Bandello.

Matteo Bandello,[1] Bishop of Agen (the woes which France inflicted upon Italy at this time were inadequately alleviated by the ecclesiastical patronage bestowed on Italians at French cost), has pointed many morals at the expense of the Italian clergy of the time (1480-1561). From a sort of defence of his it seems that he was quite aware of them, and as indifferent as Machiavelli undoubtedly would have been, if not actually was, in reference to the shocks which he gave to morality on another side. Bandello's object was to amuse; fashionable amusement in this particular kind included a great deal of indecency and not a little cruelty; so in his more than two hundred novels he dealt out a liberal measure of both. I do not pretend to have read the whole or even a very large part of them; but those with which I am acquainted, and which include all those most generally cited and specially praised, seem to me to be singularly destitute of the charms of the kind, and singularly full of its drawbacks. The chief exception is the story of Gerardo and Elena: their secret marriage, the attempt of her family to compel her to marry some one else, her apparent death, and her recovery by Gerardo, in

[1] Bandello's novels, appearing in batches from 1554, were translated into French by Boaistuau (1559) and Belleforest (1565). Painter took, through these, much of *The Palace of Pleasure*, while Fenton followed with more in 1567. There is a selection by Mr Percy Pinkerton (London, 1895).

circumstances not wholly unlike "Romeo and Juliet,"[1] with a happy ending. This is really romantic and really agreeable. But the story of Violante, who tortures and butchers her faithless husband with scissors and knives, is merely revolting, without a particle of tragic interest. And the obstinacy of Ginevra in her cruelty to Don Diego is only more satisfactorily treated than the idiotic unkindness to their lovers of the heroines of Spanish romance, because Ginevra is brought to her senses by well-deserved brutality. To read Bandello between his model Boccaccio and his successor Straparola is to form an extremely low opinion of him as a tale-teller.

Cinthio.

Bandello, in his quality of unabashed and unmitigated *amuseur*, had not troubled himself with the usual framework story of stories. Cinthio Giraldi (1504-1573) (himself a critic, *v. infra*, p. 389, but not to be confounded with the critic Lilius Giraldus) was more orthodox, and adapted his famous *Hecatommithi*[2] to the sack of Rome and the escape of certain persons therefrom. Although his novels are often yoked with Bandello's as an example of the licence of the time and kind, this is rather unjust, for Cinthio at least intended to be very particular in this respect, though his efforts may appear to modern readers not to have met with that success which the

[1] Bandello, the reader may be reminded, also tells this, though Luigi da Porto had been before him in 1531.

[2] Some in Painter, and those concerning Shakespeare in the different editions of "Shakespeare's Library," &c.

goodness of the intention deserved. On the other hand, the author of the *Orbecche* (see chap. vi., *infra*) could not and did not abstain from introducing subjects of gloom and horror. It is not insignificant that Shakespeare owed him *Othello*, nor that he has transformed into a novel-subject the historical or legendary incidents which make the house of Borgia a modern parallel to the houses of Laius and Atreus.

Firenzuola and Grazzini.

The elegant Firenzuola showed his elegance in his stories, of which, however, he made no formal collection of any great size; and for the work of Doni and others we must refer to Mr Symonds for a short account, or the native historians for a longer. "Il Lasca," Grazzini, is of greater importance, and his stories, entitled *Le Cene*, are singularly well written and gracefully framed, as well as told with that sense of dramatic and fictitious proportion which distinguishes this author. But they have usually borne the dishonourable palm among all the novels of the day for that combination of indecency and cruelty which is the most odious temper of the human soul, and which is far too much in evidence throughout the work of the kind and time.

Straparola.

By far the most interesting to literature of the whole crew (though he is said by Italian purists to be quite the worst for style) is the almost unknown Giovanfrancesco Straparola, who was born at Caravaggio somewhere towards the end of the fifteenth century, wrote some poetry, and also, early in the sixteenth, accomplished a collection of Novelle called *Piacevole Notti*, which in part or in whole were printed seven times in as many years at Venice, between 1550 and 1557, and constantly reprinted afterwards.[1] It is not at all correct to say, as has been said, that Straparola owes his charm to "oddity and licence"; and, though less incorrect, nearly as insufficient to assign his interest to "folk-lore," as is now almost universal. The literary value of Straparola is due to the simple fact that, whether he wrote an Italian style admirable to the authors of composition-books or not, whether he got his materials from other writers, from popular traditions, from sailors landing on the Venetian quays, or from any thing or person else, he managed to make real literature. The punctilious moralist will of course be justly shocked at him for the licence of some of his tales. But his naughtiness is neither cold-blooded nor cruel, and there is an extraordinary charm about some of his stories. The most romantically tragical of all is the death of the girl Malgherita, drowned through the cruel wiles of her brothers, who show false lights as she swims to her love. But this is only one of the "strange and high" excellences of this singular collection. It has a beauty and poignancy of feeling, a suitableness of setting and scenery, which are unmatched in the whole range of the Italian *novella*, and present the highest possible combination of mediæval and Renaissance gift. For what we may call the amiable fairy-

[1] The early Italian editions are, however, rare, and the later are said to be garbled. The early French version, by the dramatist Larivey, was reprinted in the *Bibliothèque Elzévirienne.* There is an admirable English version by W. G. Waters, 2 vols., London, 1894.

story, the extravagant fancy of the East, refined to imagination by the Western spirit, there is nothing better anywhere than the story of Biancabella; for the grim-grotesque variety of the same, than the story of the foolish youth who sought for Death and found Life, but in no charming guise. The fantastic legend of the speaking satyr is a vast improvement on the old story (as old as the originals of the *Seven Sages*) of the wicked queen who had for her attendants men masquerading as girls. But if any one wants to differentiate Straparola to his advantage in respect of the worst vice of the *novella*, he cannot do better than read the story of Quinquino the sculptor, and his true wife Prudence, and the priest Tiberio. This is very familiar in earlier tale-work from the *fabliaux* onwards, and there it always ends in "atrocity." Here there is nothing revolting except to prudishness rather than Prudence; the fun is good throughout; and the poetic justice not less thoroughly, though less sanguinarily, complete than in the older versions. It ought to be said that Bembo figures in these stories, and that "M. Peter," as Hoby calls him, talks in a manner much more fitting some of his extant works than the beautiful moonshine of his concluding rhapsody in the *Cortegiano* (*v. infra*, p. 170). It is good to leave the subject of the *novella* with these really *Pleasing Nights*. They are not immaculate—very far from it. But they have colour, fancy, variety, good-humour, passion; they pander to no tendency of humanity that is, *per se* and hopelessly, bad and detestable. They do not indeed close the record (for the *Pentamerone* is more than a century their junior), but they virtually close the list of the great original *novellieri* who, though they may have a certain indebtedness to predecessors, do not deliberately compile or refashion from the printed book. Even if Straparola did not invent *Puss in* (or rather *without*) *Boots*, he introduced that gracious animal to literature: and he could deal, as we have seen, with things even more gracious if less merry than Puss.

Miscellaneous prose: Letters, Dialogues.

Amongst the miscellaneous prose of the time it is perhaps less useful to attempt to specify kinds than to indicate remarkable books. The Letter and the Dialogue, however, have a certain claim to mention under the first head. The importance of the Latin Letters of the period (*v. supra*, p. 101) is almost matched by that of the Italian; and there are few of the great men of letters of the Peninsula by whom we have not more or fewer, from Machiavelli and Guicciardini to Bembo and Caro. These two kinds, indeed, joined to build the sinister fame —infamous rather to himself and his generation—of Pietro Aretino (1492-1557), the "scourge of princes," the "divine" cynosure of real or affected admiration, the pattern of despairing imitators—amongst literary bravos and gentlemen of the gutter press—from his own day to this. In comedy this person undoubtedly deserves serious attention, though his qualities are much the same there as elsewhere. Off the stage his most notorious productions are scarcely mentionable here, while the abundant works of piety with which he interspersed libel, flattery, and pornography sheer and mere, require no notice. His *Letters* extend to six volumes.

The most literary aspect of Aretino (still excepting his dramatic work) consists, first in the curious differences of opinion which have been held as to his value by critics, who are pretty well agreed as to his moral flagitiousness; and secondly, in the puzzle which most people have found in the prosperity and popularity of such a writer. As to the first point, it is perhaps sufficient to observe that no non-dramatic work of Aretino's has ever excited interest apart from some more or less illegitimate attraction of subject—licence, libel, or mere personal gossip. As to the second, there is no real puzzle. Aretino, from a safe retreat in Venice, managed to carry on with impunity a literary business which, in the circumstances of the time, was exactly equivalent to that of the more unscrupulous modern journalist. It has been observed, with perfect justice, that a personage of this kind "can make almost any man's life a burden to him," and it was exactly on this principle that Aretino worked and blackmailed. What *is* rather surprising is that the stiletto did not avenge the crimes of the stylus. Attempts at this kind of wild justice were by no means wanting; but Aretino had the luck of his vileness in escaping them with only minor damage.

Aretino.

The famous autobiography of Benvenuto Cellini [1] has always, and the *Lives of the Painters* [2] by Giorgio Vasari have sometimes, found place even in brief notices

[1] Constantly reprinted. Mr Symonds' translation (2 vols., London, 1888) is one of the best translations in any language, whether we agree or not with his estimate of book and man.

[2] The best modern edition is in 9 vols, 1878-85. The translation in Bohn's Library, recently re-edited, is well spoken of for its notes.

of Italian Literature. Vasari, however, though infinitely important and interesting to the History of Art, and indeed to the general reader, is chiefly recommended by his matter—though his form is not disagreeable—and a very copious collection of "Ana." Cellini's book is a book. The great sculptor and goldsmith, though not such a poisonous creature as Aretino, and altogether of a more human, or merely brutal, as opposed to diabolical, complexion, was nearly as much of a bravo as the "Divine" one himself. And it would be exceedingly rash to accept a single statement of his, about himself especially, without full external corroboration. But the *verve* of the book is extraordinary, and its side-lights on history, whether we regard them as really illuminative or mostly Will-o'-the-wispish, are most fascinating. It is possible, however, to exaggerate its strictly *literary* merit. Cellini's most competent translator and most uncompromising admirer has described it as "heedless animated talking." Now the *simulation* of this is literature, the mere utterance is not. Miss Austen was certainly a literary genius; Miss Bates less certainly.

Miscellanies of Gelli, Firenzuola, Bembo, Varchi, Caro.

The very curious Dialogues and *Ragionamenti* of Gianbattista Gelli[1] (1493-1563) will be best noticed in connection with his comedies. But some notice may here be taken of representatives of a curious class of work in which the sensuality and the philosophy of the Italians were helped, by the mastery of the language now attained,

[1] With the plays in Sonzogno's collection, Milan, 1887. Gelli, who was a hosier, also lectured on the *Divina Commedia.*

to express themselves, always with great ingenuity and sometimes with no inconsiderable charm. Firenzuola (*v. supra*, p. 152) puts all his lore and not a little (in not quite so innocent a sense) of that other matter which ancient Gower has coupled with lore at the beginning of the *Confessio Amantis*, into his discourse *Della Bellezza delle Donne*—a fruitful theme on which less elegant writers also expatiated. The great Bembo (who, besides many letters and other works, condescended to a formal grammatical treatise *Della Volgar Lingua*) put the considerable elegance and the not inconsiderable strength which he possessed into the Ciceronian but vernacular disquisitions on the subject of Love entitled *Gli Asolani*.[1] Benedetto Varchi's *Ercolano*[2] is, again, devoted to and written in the vulgar tongue, but composed in the manner of Cicero, while his *Lezioni sopra Alcune Quistioni d'Amore* form yet another of the documents which might justify against the Italians of the time the application of Macaulay's harsh antiphrasis on Southey's heroes, that they "make love like seraphim—or like cattle." And the work of that excellent if hardly important writer Annibal Caro,[3] includes experiments in almost every kind of prose. But before concluding the chapter we must give somewhat fuller attention to one famous book referred to often already.

Mention has already been made of Baldassare Cas-

[1] Both these, with Letters, &c., in the same collection, Milan, 1880.
[2] Both in one volume of the same, ibid., 1888.
[3] See 2 vols. of the same, *Lettere Familiari*, ibid., 1879, and *Apologia*, &c., ibid., 1884.

tiglione as not the least attractive of the Latin-Italian poets of our period. He wrote Italian as well as Latin poetry, and was a diplomatist of some importance in his day. But for none of these things can he be said to have any real share in the general European memory, though undoubtedly he has such a share. His title is the famous *Cortegiano*, which was printed in 1528, but had been written some twelve years earlier, which spread itself rapidly over Europe, reaching England (under the care of Sir Thomas Hoby[1]) in 1561, and which has been selected and praised by good wits as a sort of Bible of the Renaissance—a summary of its creed as to almost all things noble and of good report.

Castiglione and The Courtier.

That the book is itself a noble one there need not be the least hesitation in granting; and, for once, there seems to be little if any doubt that the preacher recked his own rede. None of the distinguished Italians of the time has a less questionable record than Castiglione. His book is not in the least exposed to the imputation sometimes made against it, of being a mere manual of etiquette, a successor of the "Babee's Books" of the Middle Ages, and a predecessor of the more trivial part of Chesterfield's *Letters*. The *Galateo* of La Casa, which came a little later, is obnoxious to this charge; the *Courtier* is not. Nor, further, can it be denied that the tone of the book represents an ideal which the Renaissance saw afar off and approved of too often platonically, or after the Ovidian fashion rather.

[1] Hoby's *Courtier* has been excellently edited by Professor Raleigh in the "Tudor Translations," London, 1900.

The scheme of it is but a variation on that which the genius of Boccaccio, if it had not exactly invented, had made canonical in Italy for a very large part of lighter and even of graver literary work—the scheme of conversation between a party of noble, or gentle, or learned men and women. The scene is the Court of Urbino, where Castiglione actually abode for a considerable time, and the central figure—not speaking much, but addressed by all and guiding everything—is its Duchess, whom, from the unmistakable sincerity of his lament over her death in the later-written Introduction, the author would seem to have regarded with no small share of the fantastic but generous adoration which he inculcates in his book. The subject is sufficiently close to the title on the whole—dealing with the qualities and qualifications of courtiers of both sexes. But the author permits himself considerable expatiations, though he usually brings them round to the point. Thus the Second Book is mainly occupied with jests of one kind or another, sometimes not too strait-laced, though never outstepping the decency which is the note of the whole book. A great deal of space, too, is occupied by a repetition or variation of the old slanders on women by some of the characters, and a long and vigorous defence of them by Frederico Fregoso and Giuliano de' Medici. In the earlier part there are some remarks on the vexed question of Tuscanism, which played only too large a part in Italian Criticism, and the whole piece ends by a discourse on love, in the highest Platonic altitudes, by no less a person than Pietro Bembo. On the whole, no one can deny that Castiglione does his best to outline the "very perfect gentle knight" of his own times in a spirit at once of delicate accomplishment, of manly proficiency in sport and war, and of high ethical and intellectual, though scarcely religious, sentiment. It is almost enough to say that there is no man of the century who fulfils the ideal of *The Courtier* so well as Sir Philip Sidney, and that there is not the slightest reason for doubting that Sidney himself had *The Courtier* and its ideal constantly before him.

This is very high praise, and it may be supplemented and enlarged for English readers. Very much of the best distinctive character of our Elizabethan period generally, from its earlier, more homely, and more prosaic foreshadowings in Ascham to its perfect flower of poetry and philosophy in Spenser, is closely connected with Castiglione's temper and teachings. Whatsoever evil the "Italianation" of Englishmen may have done must be regarded as compensated handsomely by the holding up of this pattern, which, by the way (we may something pride ourselves upon the fact), was nowhere welcomed and developed to such an extent as with us. Germany was too coarse and too distracted; France, though there is more than a touch of *The Courtier* in the exquisite passage—satire softening at the thing satirised—on the Court of Quintessence in Rabelais, was too confused and too careless of morality to serve as good culture for this germ. In Spain, indeed, it found a not uncongenial home: Don Quixote is a spiritual son of Castiglione, who, by the way, seems to have had not a little of the Don's guilelessness as well as of his chivalry, and was admired and cheated by Charles V. on Spanish ground itself. But England alone received the seed in a thoroughly kindly soil, and brought the flower and fruit to perfection. All the gentler and nobler side of the great Elizabethan heroes reflects *The Courtier* within its own century, and after half another had nearly passed, the typical Cavalier is the Courtier himself, ennobled and strengthened a little, that he may "keep the bird in his bosom" against a worsening world, and die with it still there. Nay, Milton on the other side, though of temper in part opposed to the ideal, still has much of it.

But in speaking of a book which is so famous, and has been so much and to a great extent so justly praised, it is necessary also to give the other side. That the atmosphere of *The Courtier* is extremely artificial—that it is hardly adapted for any but a very small section of the human race in a somewhat accidental condition of society, possessing a very large number of comparatively small courts, at which most of the men of birth or sons of learning congregate—is no fatal objection. The conditions, though complicated and artificial, were real for a considerable time, and in more than one country, and might very conceivably become real again; while it would not be destructive to the book if they were as fantastic as those of Brobdingnag or Utopia. A much more serious objection is the singular, or rather, in the Italian Renaissance, not singular but ordinary, limitation of the ethical element, and the almost entire elimination of the religious.

The Elizabethans, as we have seen, supplied the gaps, and thus made the ideal both a nobler and a more practical one. But the actual Courtier, however accomplished as a courtier, is distinctly rudimentary as a man. He is to have justice, wisdom, temperance, and so forth, just as he is to be good at the jereed and in the tiltyard, and to speak French and Spanish. But Sidney's action with the water *n'est pas dans son rollet.* And the devotion which is as ardent and as sincere in the *Faerie Queene* as in the *Lancelot,* sends neither glance nor glow through any page of the volume, unless somebody good-naturedly discovers it in Bembo's Platonic raptures.

The last name, too, brings us to another head of the Devil's Advocate's brief. We have no reason, as has been said, to question Castiglione's own character; and if his time simply had not lived up to the shining pattern he put before it, it would not be the only time which has "sinned its mercies" in such a kind. But the contrast of the book and the time is almost *too* glaring. In the book itself the highest praise is given to Ippolito of Este, a worse than fratricide from the point of view of morality, and from the point of view of taste the author (in some form or other to all but certainty) of the description of the greatest poem of the time, and one of the greatest poems of the world, as a "pack of rubbish." When Aretino and Machiavelli write they may shock us or not, but they are certainly expressing the spirit of their age and country. When Castiglione writes he may have expressed a spirit which animated himself, and Michelangelo, and Vittoria Colonna, and a few more elect souls, but which certainly animated few others. There is hardly in all literature a passage of bitterer irony than the enthusiastic anticipations of what Henry VIII., Francis I., and Charles V. are to be and to do, when we remember what each one of the three actually was, actually did. Indeed from a certain point of view *The Courtier* is the counterpart and the explanation of *The Prince.* When goodness was so limited and so unpractical, practicalness must almost be excused for being so unlimitedly bad.

Of few periods of far fewer literary histories is it more difficult to speak in brief space than of the subject of the present chapter. The "Age of Leo X.," as it used to be loosely called, was for no small length of time, and under no few changes of prevailing literary taste, extolled as one of the greatest ages of literature, as perhaps *the* greatest age of modern literature. It fell from this high estate about a century ago, and though strong efforts have been made in its favour during the past half century, it is perhaps never likely to recover its old pride of place. Of the greatness of its best authors, of an Ariosto or a Machiavelli, there never has been much, and there never should be any, doubt. By the number of names which it has to show in a rank somewhat lower it may match all but the best of other times in other countries. In polish and accomplishment of language, in clear knowledge on the part of the writers of exactly what they wanted to do, and exactly the means which would make most readers think that they had done this, it has perhaps no superior at all. But the rift within its lute has undoubtedly widened with time, and that not only from one critical point of view nor according to the shibboleth of one critical sect. From one point too much of its poetry is deficient in "cry," too much of its prose deficient in rhythmical magnificence or in racy vigour of style. From another the verse suffers equally from the occasional emptiness and the occasional frigidity of its sentiment, the prose either from its tendency to a one-sided criticism of life, whether the side be that of Castiglione or that of Machiavelli, or from an absence of any such criticism, as in the more formal and rhetorical writings of Bembo and the rest. Yet, as we shall hope to show in the Conclusion, this is but Italy's part of the burden of the Renaissance. And while acknowledging it, let us remember the charm of Ariosto, the force of Machiavelli, the real thrill and actual "cry" of Michelangelo and La Casa, the stately chivalry of Castiglione—nay, even the varied pastime of many of the novels and the wicked wit of some of the burlesques.[1]

[1] Many other writers might of course have been mentioned. Perhaps the most missed will be Ortensio Landi (1501-1560), of the *Paradossi* (1543) and other ingenious works, exhibiting, with perhaps a little quackery and fanfaronnade, a good deal of real talent. The mixture has not been unknown at other periods. My friend Mr Axon of Manchester has written some interesting papers on Landi.

CHAPTER III.

FROM RHETORIC TO PLEIAD.

SOME BACKWARDNESS IN THE FRENCH RENAISSANCE — THE "RHÉTORIQUEUR" SCHOOL—THE ARTIFICIAL FORMS OF POETRY—THE ITALIAN INFLUENCE — SUB-PERIODS — MINOR WRITERS OF THE EARLY SIXTEENTH CENTURY — COLLÉRYE, BOUCHET, JEHAN DU PONTALAIS — CLÉMENT MAROT—HIS LIFE—CHARACTER AND IMPORTANCE OF HIS POETRY—THE PSALMS' AND OTHER WORK—RABELAIS—THE PROBLEM OF HIM—HIS LIFE—'GARGANTUA AND PANTAGRUEL'—THEIR GENERAL FORM AND SCHEME—FANTASTIC NOTIONS ON THE SUBJECT —REALLY A SATIRICAL CRITICISM OF LIFE—COMPARATIVE QUALITY OF THE SATIRE — THE STYLE — SHORT RUNNING COMMENTARY — GENERAL REMARKS — CALVIN — VALUE OF THE 'INSTITUTION' IN STYLE—MINORITIES OF THE MID-CENTURY—MARGUERITE DE VALOIS —THE 'HEPTAMERON'—BONAVENTURE DES PERIERS—THE 'NOUVELLES RÉCRÉATIONS' — THE 'CYMBALUM MUNDI' — MELLIN DE SAINT-GELAIS—MAGNY, TAHUREAU, LOUISE LABÉ.

IN passing from Italy to France we pass, once for all, from the mistress to the scholars; and we enter on the subject-matter strictly indicated by the title of our volume, as far as the vernaculars are concerned. The first half of the sixteenth century, we have freely admitted, is not the period of the Early Renaissance in Italy; there is no reasonable doubt or controversy that it is the period of the Early Renaissance in France.

Some backwardness in the French Renaissance.

It is rather remarkable that the Humanism which ushered the vernacular Renaissance in all countries should have been less noticeable and later in France than anywhere else. The fact is not doubtful; the study of Greek — the Humanist *sine qua non*—was, by all trustworthy witness, much later than in Italy, later even than in Germany and in England. But this fact is susceptible, if not of explanation, of a certain amount of illustrative comment. France has seldom been very remarkable for classical—at least for Greek—studies, and though she certainly became so for a time during our present period, this was long the only exception. In the second place, the French universities were particularly powerful and particularly obscurantist. Scarcely even in Spain was there a more persecuting body, when persecution came into fashion, than the Sorbonne; scarcely at Cologne under the greatest flourishing of Ortuinus was there, to say the least, a greater resistance of *inertia* to the new studies than at Paris. And, still further, something must be set down to the fact that France had not only the oldest and most celebrated university teaching in Europe, but also a literature which, though Italy could outshine it with her best examples and with the state of perfection reached by them, was far older, immensely more voluminous, and more varied than the Italian. Yet of this literature, as the conquered Italians notice with some contempt, the French nobility and gentry of the fifteenth century took very little heed; while it further happened that French had for some time fallen into grooves of both verse and prose, which were likely to hold the wheels steadily.

The Rhétoriqueur *school.*

These grooves are those of what, with more convenience and logical reason than positive historical authority, is called the "Rhétoriqueur" school.[1] The term is derived from a chance gibe of the late fifteeenth-century poet and satirist Coquillart at the versifiers his contemporaries as *grands rhétoriqueurs;* and the justification of it as denoting not merely the style but the literature of a whole period is strong. Not merely had Rhetoric in France and all over Europe, as it were, subsumed poetry, but the very word had begun to be used as equivalent to poetry itself. The praise of Chaucer's "Rhetoric" is familiar in English work of the time, and the habit was at least as common across the Channel as this side of it.

Now the association of Rhetoric with exceedingly ornate ("aureate," as it was called in English) language was an old one enough; in fact it had become and had remained inveterate in ordinary speech, while it was sanctioned, if not by the great old authorities such as Aristotle (which were only now again going to be known directly), by those with which the Middle Ages were most familiar, such as Martianus Capella. That barbaric but not despicable writer's description of Rhetoric herself—with her bright coloured dress, her gemmed and various-figured baldric, her rattling and clattering armour, the resounding of her very kisses—was thoroughly adopted and enjoyed.

[1] See *The Transition Period*, p. 114.

And it has perhaps never been more thoroughly carried out in prose or in verse than by the French writers from Christine de Pisan and Alain Chartier to Crétin and Le Maire de Belges, and by the Burgundian school, such as Chastelain and Robertet. But for these reference may be made to the preceding volume of this History.

The artificial forms of poetry.

It happened further that the tendency was intensified by the equally inveterate popularity of the artificial forms of verse—*Ballades, rondeaux, chants royaux*, and the rest—which had come into favour at a rather uncertain period in the late thirteenth or early fourteenth century, and had held it with singular tenacity, and with the redoubling of technical refinements usual in such cases. These forms, in the hands of the best of their earlier practitioners, such as Jehannot de Lescurel, had shown themselves able to embody, in a very charming and adequate fashion, the fresh gaiety and genuine sentiment of the Middle Ages; while in at least two writers of the mid-fifteenth century, Charles d'Orléans, and still more Villon, they had served as vehicles to poetry of the truest, and in the latter case all but the most universal, character. But they were now very old and very much hackneyed—the bloom was off and the juice out of them; while, unfortunately, their very formal perfection, and the almost automatic music with which it provided those who used them, made it specially easy to obtain the semblance of poetry without the reality.

If this applied to verse, prose suffered not only from

Rhetoric, but from a complication of minor drawbacks and deficiencies. A new kind, of immense promise, either in the hands of Antoine de La Salle or in those of somebody else, had indeed been founded by the transformation of the old verse *fabliau* into the new prose tale; but it is probable that this itself owed a good deal to Italian influence. The vernacular Sermon had advanced in familiarity and liveliness, if not exactly in dignity. But the Chronicle, which had always absorbed the chief energies of French prose-writers, was specially infested by Rhetoric; and in its one great practitioner, Comines (who continues over not a little of our own period, though he is more representative of the last), it had a man whose genius was very much more of thought and matter than of style, who had a great deal to teach thoughtful French readers, but very little to set before ambitious and docile French writers by way of pattern. All this made at once for some delay in the reception of a foreign influence, and for a powerful effect of it when it once began to work.

The Italian influence.

The actual beginning certainly coincides more or less with the Italian wars of Charles VIII. and his successors. This coincidence is indeed so natural and so certain that there is no need to haggle over any difficulties of date or detail. These French invasions coincided with the very flower- and fruit-time of the Italian literature of the Renaissance, and there could be no question of the literary faculty of the race which was brought into contact therewith. Yet the effect (for the reasons doubtless which have been given) was by no means shown very early. The first French sonnets, those of Mellin de Saint-Gelais, only date from *c.* 1530; the Italian influence, though it exists, is by no means very strong, in Marot, whose forms are chiefly of an older kind; and though Italian as well as French romances may have had their influence on Rabelais, the Italian work which affected him most was the Harlequin-Latin Macaronic of Folengo. Not till quite towards the end of our time, and in that work of the *Pléiade* with which we do not directly meddle,[1] is the Italian influence triumphant or full.

Sub-periods.

The literary interest of our own time, therefore, may be divided into three parts. First, the earlier and older fashioned work which is specially representative of the first quarter of the century; then that of two or three writers of the transition (one at least also one of the principal writers of Europe); and last, that of writers such as those just mentioned, Mellin de Saint-Gelais and others, who touch "Rhetoric" with one hand and the *Pléiade* with the other, who are mainly contemporary with Marot, and would have been so longer, had not that luckless, though not graceless, bard's life been cut so short.

Minor writers of the early sixteenth century.

For the first batch, however, we need spare no very extensive space here: its most important representatives indeed have already been dealt with in the preceding volume. Comines, as has been said, lived into our period, indeed, outlived its first decade; the poet-chronicler Molinet—

[1] For it see the vol. on *The Later Renaissance.*

heavy as poet, heavier as chronicler—saw its first seven years. The life of Guillaume Crétin covered the first quarter of the century, so that Rabelais could represent his death-bed without violence to possible chronology, and in a spirit which is not so certainly scoffing as some have thought.

Although Master Francis also borrows Geoffroy Tory's mocking at the extreme *rhétoriqueurs* in the matter of the Limousin student, Tory (1480?-1533) was more classical than Italian in his tastes, and would probably have regarded sonnets and *rondeaux* in the mood of "fight dog, fight bear." The shrewd and clear-headed (nor thick-voiced) Coquillart himself did not die till 1510, and the great lights of the later Mediæval theatre, the brothers Gréban, had scarcely gone out. But the chief poets of the time (for Octavien de Saint-Gelais but just outstepped the limit of 1500) were Jean Marot (the certain, as Octavien was the probable, father of a poet greater than himself), the agreeable light singer, Roger de Collérye, and Jean Le Maire de Belges, who, though a long liver, was distinctly of the earlier school, and has from some received the credit of being by far its best writer. If we add the shadowy Jehan du Pontalais, and the laborious Bouchet, a still longer-lived man than Le Maire de Belges, the utmost demands of proportional representation for the period will be satisfied.[1]

[1] It is unpleasant to have to find fault with predecessors. But it is necessary to say that the great collaborative *History* of M. Petit de Julleville gives a treatment of the minor French writers of the present period which is inadequate and perfunctory to an astonishing degree, when it is remembered that the book extends to eight very

Colléry, Bouchet, Jehan du Pontalais.

Colléry, Bouchet, and Pontalais may have a little longer notice. Roger de Colléry, an Auxerrois, and a writer of verse much lighter than anything of the time before Marot, is not only commendably free from the worst vices of the style of the *Rhétoriqueurs,* but occupies a place of some importance as the first named modern representative of the famous French school of joyous song. He keeps the allegorical personage to some extent, but avoids its atmosphere of tedium, though he is a little conventional. There could not be a greater contrast to him, save in this one point, than Jehan Bouchet, "Traverseur de Voies Périlleuses," friend of Rabelais (who did not dislike his verse) and author of an enormous amount of *rhétoriqueur* poetry. Jehan du Pontalais, on the other hand, is a contrast, partly in the same, partly in a different way, to the solid Bouchet himself. For he is only personally known as a sort of minor Villon, or French George Peele—the Peele of the Jests, not the Plays. But there has been attributed to him a really remarkable anonymous book of Louis XII.'s time, *Les Contredits du Songecreux,* partly farce, partly direct satire on classes, if not (which was as yet too dangerous) on

large volumes for French Literature only. Fortunately nothing can be better than the treatments in MM. Hatzfeld and Darmesteter's *Seizième Siècle en France* (Paris, 1878), and in the first volume of Crépet's *Poëtes Français* (Paris, 1861), where the subject was mainly in the most competent hands of M. Ch. d'Héricault. In these the necessary amplifications of the text must be sought. Modern editions of Colléry, Bouchet, and one or two other writers exist ; but most are only in the older forms.

individuals. But these and others must be sought in special histories; even far-fetched and dear-bought old acquaintance must not obtain for them more than a representative position here. It is sufficient that in this twilight of modern French they illustrate already tendencies which have been more fully developed since. The special and peculiar glory of the language, the polishing of the plain style till it has the supremacy of Pascal or Malebranche, of Courier or Mérimée, they indeed show not. But the light *gaulois* manner, which has of late almost disappeared in anything like perfection, is very fairly in evidence; and even the *ampullæ* of the *Rhétoriqueurs* may be charitably regarded as attempts at that grandeur which, though far less characteristic of the literature, was attained later in this century by Dubartas and Aubigné, and three hundred years afterwards by Lamennais and Hugo.

Clément Marot.

In all these writers the late mediæval character is still uppermost, and it has hardly lost its place in Clément Marot. His father Jean, a Norman by birth, had moved southward and married a Cahorsine girl, or rather two in succession. The second (her name is unknown) was the mother of Clément, who was born in the winter of 1496-97. Jean, who was secretary or scribe to Anne of Brittany, was himself a versifier of merit in the recognised forms, and even something of a poet; and when he introduced his little son to the court of France at the age of ten years only, both he himself and divers of the lettered court of Louis XII. taught the boy rhyming in fashions which, like some, though not all good men of the time, he did not forget or rebel against. Clément was busy at first with the usual fifteenth-century things, "Judgments" of this, "Temples" of that, exactly as if he had been a Lydgate earlier, or a Douglas in his own time. He presented a poem to Duke (not yet King) Francis about 1514, that is to say, in or about his own eighteenth year. Five years later he was *facteur*, "maker," poet, to Francis' Queen Claude, and gentleman-pensioner of Francis' sister Margaret and her husband the Duke d'Alençon. To Margaret he was in more senses than one attached for the whole of his life; and the usual half-natural and half-fatuous pains have been taken to define the exact limits and character of the attachment. That it was something more than that of courtier to queen, or the still lower one of pensioner to patroness, no one who reads his work can have much doubt; but there is a third relationship, that of professional poet-lover to mistress "in title," which is far more difficult to characterise with any certainty. Some excellent folk have, in this as in other cases, tried to clear Queen Margaret of any scandal. Let us do better: let us not even consider the question.

His life.

What is certain is that Margaret was not only his mistress in the noble senses, but his sincere, and, as long as it was in her power, his effectual protectress; while Francis seems also to have been as sincere a friend to Marot as his *métier* of king, and his temperament of selfish sensualist, permitted. The poet went with him to Italy in 1524, the year of his pension, was wounded and taken at Pavia; but returned to France next year. There was a "Diana" (possibly but not probably she of Poitiers) who had been kind and now was not. He thought she had something to do with the troubles which soon came on him in the shape of imprisonment for heresy. It is certain that, if Diana was his evil angel, Margaret was his good one, and obtained his release. He not only escaped this danger in 1526, but soon after became a pensioned servant of the king himself. In 1530 he married.

But his troubles on the score of heresy were not over: in fact they were but beginning. He was called to legal account in 1531, when he escaped by the suretyship of the King and Queen of Navarre, through their secretary, and again in 1535. Then he thought not even Béarn a safe refuge, but escaped to Ferrara, where he had the protection of the duchess, Renée of France, who, like all the Valois princesses, protected letters.

He had three years before collected his earlier work under the title (one of the delightful conceits for naming men and books which redeem the *rhétoriqueur* school) of *Adolescence Clémentine*, and at Ferrara he wrote *blasons* and half-nonsense epistles, which had a great vogue. But Renée's husband was less well inclined to the Reformation than his wife, and Marot had to leave Ferrara; though after a sojourn in Venice he was permitted to return to France. He was still patronised and favoured by the king. But it is possible that he did himself no good by a quarrel (not the least "be-inked" of those tedious things, the "Quarrels of Authors") with another poet, François Sagon; and certain that he stirred up his old enemies by his translation of the Psalms. So once more he had to fly, this time to Geneva. But, like others, he found the capital of the Reformation as intolerant as any stronghold of the Pope, and infected besides by a fanatic sourness more detestable than any "decretalism." He is said to have been condemned to death, and actually whipped; he seems certainly to have been turned out of the city in the most insulting fashion. Francis, however, was still well inclined towards him personally, and he was allowed to die quietly in Piedmont, under French protection, if not in France. The event occurred in 1544, when the poet had not yet reached the age of fifty. His days had been few; and many of them, especially the last, when the "browner shades" require most alleviation of circumstance, had been evil. Of the two famous epithets of the poet, Marot certainly deserves that of "light" if not exactly (despite his *Psalms*) that of "holy." Neither shall the reproach of *un*holiness be by any means attached to him. His seems to have been altogether a fair-weather nature: entirely free from all the more detestable vices, but not abundantly furnished with the more stalwart virtues, and very particularly destitute of that—highest of all, or rather transcendent over them all—which is called Wisdom.

Something, though not so much as is generally thought or said, of this levity of character, reflects itself in his poetry.[1] With rare exceptions, among which are some pieces, probably or certainly, to Margaret, his lightest things are by far his best. His earlier allegorical poems display almost all the numerous faults which beset their evil kind; his *Psalms* excite the merest historic interest; and his *Blasons* or elaborate pieces of eulogistic or abusive description share, while they are much less amusing, the tedium which attaches even to a certain part of the grotesque of Rabelais himself. Only, perhaps, in the easy flow of the Epistles to the King, and other similar pieces, do we come upon things in Marot which do not require to be praised by allowance.

Character and importance of his poetry.

Yet, to us at least, he is of all but the first interest. This interest is derived in the first place from the surviving mediævalism which made him admire and edit not merely Villon but the *Romance of the Rose* itself, and which is obvious almost throughout his work, side by side with characteristics which are those of the Renaissance and almost of modernity. In the second place, he is interesting because he carries high the banner which it has been the special boast of literary France to wave—the banner of the lighter as opposed to the graver literature—and because in doing this he has almost entirely shaken off the somewhat elaborate and ponderous jocularity which had become fashionable in the later Middle Ages, and which, though his gigantic strength enables him almost always to avoid heaviness, is by

[1] Ed. Jannet and C. d'Héricault, 4 vols. Paris, 1873.

no means imperceptible in Rabelais. Lastly, he is interesting because he has done some things very delightful in themselves.

It has been said that few modern readers will find these points of interest in the once famous *Psalms*.

The Psalms

To estimate the popularity of these we must of course allow for the fashion (and something more) which recommended them, but even then it is not quite easy to understand. No verse translations of the Psalms have ever been satisfactory, the best being perhaps that in Northumbrian Middle English. The English Prose Authorised Version is indeed magnificent; but its magnificence arises from the very qualities which French was losing rather than gaining at the hands of Marot himself and his successors. Neatness and grace, though they are well enough at home in some of Marot's shorter religious pieces, the so-called *Oraisons*, are things useless if not positively dangerous in the rendering of Hebrew poetry. Very rarely will even the subdued but poignant passion which he sometimes could command come into play, while splendour, sublimity, colour, indignation, passionate sorrow for sin, are not his trade at all. To take the very beginning—

> "Qui au conseil des malings n'a esté,
> Qui n'est au trac des pêcheurs arresté,
> Qui des mocqueurs au banc place n'a prise,"

is not very much above

> "How blest the man who ne'er consents
> By ill advice to walk,"

while it is perhaps even more prosaic. Not only does

Marot scarcely ever achieve that grave melody of which the later Huguenot poets were masters, but he makes little of subjects such as the "King's Daughter," which might have seemed likely to appeal to him. He is perhaps better in the mild and plaintive line, such as *Qui Habitat in adjutorio* (Ps. xci.) than on the greater occasions of the *Cœli Enarrant*, or the *De Profundis*, or the *Super Flumina*, though he does no ill justice to this last. His prose, as shown in the prefaces of the *Rose*, the *Villon*, and the *Adolescence Clémentine*, is pleasant and useful to compare with that of Rabelais. There are agreeable things also in many of his Epistles, besides the famous and universally known one to the king about his larcenous valet. But for the real Marot—the poet—we must go to the "little people" of his flock, the epigrams, and the *rondeaux*, and the songs, to the exquisite

and other work.

"Un doulx Nenny avec un doulx soubzrire,"

which has been glanced at above as having been thought to be addressed seriously or in character to Margaret, to the famous *ballade* of *Frère Lubin*, to the delightful *rondeaux* "Dedans Paris" and "En la Baisant." Not that these are the only good things of the kind in him, but that they are the best where many are good.

There are few of the greater writers of the world of whom it is more difficult to take a purely achromatic view than it is to take such a view of Rabelais; and there is perhaps no one in whose case it is so difficult to get that view, when

Rabelais.

once taken, accepted by others. He appeals, indeed, if not quite on the same side, to Frenchmen and Englishmen almost equally, and is in not a few ways even more Teutonic than Latin. But, except the national *idola*, there is hardly one of the great classes of disturbing prepossession which does not here come into play:—the religious, the moral, the æsthetic, others equally or almost equally powerful. Nor is the matter made any better by the fact of the difficulty (or at least apparent difficulty) of his language; for, small as this difficulty really is, it is great in appearance. As he has been generally praised, the praise has almost always been of that controversial, not to say directly provocative, character which makes two enemies for one friend. The apostle of free-thought and assailant of superstition cannot recommend himself to those who prize orthodoxy and religion; the advocate of Humanist apolaustics is horrible to the severe moralist; the amasser of images and expressions which are not only loose but coarse in the extreme must shock the person of refinement. And the worst of it is that Rabelais—very little read, and read not least it may be feared for the least good side of him—is apt to be regarded from one or other of these points of view before he is read at all, and the prepossession hopelessly colours the reading.

The problem of him.

Perhaps the fallacy which is at once most necessary and hardest to remove in his case is the almost universal notion—contradicted by every man's knowledge of himself, but recurring in every man's judgment of another—that human nature is consistent; the notion of "ruling passions" of the homogeneous type. This fallacy is apt to pervade attack and defence alike. "No decent man," cries one side, "could possibly use such language or put such ideas," and the other side replies that he used the language and the ideas merely or mainly as a screen or a blind, to make his more serious conceptions agreeable or safe. So with his free-thought; so with other things. It seems almost impossible to get people to accept the obvious truth that in most cases, if not in all, the strands of life and thought are double; that there is what we are pleased to call an animal as well as what we are pleased to call a spiritual side in man; that it is possible—nay, common—to laugh at what you both love and respect. That is to say, though perhaps nobody but a fool would deny these propositions in the abstract assertion, it is the hardest thing to get even wise men to accept them in the concrete application. A little hypocrisy, a little false modesty, and a great deal of false logic combine to prevent this acceptance. If people would only remember the whole, as some have actually remembered a part, of the following simple truths, Rabelais would cease to be either a horror or a puzzle. These truths (as one may hope they be) are: That Rabelais was a man of the sixteenth century, with the semi-rational admiration for antiquity and the semi-irrational contempt of the Middle Ages, which belonged to the men of his time, intensified by genius and only partly corrected by humour: That he was an escaped monk: That the association of light literature and loose language is a very old thing, and in fact has but recently ceased to be the order of every literary day: That the light literature of France in *fabliau* and farce had been as exceptionally coarse as her serious poetry and romance had been exceptionally chaste: That the kind of the *fatrasie*, or miscellany of sense and nonsense, was established and popular: That Rabelais was (and no shame to him) sincerely fond of the good gifts of God—the beauty of woman and of art and of literature, the gladness of the wine, the pleasant savour of flesh and fish and fowl and fruit: That he was an equally sincere devotee of religion as he understood it, and that if there was too much revolt from the mediæval view in his understanding, there was good sense too—sense of the welfare of mankind, of the establishment of a noble theory and practice of living: That he shared not ungenerously in the hopes (let us be frank and say the delusions) of perfectibility, which were common in his time. And lastly (for we must allow for this, though not quite to the same extent as some of his maladroit defenders have allowed): That he was a man of extraordinary shrewdness, who had run great risks already and was not too anxious to run more, and that his time was an exceedingly dangerous time. If spring and escapement be adjusted with a due heed to these facts, there will not be so much difficulty, as there has generally been assumed, in the way of "knowing our Rabelais."[1]

[1] The minor genuine or probably genuine works of Rabelais are inconsiderable. They consist of a burlesque or "Pantagrueline" *Prognostication*, which has been frequently imitated, and is not itself quite original, but amusing and characteristic enough ; of *La Sciomachie*, a description of the festivities at Rome in the palace of the Cardinal

Francois Rabelais—"Maître Alcofribas Nasier" by one of the anagrams dear to his day—"Caloyer des Iles Hyères," by another fantastic *alias*—was born at Chinon, probably about 1495. A much earlier date, 1483, used to be assigned. He was sent "into religion" at the early age which equally excluded all possibility of real vocation, and all opportunity of resisting if there was none; and it was particularly unfortunate that his order was that of St Francis, which had sunk to the extremity

His life.

Ambassador du Bellay on the occasion of the birth of the Duke of Orleans; of a verse-letter to the "Traverseur de Voies Perilleuses" (*v. supra*); and of a few epistles, some in French, some in Latin. There is no reasonable doubt about any one of these. Of the Apocrypha the most important is a curious collection of fantastic woodcuts entitled *Songes Drolatiques de Pantagruel*, which have the extravagance and the obscenity of the more questionable parts of "the Book," but necessarily want its higher qualities, and indeed are little more than caricature-puzzles of a low type. The bibliography of the earlier editions of *Gargantua*, &c., is a complicated subject; and the variations during the lifetime of the author were considerable. In the almost endless task of annotation that of Le Duchat (Amsterdam, 1711) was the pioneer, and is still to some extent a source. Of later editions that of Esmangart and Johanneau (Paris, 1823-26), which includes the *Songes Drolatiques*, is still more or less indispensable for the thorough student. But the two most generally recommendable of the text are those of Jannet and Moland in seven pocket volumes, which has the more certain minor works, and a useful glossary (2d ed., Paris, 1873), and the more stately one of Marty-Laveaux (1870 onwards). The English translation of Sir Thomas Urquhart is almost a classic in itself, and it was not ill-continued by Motteux. It has been more than once handsomely reprinted recently; while in 1893 Mr W. F. Smith of St John's College, Cambridge, gave a new English version with commentary representing recent French study. The literature of articles, &c., on Rabelais is enormous; that of entire books not small. The best of the latter are those of M. Jules Fleury in French and Sir Walter Besant in English.

of uncouthness and corruption. He took priest's orders; but was ill at ease himself and unpopular with his brethren. Nor was he, the most unmonkish of mankind, much better satisfied with the Benedictines (the most scholarly and polished of orders, as the Cordeliers were the most ignorant and clownish), to whom he was transferred by the Pope's licence. He unfrocked himself with the connivance of the Bishop of Maillezais, studied medicine and practised it, besides acting as printer's reader, and thus using as well as acquiring his considerable classical scholarship. He had a still more powerful protector in Cardinal du Bellay, in whose suite he went to Rome, and who, when the tolerance of Francis the First changed to intolerance, restored him for a time to convent life. But the king was always personally well inclined to Rabelais. A benefice at Meudon was given to him by another cardinal, Châtillon, but he held it for so short a time that the stock phrase, "Curé de Meudon," is something of an absurdity. He had another in Maine, but resigned both two years before his death in 1553. These main facts are pretty certain; but the usual lives of Rabelais are chiefly legendary, and not a few things (such as the supposed enmity between him and Ronsard, on which large structures have been built) rest upon no evidence, and are more probably false than true.

All such things are, however, whether false or true, more or less immaterial to literature; and it may be doubted whether we need care to know anything more about Rabelais personally than that he was a monk, unfrocked by his own act, who turned to Humanism and to Natural Science. And that could be discovered from his great book or books. This, for it is practically one, though it is generally (and in strictness correctly) known by the double short title of *Gargantua and Pantagruel*, was preluded by a new edition or version of an old burlesque romance concerning one of these personages, the good giant Gargantua. Rabelais seems to have first thought of simply continuing this, and published in 1532 the first book of the history of *Pantagruel*, Gargantua's son. Then, either changing his mind, or, as is at least equally probable, following out a design purposely eccentric, he went back and produced his own *Gargantua* in 1535. The second book of *Pantagruel* did not appear till many years after, in 1546, nor the third till 1552. The conclusion did not see the light till twelve years later, and eleven after the author's death, though part of it, the *Ile Sonnante*, had appeared a little earlier. This delay, with some alleged differences of tone and temper, has led to its being considered spurious; but the present writer has, after many years' study of the question, hardly the smallest doubt that it is genuine, though it was pretty certainly not finally revised by the author, and may have been rehandled by somebody else. The external testimony against it is of no weight, and the internal is all in its favour.[1] It may without rashness be said

Gargantua and Pantagruel.

[1] During the summer of 1900 it was stated in the newspapers that a new version of Book V., dated 1549, had been discovered in print. But I have seen nothing more about this.

that nobody in Rabelais' time, or near it, except Rabelais, could possibly have written the book, which contains some of the very best things of the whole. If the satire on monkery is a little fiercer than before, there is nothing fatal in that.

Their general form and scheme.

The apparently complicated and desultory character of the whole work can be greatly simplified by a little thought. In general form it is, as has been said, a burlesque romance—a greater part of the fun being drawn from the gianthood of the heroes in *Gargantua* than in the longer and more serious *Pantagruel*. The former book deals successively with Gargantua's birth, with the two stages of his education—the first sensual, disorderly, and ignorant, the later in the full strenuous tone of Renaissance Humanism—his sojourn at Paris, and his victorious intervention in the war between his father, Grandgousier, and the petulant invader, Picrochole. The character of Friar John—a very muscular Rabelais himself—and the Abbey of Theleme, of which he is the first superior, and which is established on principles diametrically contravening those of the ordinary convent, are the chief episodes or minor parts of the plot.

Pantagruel, much longer, is also more diversified. It falls generally into three parts—the education of Pantagruel (a variant of the second part of his father's), his war with the Dipsodes (which in the same way corresponds to that with Picrochole), and the voyage in quest of the Oracle of the *Dive Bouteille*. This is undertaken partly to solve the doubts about marriage of the most famous character of the whole book,

Panurge, who occupies in this part more than the place of Friar John in the earlier, though that redoubtable monk is great here also. Panurge, who becomes one of Pantagruel's companions at Paris, and governor of one of his provinces after the conquest of the Dipsodes, has been the subject of much inkshed. He is an audacious but successful compound of divers bad qualities — cowardice, evil concupiscence, spite, and others—with one saving grace, that of extraordinary ingenuity and wit; for, full of humour as Rabelais himself is, Panurge is witty rather than humorous. As for the Oracle of the Bottle, it is, of course, *Tringq!* How could an oracle of a bottle be anything else?

Fantastic notions on the subject.

As nearly all books of any importance have given temptation to the besetting fancy for discovering mares' nests, it would indeed be surprising if such a book as this had not done so. And the quest for these is itself a main cause of the puzzlement and the disgust which readers of this class have experienced. The wiser mind is aware that, in most cases probably, no single elaborately devised plan has ever been present to the mind of the greater authors: and that, in nearly all, such authors are led by their own genius to vary and alter any plan with which they may have started, until it is at best a trunk with infinite branches, and not seldom a mere central cottage round which a palace has grown. It is the business of special editors or critics of Rabelais—if indeed it be even theirs—to enumerate and, if they choose, to discuss the conjectures which have followed upon this initial fallacy. The wildest allegorical debauches of the great Fulgentius Planciades (an author whom Master Francis knew, quotes, and beyond doubt appreciated with no small relish) have been equalled by the suggestion that the voyage to Bacbuc's oracle is an allegory of the processes of making wine. The "key" craze (a little excused by the fact that Rabelais openly introduces some real personages, and very probably adumbrates others) has been active to the fullest: and King Francis, his son Henry, Diane de Poitiers, Luther, Calvin, almost every distinguished and not a few undistinguished personages of the time, have been identified with this and that personage of *Gargantua and Pantagruel.* The unmistakable fact that Rabelais, though probably in no sense a Protestant by sect, was a protester against the abuses of the Roman Church, and in particular against the degradation of monachism, while he as undoubtedly shared, though to an uncertain extent, the dislike of his nation and his time for mystical dogma, has, again unavoidably, tempted many to see in his work a deliberate and formidable assault on Catholicism or even on Christianity. And a great deal else has been read into a book which, in the form and on the face of it, certainly rather invites indulgence of an intemperance of this sort.

Really a satirical criticism of life.

Let us on this point, without fear of losing the smiles of Bacbuc, be all but total abstainers. The side which Rabelais would have taken—which to some extent he actually did take—in the great quarrel or quarrels of the time is clear enough, and has been sufficiently indicated already.

He is against almost every form of that corruption of mediæval religion, literature, manners, philosophy, which manifested itself in the Fifteenth Century; he is for the renewed and intelligent study of the classics, the purification of religion, the rejection of the mere formalisms of scholastic philosophy and canon-law, the pursuit of natural science. That he shared to some extent the excessive and unintelligent contempt of things mediæval, which is one note and one blemish of the Renaissance, is extremely probable and in fact evident. But it is absolutely impossible to hold the extremest view of his free-thinking tendencies without shutting the eyes to not a few (and these of the very best) passages in the book. To take it by itself (and as a matter of fact it has goodly company), the counsel of Hippothadée to Panurge can be read by no one not hopelessly prejudiced without his seeing that the writer had at any rate his moments of the truest and almost the sublimest piety, of the most wholesome moral sense, of the kindliest and most natural human sympathy. The same (with a variation due not wholly to the admission of humour) is the lesson of the advice of Rondibilis on the preventives of Cuckoldage. The education passages in *Gargantua* have extorted admiration, or impressed silence, in the case of all but fanatics of anti-Pantagruelism. And though it has been less generally recognised, the picture of Quintessence fantastic, but adorable, with her *bouquet de rose franche*, mixes delicate poetry with pretty sharp satire in a way which few writers since Aristophanes have ever equalled. As for the strong shrewd sense of the criticism of life with which the book is saturated, we again find few deniers; while denial when it occurs is so evidently the result of prejudice on other points that it may be politely neglected.

It appears most probable, from an unbiassed reading of the book, that Rabelais, like more than one other of the greatest of satirists (notably Fielding), began merely or mainly with sportive burlesque and parody, and was enticed by his own genius and the "grace of going on" to continue his work, to enlarge it, and to make it the vehicle, not merely of satire on the windy ways of men, but of some serious doctrine and expression of opinion, often indirect, sometimes straightforward and unveiled.

So far as general tendency goes, this satirical criticism of life sums it up, and we need go no further. But the criticism itself is of a very peculiar character, and possesses all the idiosyncrasy of genius. It is as agreeable as it is instructive to compare it with that of Lucian (from whom it unquestionably derives to a great extent), with that of Swift (which in a similar but less degree is derived from it), and, if anybody pleases, with that of Voltaire. This last may be dismissed almost at once. Witty as is the much lesser Francis, always sharp-edged and very often true-aimed as are his weapons, commendable as his object is on occasion, though only on occasion, there is a thinness as well as a negativity about his satire which shows disastrously beside the full-blooded generous manhood of Rabelais. In the most debatable feature of both, the lusty licence of the Tourangeau looks almost clean beside the sniggering

Comparative quality of the satire.

indecency of the Parisian. But the contrasts with Lucian and Swift are far more valuable and satisfactory, for here the things compared are more on an equality. How much Rabelais owes to Lucian must be apparent even to those who do not know the Samosatan well, while to those who do it occurs on every page. But while Lucian is free from some of the faults and many of the extravagances of Rabelais, this very freedom arises from a defect. The sin of the greatest of Post-Christian Greeks in literature is, as Photius long ago saw, that he is too negative—indeed, though he is less thin, he is more purely negative than Voltaire himself. He has absolutely no enthusiasms; even his keen appreciation of sensual pleasure does not rise to passion, while his almost equally keen taste for art still falls short of anything like *furia*. He believes in nothing, wishes for nothing very much, can excite himself about nothing. With Rabelais, on the contrary, the steam is not only always up, as modern slang says, but up with a full head, and escaping through every safety-valve. His portentous catalogues are less calculated buffoonery, mere followings of mediæval precedent, than waste-pipes for superfluous and exuberant thought and language; his giantries and arithmetical fantasies are the same; his very foul language and foul imagery are but as the smoke of the furnace. And the same enthusiasm, contagious to all but those incapable of it, enables his readers to go through with what he himself has written under its influence. Humanitarian sympathy is apt to be disgusting because it is apt to be mawkish. There is nothing mawkish about Rabelais; he is good fellow and good Samaritan at once; a visionary as well as a voluptuary; a genuine believer in the possibility, if not of perfection, at anyrate of amelioration, as well as a lover of the Septembral juice and of "pretty maids all of a row."

And as there is nothing in him of the Lucianic poco-curantism, so there is even less—*Si Peu Que Rien*, as he would say himself—of the Swiftian indignation and despair. The Oracle of the Bottle reads almost like a designed counterblast to the moral of *Gulliver's Travels*. That there are fools in the world Rabelais would admit with the utmost cheerfulness—in fact, he states the fact genially on every page. And he would probably by no means deny that there are rascals in it. But in his view most of the folly, and probably a large portion of the rascality, come simply from not "following nature"—not enjoying and letting enjoy the good things of God. If you do what you like, letting, of course (as is practically involved in the law), everybody else do what he likes under the same caution, the world will go very well. With Swift it is an impossibility that the world should go well, because, unfortunately, folly and roguery are themselves nature, and the more men follow her, the more they will be guilty of them. Less majestic and terrible than the Englishman, as he is less accomplished and (within limits) consummate than the Greek, Rabelais is very much more inspiriting than either. His humour has infinitely more of good-humour about it: and that good-humour by no means arises, as has been too often unjustly thought, even by those not ill inclined to him, from ribaldry or even from nonsense —great master as he is of the latter and only too prone to indulge in the former.

To these advantages we must add an extraordinary gift of felicitous and rememberable phrase, and a command of French prose which would put him in the first rank of writers whatever had been his subject. Few probably, even among Frenchmen, realise the extent to which the phrase of Rabelais has penetrated the language: no one who does not know the older language can imagine the advance that he made in handling it. Quaint spelling, humorous exaggeration, fantastic word-coining, these things, no doubt, characterise him to no small extent; but if it were possible to cut them all out of his work, its simpler and more unaffected passages would still give him the very first rank. Still, there is no doubt that the union of these different appeals is what constitutes his special strength. There is hardly another writer who combines the wildest farce and the most serious sense in a manner so successful; nor is there any, except Shakespeare, who has made his farce and his seriousness go so fraternally together. The hodge-podge of his subject, while it exposed him to greater danger of failure, gave him at the same time, no doubt, greater chance of success. And for this reason a slight notice of passages and episodes may fitly close our handling of the greatest book—the only book, perhaps, except the *Orlando*, of absolutely the first class—that we have to notice in this volume.

The style.

Rabelais himself, in the Introduction to the Fourth Book, defines "Pantagruelism" as "a certain gaiety of spirit, saturated with contempt of the things of chance." This is the old *contemptus mundi* turned a new way. It is neither the self-sufficient superiority of the ancient philosopher, nor the sardonic-despairing "Vanity of Vanities" of the preacher, nor the half-childish frolicry of the mediæval droller; but a combination of the three, altered and fortified by what (if the word had not been so foolishly and tediously abused) one might call the Modern Spirit. As an example of the difference given by this latter element, nothing better perhaps can be found than the delicious remonstrance of the Amiens Monk with the æsthetic ecstacies of Rabelais and his companion over Florence. The bulk of this, the charge against the "flower-town" that it contains not a single *rôtisserie,* is exactly what we might find in Aristophanes and still more in Lucian. But the first three or four lines strike the note of variance, "I don't know what the devil you find here to praise so much. I have gazed at it as well as you, and am no more blind than you are. Well! What then? Here be fine houses and that's all." In these few words the loss and the gain of the modern, as compared with the ancient, world appears marvellously. The most matter-of-fact Greek could never have been simply insensible to the beauty of "fine houses," though the most transcendental Greek might affect to set that beauty lower than the beauty of the "things of the soul." But for this very reason

Short running commentary.

the most ingenious Greek satirist was unlikely to think of the particular form of humour invited by vulgarity of this kind. And while the example is valuable in this way, it is perhaps more valuable as showing the strength, and at the same time the delicacy, of Rabelais' command of this humour. Only Pascal, among other Frenchmen, would have left it so artistically alone. Even Molière, even Courier, much more Voltaire, would have been tempted to elaborate it, to force the note, to show some sign of fear that by itself it would not produce its effect. This highest—this Shakespearian—simplicity of humour is by no means uncommon in the writer whom critics have delighted to represent as incapable of uttering his jests without grinning at the same time through a dirty horse-collar. Not of course that Master Francis was at all squeamish about indulging in this latter exercise also; while occasionally he could, as has been said, drop comedy and satire altogether, and be simply and nobly serious.

These characteristics, with his astonishing literary versatility and accomplishment, achieving the expression—the frequently consummate expression—of them all, are displayed throughout the book, in manners and degrees conditioned to some extent necessarily, but to a less extent than might seem necessary, by the varying nature of the subject. In *Gargantua* and in the First Book of *Pantagruel*, the pure burlesque extravagance of the original design—so far as (see above) there is likely to have been any such—is perhaps more prominent than anywhere else, though it is noticeable that *Gargantua* itself contains, in the education passage and the description of the Abbey of Theleme, two of the most important and substantive pieces of seriousness in the whole book. It is probable that such things as "The Antidoted Fanfreluches" at the very beginning are sheer mystification, except in so far as a parody may be intended, on the one hand, of the prophecies so popular in the Middle Ages—on the other, of the obscure and affected language of the *Rhétoriqueurs*. So also a very large, perhaps the largest, part of the adventures of Gargantua, from his birth (and before) upwards, is mere parody of the details of *Enfances* given in the Romances. Very frequently—too frequently for modern taste—the author gives the rein to the pure or impure fancies of the *fatrasie* and the *fabliau*; while in such passages as the descant on Gargantua's livery-colours he mingles jest and earnest. The war with Picrochole, and the feats of Gargantua and Friar John, are once more parody of Romance, with a by no means unnoticeable side-glance at the elder and more stately muse of History herself.

In *Pantagruel* the parodist and parasitic vein is by no means abandoned; indeed, the old sequence of "*Enfances*," "War," and "Quest" is the connecting canvas of the whole. But the author begins to give much freer play to his own genius. Friar John, the secondary hero of *Gargantua*, is only a livelier presentment of the comic hero of apparently lower class, who goes back to the very first age of romance in the Rainouard of *Aliscans*. Panurge, who occupies the same place (if indeed he be not promoted to first rank) in *Pantagruel*, is a very much more complicated and subtler creation. If there be one possible allegorical interpretation which is less of a Will-o'-the-wisp than another, it is that Panurge is a sort of satirical incarnation, not, as some would have it, of the more sensual and lower side of humanity generally, but of that of the French character, as it appeared to a typical but in some ways transcendent Frenchman. And the author seems to be in a hurry till he has reached this favourite companion and contrast to the *bon Pantagruel*, the prince of few words, shrewd but kindly thoughts, unblemished valour and sincere piety. Pantagruel's youth is very briefly treated: he escapes altogether his father's disorderly nonage. The jargon of the Limousin scholar, the fantastic-satiric catalogue of the library of Saint-Victor, the Pantagruelic Judgment of Solomon between Baisecul and Humevesnes are in the old kind; but little time is spent over them. And after the advent of Panurge himself, or at least after his full production—for his first appearance precedes the Judgment—the flights of fancy become ever more daring and more original. The sign-duel of Panurge and Thaumast would have delighted Lucian, that "knower of old things and vain." And though the war with the Dipsodes is, except as a mere carrying out as above of the general romance-plan, one of the obscurest and least interesting parts of the book, the boldness with which Rabelais, Humanist as he is, casts ridicule on the heroes and heroines of classical antiquity at once gives us his differentia from the mere "atavists" of the Renaissance, from the men who would if they could have simply put back the clock to Greek and Roman times.

But we do not reach the full expression of the mingled wit and wisdom of our author till we come to the Third Book—the Second only of *Pantagruel*, but the more canonical as well as convenient numeration always regards *Gargantua* and its sequel as continuous. In the preliminary history of the marriage of Panurge it is of course possible, as elsewhere, to discover considerable borrowings; in that matter Rabelais follows the practice of all the great masters before, during, and since his time. But the whole is as distinctly his own as is also usually the case. And here, better perhaps than anywhere, we can trace the working of "Pantagruelism" on the general *données* of Romance. The hero must have a lady-love; and Master Francis at once accepts and evades the necessity in his quaintest and most wayward fashion. Nowhere has he brought in more out-of-the-way learning, keener satire on the ways and wishes of mankind. Nowhere has he indulged so little in mere extravagance, in mere nonsense. Nowhere does his satire on professions and schools of thought fly wider or on stronger wing. And nowhere has he coined rememberable phrase with greater abundance and greater felicity. The advice of Hippothadée and Rondibilis has been already noticed from one point of view; but the latter is remarkable from many others. And all the scenes or chapters —the *Sortes Virgilianæ*, the dream, the consultations with the Sibyl of Panzoust and the necromancer Her-

Trippa, with the old French poet Raminagrobis and the dumb Nazdecabre, with the ephectic philosopher Trouillogan and Triboulet the fool—form a close-knit chain of sense and satire, made more complete by the unbated and invincible resolution and ingenuity of Panurge, who explains everything in the teeth of its clearest meaning, so as to suit his wishes. Moreover, it is fitly continued by the episode of Judge Bridoye and his infallible method of judgment by dice—the most good-humoured, as the later account of the *Chats Fourrés* is the most ferocious, of Rabelais' many attacks on lawyers—leading up to the resolve to visit the Oracle of the Bottle. Nor perhaps—though the grim satire of the "Herb Pantagruelion" (hemp), anticipating Joseph de Maistre, and showing that Rabelais' humanitarianism was of no foolish or milk-sop order, may seem purely episodic—could anything better terminate a book which, if not containing the absolutely best things, has the most uniformly sustained excellence of all the Five. Nor have judges missed the curious effect of the last appearance in person of the good Gargantua, and the pleasant contrast of this appearance, as of a grave and gracious monarch solely busied on the welfare of his people and his son, with the former picture of the spoilt darling of the hoyden governesses and the clownish pupil of Master Jobelin.

There is no falling off in the Fourth as far as details go; but as a whole it has less unity, less clearness, and less attraction. Many of the islands and countries visited are difficult to interpret, and some, probably, have no definite counterparts in the world of sense or of thought. Nowhere perhaps has the Rabelaisian enumeration gone nearer to the tedious than in the chapters on Quaresme-prenant, while nowhere is the sheer partisan more evident than in the description of the islands of the Papefigues and the Papimanes. As for the section of the Andouilles, it is partly unintelligible, and perhaps had better not be understood. Yet it is difficult to find many chapters—short as they are and long as is the book—which do not sparkle with the true Rabelaisian rock-salt. The quaint, if slightly inhuman, *fabliaux* of the drowning of Dindenault and the vengeance of the Lord of Basché, the immortal storm,[1] the inimitable, if slightly unfair, personage of Homenas, the frozen winds, and "Messer Gaster," could not be spared. If on the whole the spirit is less kindly (a strong argument in favour of the Fifth Book), the construction more casual, the satire coarser, yet the hand is unmistakable, and has lost hardly any of its cunning.

To the present writer at least, as has been already remarked, that hand is quite as unmistakable in the Fifth. Nor would he admit any diminution, but rather contend for an increase in some parts of power and interest. The final exhortation of Bacbuc, with the more than Baconian splendour of its celebration of science and material progress, would by itself make the reputation of a great writer and a great thinker in his own way: and the fantastic

[1] *V. supra*, p. 71, for the connection with Folengo.

alternations of the grave and the gay which precede it are in Rabelais' most characteristic manner. I have already spoken of the Entelechie or Quintessence part; but I may repeat that, not merely in reference to the figure of "Queen Whims" herself but to much else, it is one of the most characteristic passages of the whole. It has been said that the satire on the "Furred Law Cats" is savage, and perhaps that of the Ringing Island itself is not less so. But we have observed that Rabelais' method in this kind hardened throughout — that the last undisputed book, the Fourth, is itself much less kindly than the First and Second, while there is a certain though not a very great darkening of tone even in the Third. The *Ile Sonnante*, moreover, is quite of the same archipelago as those of the Papefigues and Papimanes; while the *Chats Fourrés* themselves are but a climax, part of the lower steps of which are noticeable enough in the earlier books. Moreover, it cannot be too often repeated that, while these things, as well as the crudities of the *Iles des Ferrements*, of the dialogue with Frère Fredon and other things, are simply extremes of a scale equally noticeable elsewhere, there is even reason to believe that the master's last touches, which would or might have harmonised and humanised them all, were never given. Nor will some at least refuse weight to the argument that while at the close of the Fourth Book the scheme is obviously incomplete, the Fifth brings it to quite sufficient and satisfactory end. Not thus do the forgers and continuators of literature work. The speech of these invariably bewrayeth them; the speech of the Fifth Book is the true voice of our Esau.

General remarks.

But of this great book, almost more than of other great books, it may, or rather must be said, that no account by abstract or critical summary, though of far greater extent than any here possible, can be in the least satisfactory. Even extracts will not do; for the variety of the book, whether in all cases deliberately calculated or not, is of its essence; and when this variety is in any way hidden, the essence disappears. On the other hand, the humble office of the critic and literary historian recovers its importance, and is here, more than in most instances, in place, from more than one point of view. In the first place, even a candid reader who honestly attacks the book itself, is likely to be prevented from fully appreciating it by its outrageous desultoriness, by its daring, and, as it may well seem, wanton disregard of convention, by its constant direct or indirect dependence on previous models or butts, and, lastly, by some almost mechanical eccentricities of form and dress. Strange as it may seem to those who are superior to the weakness, dialect or obsolete spelling undoubtedly does offend some tastes almost as if it were a personal insult. And when such a man of letters as the late Mr Lowell could confess that the quaint English of the Scottish Fifteenth-century poets stood in the way of his enjoyment of them, it would be unreasonable to quarrel too much with those unfortunate persons, whether French or English, who are similarly offended by Rabelais. How much of his orthographical caprices was due to himself, and how much to the habits of his printers, it would be difficult to say. But what is certain is that late fifteenth and early sixteenth century printers in French, almost more than in any other language, did take liberties with orthography. Some of these liberties were sprouts of the exaggerated Humanism of the time—endeavours to get nearer the real or supposed etymology; some of them are mere fantasies, of the kind which has been summarised as the "putting of as many letters into a syllable as it will possibly bear."

But the office of the critic may be legitimately promoted in this case upon another consideration—which is, that it has been very freely and very recklessly exercised before. Few people who take an interest in literature at all are likely to come to the reading of Rabelais without very great preoccupation, which is quite as likely to be injurious in one direction as in another. Such an epithet as the old Elizabethan one of *dirty* Rabelais is not more misleading than the Augustan ticket of "Rabelais' easy-chair"; and there is some danger even in such a more laudatory description as Kingsley's "age when Rabelais was compelled to hide the light of his great wisdom not under a bushel, but under a dunghill." One does not think highly of any one who resorts to a dunghill to hide even wisdom.

Therefore there is still room—and more than mere

room—for a critic who will face the facts, disown altogether the "accusing excuse," and present Rabelais, as Rabelais wished to present his own hero, *dans son naturel.* That nature is the nature of a man of extraordinary genius, who is of fibre both coarse and fine, and who, in carrying out the principle that nothing human is out of his way, occasionally accepts the coarser humanities as well as the finer. The one defence for Rabelais in his weaker parts is, after all, that universal one of the time — the fact that, if he offends us, he acts and speaks with zest and relish to himself. There is none of the calculated and cold-blooded indecency in him which is sometimes so nauseous in Voltaire and Sterne; nor is there that sense of forcing, of labour, of hypocrisy with the wrong side of the mask outward, which is so nauseous in at least some plays of Dryden. In mere nastiness Rabelais delights, as children and common folk delight in it: in what we widely call impropriety he delights, because the instincts to which it gives uncomely expression are natural instincts, and, if duly governed and refined, better than natural. Again, the imputation of atheism, or even of free-thought in the worse sense, is certainly false; while, audacious as his criticism is in almost every respect, he can no more be justly termed an anarchist in politics than he can be called an atheist in religion.

On the pure credit side his assets are so great that one can only marvel at the undervaluation of them by any competent auditor. A wonderful fertility of fancy, which not seldom rises to actual imagination; an astonishing vigour, *brio*, "race"; learning which is not so much carried lightly as itself made a means of progress — wings, not weight; a purely literary gift or faculty of making language do what the user wants to make it do, which is hardly excelled by the greatest in literature. And for those who want something more still, who must have motive and moral, substance and subject, that real and intense desire for human happiness and welfare which has been more than once glanced at already. Some, of course, may question whether this is such a good thing — whether the "Verdammte Race" deserves sympathy, is capable of improvement, can produce any progress which is worth anything. These can, no doubt, make something of a case for their view; but it is not so commonly held that the fact that Rabelais held the opposite one can fairly be counted to his discredit. You *may* say some things against him, and some of these some things truly. But three things will remain. He is (let the competent gainsay if they dare) one of the greatest writers of the world; he is one of the great satirists of the world; and he is—as not all great writers and very few great satirists have been — one who sincerely and strenuously loved his fellow-men.

The contrast—a contrast obvious, hackneyed, and in fact clearly felt by the men themselves—between Rabelais and Jean Calvin (1509 - 1564) is not least remarkable in the point referred to by the last words of the preceding paragraph. Calvin's love for his fellow-men was exclusively devoted to their souls, and even in that respect of a very limited extension and a very peculiar kind. But with his character and his doctrines, we have, most fortunately, nothing to do. We have only to do with him as a writer—especially as a writer in French; and more than one of his contemporaries, besides Servetus, might have been glad to escape further intercourse.

Calvin.

Born at Noyon, in Picardy, of a family which had something to do with the Church and something with the law, he tried both professions; but his adoption of the Reformed opinions of course closed both careers to him in France. Basle, Ferrara under Renée, and Geneva successively received him; and at the latter place he lived, with some intervals, for many years as a sort of anti-Lorenzo de' Medici, hating all vices but his own, all beliefs but his own, and all the softer arts and graces of life without exception, till 1564, when he went to his own place. His work is considerable both in French and Latin. But the Latin need only concern us in so far as it exercised an influence on the French, while of the French the *Institution Chrétienne* alone need receive detailed criticism. It was first written in Latin and published at Basle in 1535-36. But the author himself translated it into French, and issued it in that language in 1541; while, nineteen years later, he revised it, with some changes of style about which there are differences of opinion not necessary for us here to discuss.

Value of the Institution *in style.*

Opinions differ also, it is believed, about the literary merits of the French *Institution* itself. But some at least who are certainly not biassed in its favour by agreement with the doctrine or admiration of the man, think it by far the greatest literary book of the early Reformation. In beauty it cannot vie with the liturgical work of the Anglican reformers; but that work is, as will be seen, extremely difficult to assign to any one person, and, besides, does not take form in any single original book of great merit. Nor is it such a contribution to French language as Luther's work was making to German; but as a composition it is much better literature than anything that Luther produced. The nearest literary analogue to it, both in character and in the means by which that character is achieved, is the work of Ascham and some of his friends in English; but Calvin's is far above this in positive merit of style. To appreciate this fully, it must be remembered that French prose, as usual, is much later than French verse, and that though in Calvin's time it had actually been practised and produced for more than three centuries, it had made rather surprisingly little progress. In only one of its kinds—history, or rather chronicle—had really great work been turned out, and this had exchanged the charming naïveté of the best artists, from Villehardouin to Froissart, for the bombast of Chastellain, or the formless form that encloses the shrewd sense and wide range of Comines. Except in the comparatively young and limited short prose tale, no other kind had done really well. Nor even in their very best examples did memoir or chronicle, tale or story, provide the writer of graver prose with a style flexible, varied, effective. Calvin did provide this. He did it by the only possible means—by the same means which Ascham adopted, but which were naturally more suitable to French than to English, and which were further facilitated in his own case by the circumstances. He was translator of his own Latin into his own French, and he had only to adapt, with judgment and discretion, the style of Latin to the uses of her eldest daughter. In doing this he did not adopt that corrupt following of the older tongue which had been very mainly responsible for the disgusting frigidities of the *Rhétoriqueurs;* he did not attempt further to "despumate the Latial verbocination" into French. And he neither imitated the declamatoriness of Latin, to which French is only too well inclined of itself, nor fell into that other pit which has decoyed many great English writers—the construction of relative and other clauses, which, perfectly clear in the ancient language, become obscure in a modern one. Calvin's French style stands to Latin—by happy accident or deliberate and successful attempt—almost exactly as the French language itself stands towards its mother. And his greatest triumph is the attainment, by sedulous imitation of Latin, of a real prose clause—*colon,* "limb," as the Greek term more happily has it—capable of constructing in its turn a real sentence or body, whether long or short. All who know Old French well know that this is precisely the point in which it is deficient. Even in verse—though the line and the couplet and the stanza help the writer almost automatically there—a tendency existed towards the merely natural arranging of words. In prose, without such help, and after the half-poetic turn of Villehardouin, the native grace of Froissart, had been lost, the tendency was either to ponderous word-heaps like those of the *Rhétoriqueurs,* or to clumsy locutions like those of Comines too often. Calvin changed all this, and the highest praise that can be given to him is that he not seldom approaches the still greater but rare achievement of that one of his contemporaries whom he pretty certainly regarded with the bitterest loathing, and who, with as much probability, returned the compliment by sovereign contempt—that is to say, of Rabelais himself.

Minorities of the mid-century.

As we might expect, the "minorities" of the second quarter of the century are of more importance than those of the first. In verse, many writers of some, and a few of remarkable talent, group themselves (not always in friendly fashion) round Marot. In prose, at the other end of the scale from Calvin, not a few writers of *Contes,* with the interesting figure of Queen Margaret at their head, cluster round Rabelais, and to a great extent imitate him.

Marguerite de Valois.

Marguerite de Valois (1492 - 1540), also styled d'Angoulême from her father, d'Alençon and de Navarre from her husbands, is one of those persons, not too common in life or in literature, who are the better liked the more they are known. She belongs to history; and though her lot was what is called in the hackneyed phrase "brilliant" enough, it was scarcely happy. Her love for her brother, the showy but rather worthless King Francis, seems to have been deep and sincere; but it was rewarded by the ribaldry of the time with a base slander, and by its object with ingratitude and neglect at the last. It is pretty certain that both her husbands were unworthy of her, and it is not clear that either cared for her much. On the other hand, though not exactly a beauty, she seems to have been able to excite in courtiers, literary and other, not merely the lip-worship common from courtiers to queens much less attractive than herself, but something like a real passion. And though at last she was check-mated and thrown aside, she was able earlier to exercise a great deal of political influence with good effect, and to bring about some excellent literature.

How much of that[1] which goes under her name (and which in the poetical division has been even increased lately) is wholly hers, it is very difficult to determine. That the French royal house had the spirit of letters in it, at least before the Bourbon blood came in, is sufficiently proved by Charles of Orleans. There is no reason to grudge her her verse, which is varied enough, comprising farces, mysteries, allegorical religious pieces, and much else. The merit of all is average, of some

[1] The *Heptameron* has been repeatedly printed; most accessibly in the Garnier collection. An essay on the book was contributed by the present writer to a recent translation in English, which has appeared in several forms. The best edition of the Poems, *Les Marguerites de la Marguerite*, is that of Franck, 4 vols., Paris, 1873; but additional pieces have since been discovered.

a little above this; and it is fair to Marguerite to say that she frequently hits upon the melancholy resonance which was to be the note of the best Huguenot verse, though she herself was not much more than half a Huguenot. This melancholy, which in nations outside Italy is a mark of the Renaissance, quite independently of religious motives, and is in fact a sort of raising and philosophising of mediæval tones, reappears eminently in some stories about her, and to some extent in the *Heptameron* itself.

The Heptameron.

This very remarkable book, which has as a rule been undervalued, presents almost equal attractions to those who read for mere amusement, to those who appreciate literature as literature, and to those who like extra-literary puzzles of various kinds from authorship to allusion. Combining, as we have a right to do here, the two first points of view, we may say that it is the best of all collections of *novelle* on the Italian plan, except the great original, and that in one respect Marguerite has surpassed Boccaccio. The framework personages of the *Decameron* are notoriously very shadowy; except the naughty audacity of Dioneo, and to some extent of Neifile, there is hardly anything characteristic about them. But Oisille and Saffredent, Nomerfide and Emarsuitte, Parlamente and Hircan, especially the two last, are real people, with parts and characters very distinctly and dramatically outlined. This distinctness and dramatic character have aggravated the usual temptation in such cases to "key"-making—to the attempt to identify the personages. It is sufficient to say that this always idle game is here rather more idle than usual. The attraction of the actual arrangement, however, is very great, and it is partly due to the contrast—also wanting in Boccaccio—of the merriment (not seldom passing the bounds of strict decency) of many of the tales with the polished manners and character-interest of the framework, with the constant undercurrent of melancholy though voluptuous meditation above referred to, and, lastly, with a very real religious feeling, which has seemed dubious or impossible to those who will persist in ignoring time and place, but which was natural enough in the Renaissance. Doubts, however, may be raised about the actual authorship of the book as a whole, with more reason than usual in such cases.

Bonaventure Desperiers.

It was never published by the Queen or in her lifetime, and, when it did appear, it was in an incomplete form, under the not-at-all appropriate title of *Les Amants Fortunés.* Further, many of the men of letters of the time were members of her court, and there was one who is especially noteworthy. This was Bonaventure Desperiers,[1] a short-lived and ill-starred writer of great talent, whose exact birth and death dates are both unknown. But the whole of his days were pretty certainly included within our half century, and he seems to have committed suicide, either in a fit of madness, or to save himself from slaughter for unorthodox opinions, rather of the char-

[1] For the *Nouvelles Récréations et Joyeux Devis* I use the edition of Gosselin (Paris, 1843), with preface by Nodier and notes by the Bibliophile Jacob; for the *Cymbalum Mundi* the Amsterdam edition of 1732.

acter of free-thought than of Protestantism. Of opinions of this kind there is no trace in the *Heptameron,* and we may be certain, from all the Queen's other work, and from all really recorded testimony about her, that she would have sanctioned nothing of the kind. But Desperiers left another book, also not published till posthumously, which is curiously like and yet curiously unlike the *Heptameron* itself. This is the so-called *Nouvelles Récréations et Joyeux Devis*, a work consisting of a large number of mostly very short tales. Although told with such brevity that in some cases one cannot but suspect an intention to rewrite and expand, they are singularly effective, sometimes superior in vividness and force of style to the *Heptameron* itself, and here and there displaying that same melancholy note which has been spoken of above. Now, did Desperiers help his mistress? did she inspirit her servant? or can the two be quite independent? We can only guess the answer.

The Nouvelles Récréations.

However this may be, the *Heptameron* itself is, if not a great, a singularly attractive book, and the *Nouvelles Récréations* are not unworthy to keep it company, always remembering that they are in a different style. They are far less finished, nearer to the old popular *fabliau*-spirit, and in most cases, though not in all, destitute of the urbane and polished tone which makes itself felt even in some pretty coarse chapters of the Queen's book. We are —to take imagery from Rabelais—not so much in the Court of Quintessence (with which gracious image one is not seldom tempted to associate Margaret herself), as in the society of Panurge and Friar John. But these two atmospheres were at the time so constantly close to each other, if not so subtly and inextricably blended, that little sense of incongruity need be felt by those who have really appreciated the Renaissance either in Italy or in France.[1]

The Cymbalum Mundi.

The *Cymbalum Mundi*, on the other hand, is one of the examples of the truth of a certain proverb about dogs and bad names. It seems, or has been said, to have been the cause, direct or indirect, of its author's death. It was constantly spoken of as on a level with the mythical *De Tribus Impostoribus*, as a blasphemous attack on religion in general and Christianity in particular; it was all but utterly suppressed, and when, at the beginning of the eighteenth century, Prosper Marchand reprinted it from a nearly unique copy and defended it from the charge of atheism, its enemies resorted to the not unusual stratagem of declaring that if it was not wicked it was dull. The truth is, that, though not a pious work, it is by no means very wicked; and that, though by no means very witty, it is not open to the charge of dulness. It is a direct imitation of Lucian, and people do not often imitate Lucian in a spirit of

[1] The *Heptameron* and the *Nouvelles Récréations* are the chief examples of this *Conte*-literature, which continued throughout the century and into the next. But the Court of Marguerite was a very nest of the form — for instance, Boaistuau and Le Maçon, the translators of Bandello and Boccaccio, were of her train. The chief minor works are the earlier ones of Noël du Fail (1520-1591), *Propos Rustiques* and *Baliverneries*, and the odd *Pierre Fai-Feu* of Charles de Bordigné, of whom not much is known.

ardent piety; nor is it at all impossible that, in an age when the scandalous controversies of Catholics and Protestants were aggravating the Humanist indifferentism into positive anti-religion, Desperiers may have written in a spirit at least Voltairian. But a good deal, not merely of rather arbitrary dotting of the i's and crossing of the t's, but of italicising and underlining, not to say glossing and garbling, is needed before the book becomes in any sense anti-Christian.

It consists of four short dialogues. In the first, Mercury, sent down to earth to get the Book of Destiny rebound because it is loose in its covers, is outmatched in his own trade of cheat and thief by two Athenian rascals whom he meets at a tavern, and who steal the Book, substitute a volume of earthly statutes, and set up as fortune-tellers with their prize. The second is a satire on the Philosopher's Stone (Truth broken into fragments by sects). In the third, after Mercury has accidentally made a horse speak by pronouncing the words of power, the animal tells his master some home-truths; and the fourth is a dialogue of two dogs, adjusted to the same obvious purpose of satire on humanity. It needs, of course, very little ingenuity to turn the Book of Destiny into the Bible, to make the talking horse a satire on miracles in general, and Balaam's Ass in particular, and so forth; but it is at least a question whether the intelligence which is thereby shown is much greater than the ingenuity which is therein required.[1] At

[1] Even Charles Nodier was misled, and has misled others on this head, by that curious anti-clerical tendency which has always been so

any rate, the book, disregarding alike its reputation of scandal and its disrepute by partisans, is a much less remarkable literary achievement than the *Nouvelles Récréations.* It is, in fact, little more than one of the many proofs of the vast influence which Lucian exercised over the Renaissance, an influence which up to the present time has been rather underrated. Desperiers is indeed much less at home in the form of the dialogue than in that of the *conte.* If the *Cymbalum Mundi* be compared with the *Colloquies*, or even with such a minor example of Latin dialogue as *Eckius Dedolatus*, the unreadiness for this particular form, even of French, the most accomplished, next to Italian, of the vernaculars, will be almost sufficiently demonstrated. For that Desperiers was a man of keen wit, and a master of such French as was at his disposal, cannot be doubted.

We must now turn to the poets, and of many mention at least four. Mellin (*i.e.*, Merlin) de Saint-Gelais[1] (1487-1558) has not been a very great favourite of late years, either in other countries or even in his own. But he can be read with pleasure still; and he has his special interest for the historian because he is a link of union between the school of Marot and the Pléiade, between the older French style of poetry and the new Italianated singers. He was actually an older man than

Mellin de Saint-Gelais.

strong in Frenchmen of letters. It is odd to see how the inquisitorial habit of discovering mare's-nests infects these anti-inquisitors.

[1] In the Bibliothèque Elzévirienne, ed. P. Blanchemain, 3 vols., Paris, 1873.

Marot himself, and survived him by many years. If his father was really Octavien de Saint-Gelais, he had both good blood and fair poetry by inheritance. It is certain that in his younger years he not merely visited Italy, as did many Frenchmen then, on warlike errands, but actually studied at her most famous universities —Padua and Bologna. He entered the Church, was freely patronised, and obtained a considerable position by his verse—a position which he did not lose, though he set himself against the rising stars of the Pléiade, and which (more remarkable still) was actually at last accepted by themselves.

Some histories of literature gave a great deal of space to these literary quarrels, with which the present period was much infested, from that of Marot and Sagon, with "Marotiques" and "Sagontiques" on each side, to the probably imaginary one between Rabelais and Ronsard; while Italy is at least equally full of them, from that between Aretino and Berni to the wrangling, after our time, over the *Gerusalemme Liberata*. But all such things had better be banished, as very many of them have been already, to their special valley in the Moon; and it is devoutly to be hoped that no Astolfo will ever bring them back again.

Besides being something of a scholar, Mellin was also much of a musician, and his double studies are perceptible in their result, the remarkable harmony of his verse. It cannot be said to be of extraordinary vigour, or to possess great depth of meaning. But it is always graceful and polished in style, as well as singularly satisfactory to the ear. And it shows "the meeting of the waters" as does no other verse of our period. Side by side with the sonnets, which Mellin almost certainly introduced into French literature, and which in turn he helped to hand on to English,[1] are a crowd of pieces in the ancient forms, *rondeaux*, &c., and in those more modern and simpler *dixains*, *huitains*, &c., which Marot had made fashionable. In all these, and especially in his epigrams, Mellin de Saint-Gelais ranks fairly with Marot at all but the latter's very best: and while he has not Marot's usual grace, he often escapes his occasional triviality.

Magny, Tahureau, Louise Labé.

Three poets, or rather two poets and a poetess, of curious grace, if not of much strength, may close the tale. These are Oliver de Magny (?-1560), Jacques Tahureau (1527-1555), and Louise Labé (1526-1566). Magny and Tahureau show something of Pléiade influence; but the first died only ten, the second only five years later than the middle of the century. Magny[2] was a townsman of Marot by birth, a lover of Louise Labé by choice. He died very young; but his genius rather than his youth should be credited with his escape from the stiffness into which Ronsard and his school sometimes relapsed

[1] Wyatt (*v. infra*, p. 265) translated some of his. Mellin's competitor for the honour of introducing this form (which has indeed never given such good results in French as in English) is Ponthus de Thyard, one of the outlying members of the Pléiade, and now and then certainly a better practitioner than Mellin himself. But dates and other things give a probable, if not an absolutely certain, priority to Saint-Gelais.

[2] Ed. Courbet. 5 vols., Paris, *s.d.*

after Marot had got rid of it. Tahureau,[1] even sooner taken from the world, had given still better poetry before he left it. His delightful title of *Mignardises Amoureuses de l'Admirée* gives the very savour of his work—a little not ungraceful affectation, a great deal of genuine sweetness, and not a little real passion. He had the good sense not merely to admire but to marry his beloved. Louise Labé,[2] "La belle Cordière," is one of the most considerable poetesses, perhaps the most considerable poetess, of France, and inspires her work with that touch of melancholy passion which is so rare in French writers of the male sex, but which in at least two other instances, of prose and verse respectively—Julie Eléonore de Lespinasse and Marcelline Desbordes-Valmore—has been attained by French women.

And so we may leave a part of our subject which—in one instance of the highest, in two or three others of high interest—is not, either in the whole history of its own division of literature, or in that horizontal survey which we are pursuing, of the very first importance. Without Rabelais, France, though above England for the time, would not be so very far above her; both countries would present pretty equally the spectacle of a transition not yet finished, of school-work, of the experimental and the immature. With Rabelais she has no country to envy; but then Rabelais, intimately as he is connected with his time, is one of the great chance-medleys of literature in his real and essential quality.

[1] Ed. Blanchemain. 2 vols., Geneva, 1869.
[2] Ed. Tross. Paris, 1871.

CHAPTER IV.

THE SCHOOL OF ELIZABETHAN LITERATURE.

OPENING AND GENERAL CHARACTER OF THE PERIOD IN ENGLAND—CAUSES OF THESE—IN LANGUAGE, GRAMMAR, AND METRE—IN PROSE STYLE—IN DRAMA—MORE—ELYOT—THEOLOGICAL POLEMIC—LATIMER—THE TRANSLATORS AND LITURGISTS—PUZZLES OF THEIR WORK—ITS UNSURPASSED LITERARY QUALITY—THE CAMBRIDGE PROSE-MEN—CHEKE—WILSON—HIS 'ART OF RHETORIC'—"INK-HORN TERMS"—ASCHAM—THE POSITION AND WORK OF WYATT AND SURREY—THEIR POETIC VALUE—THEIR MODELS AND MASTERS—THEIR MEANS AND METHODS—THE ENGLISH SONNET—THE "POULTER'S MEASURE," ETC.—BLANK VERSE—SOME OTHERS—TUSSER AND HEYWOOD—THE 'PROVERBS' AND 'EPIGRAMS.'

Opening and general character of the period in England.

It is by no means out of accordance with the rule of things in literature and life that the English Renaissance, which was to produce by far the greatest literary results of the whole movement, had an overture, and even something much more than an overture, of portentous and almost unexampled length and dulness. At the beginning of the sixteenth century the Scottish division, with men like Dunbar and Douglas, was indeed more than respectably furnished; but this has been dealt with already,[1] and was in fact an almost entirely isolated phenomenon, due less to natural growth than to intelligent but artificial imitation. It had next to no sequel, or such as may best be briefly despatched at the end of this chapter. In England, at first sight, there is nothing at all to show but men like Hawes, Barclay, and Skelton in verse[2]—the first, a swan-singer of mediæval music, half graceful, half awkward, as swans are on earth and in water respectively; the second, a plodder of no genius and not much talent; the third, an eccentric exception:—in prose, men like Berners and Fisher,[3] whose real importance it requires no little study fully to realise. But the most remarkable thing is not so much that the curtain rises on so weak a cast, as that the stage remains for so long inadequately occupied. More than three quarters of the century — nearly the whole of three conventional generations—has to pass before any real substantive progress is made: our own period proper closes as it had begun, *re infecta*, or at best with such comparatively slight advance—itself to be for long not much further advanced upon—as the work of the later Tottel's Miscellanists in verse, and that of Ascham in prose.

This phenomenon is at first sight so odd that some, either wilfully or for lack of eyesight, have declined to recognise its existence; exaggerating the positive—it is not easy to exaggerate the transitional—importance of Wyatt and Surrey, and finding a "Father of English Prose" in an estimable practitioner like More, who

[1] See *The Transition Period*, chap. ii.

[2] Ibid., chap. i.

[3] Ibid., chap. x.

did his best work in Latin. Others, following the usual line, have laboured to the utmost the theory about Literature being an "expression of national life." The nation, it seems, was too busy with religion, politics, social changes, to have leisure for literature; just as, if these three quarters of a century had been an active literary time, we should have been told that this activity was a reflection of the other. It would be wiser to take the merely devout line of Grandgousier, and to say that at this period England had not a great literature because it did not please God that she should have it. And, undoubtedly, there is very much to be said for that point of view. Yet we may, perhaps, before beginning the actual survey of what was, and in order to clear our eyes for that survey, submit some of the considerations which to some extent account for the absence of what was not—reasons which ought to be familiar, but which, if one may judge from the evidence at hand, are perhaps not so generally comprehended or accepted as they should be.

Causes of these.

The first, the most obvious, the most important, of these reasons, but perhaps still one not quite completely recognised, is the peculiar character of the English language — a character on which mere philology throws very little light, if, indeed, it does not distinctly obscure the field and distort the vision. Modern English is, of all great literary languages, the least of a natural growth or even a chemical compound, the most of a mechanical blend or adjustment. The purely English or Anglo-Saxon, the

French, and the Latin elements in it, not to mention the smaller constituents, have simply taken their shapes by a secular process of rolling and jumbling together, like the pebbles on the sea-shore or the sweet-meats in a confectioner's copper basin. From this mere attrition, this mere shaking together, English grammar, English prose style, and English prosody have resulted. And this process took—could not but take —centuries before it could turn out results suitable for a Spenser or a Shakespeare, a Hooker or a Bacon. The real reason why the results of a method so apparently accomplished as Chaucer's were mere botch-work in the hands of his purely native followers, was that Chaucer came too early, and when this process of attrition had not gone on long enough. Dante, dealing with a language like Italian, homogeneous in itself, however various in dialect, was able to do his work once for all—not that Dante gives us complete modern Italian, either in grammar or even in prosody, but that there are no fundamental differences. Chaucer could do nothing of the kind. The philologers who ask "Whether Chaucer did not know his own language?" and so force on him chimerical uniformities of rhyme and syntax, may be asked in turn, "How, then, do you account for what followed?" They cannot account for it. The literary historian can.

In language, grammar, and metre.

In other words, Chaucer, by main force and gigantic dead-lift of individual genius, had got the still imperfectly adjusted materials of English into a shape sufficient for architecture of permanent and beautiful design. But when this force and this skill were taken away, the rough-edged or crumbling materials of language, the not fully organised devices of grammar and metre, were insufficient to make anything but more or less shapeless heaps. Skelton may have evaded the difficulty by adopting rococo forms; Surrey and, earlier still, Wyatt, by taking liberties with accent or quantity on the one hand, improving grammar on the other, and borrowing the constraining stay of the sonnet or the liberty of blank verse from more accomplished languages like Italian, may have made actual progress towards the true English style. But all this demanded time, experiment, unsuccessful as well as successful, and an amount of individual genius which simply did not happen to be available for the moment, or for many moments.

In prose style.

The prose-writers had an apparently more difficult but really easier task. They were not misled, in the very act of being assisted, by intrinsically consummate, but relatively premature and exceptional, work like Chaucer's. Chaucer's own prose, interesting and important as it is, has nothing of the exceptional and almost portentous character of his verse. It fits (with due allowance for the exceptional talent of its author) easily and naturally into the succession of its kind, from the *Ancren Riwle* and the various theological exercises of the thirteenth and early fourteenth centuries. It is itself succeeded as naturally by fresh applications and developments. The prose-writers of the fifteenth century are not, like the verse-writers of it, endeavouring to draw a bow which is not only too strong for them, but of which the yew is dry-rotted and the string frayed by time and weather. They have a great deal to do; they have not done very much as yet. But they are putting prose more and more to its naturally multifarious or rather infinite uses; they are accumulating the vocabulary; they are discovering, either by mere practice, or by borrowing, sensibly or insensibly, from the French and Latin originals, whom they almost inevitably follow, the varieties of style; they are shaping grammar by using it. In one great instance—that of Malory—they have already done a great deal more than this: they have actually made, once for all, a style that cannot be surpassed for its particular purpose. And now, in our own period, in Fisher and in Berners, we find them achieving something only less great. Berners, indeed, like Malory, "comes to the end": of the myriad purposes of prose he has found one which he can discharge excellently, but which will not need, in that particular way and style, to be discharged again. Fisher is much less positively satisfactory and interesting to us; but he is even more important to history, because he is trying the rhetorical devices, forming the tools of style, for purposes other than his own, as well as for his own itself.

In drama.

Nor perhaps does this at first sight humdrum and disappointing period show less well, when it is examined in the third great division, hybrid between prose and poetry, that of drama. Unfortunately we are here in a difficulty which does not beset us either in regard to poetry or in regard to prose: to wit, that we are in many, if not in most cases, almost wholly ignorant not merely of the personality of the writers, but even of their approximate dates. What we do know is that at this time, partly as a matter of natural development of or from the kinds of the mediæval mystery, morality, and farce, partly as a direct result of the study of the classical drama, especially Seneca on the one side and Terence on the other, dramatic attempts are made which, though not in a single case resulting in a perfect comedy or tragedy, yet express a distinct advance towards the two great types of modern drama. But the detailed items of this will be for the general dramatic chapter. The present will be limited to the accomplishments—a poor thing, but our own—of English poets and prose-writers proper between the rough limits of 1500 and 1550.

This poverty is aggravated by the ordinance which has handed over the most important writers of the earlier century to the preceding volume. Of the three poets who alone, for this period, have substantive claims, Barclay actually outlived the strict limits of our own time by a year or two. Skelton saw nearly the whole of its first three decades, and Hawes probably more than its first two. Yet are they distinctly representative of the past, if in Skelton's case partly of dissatisfaction with that past; inheritors of almost wholly Chaucerian tradition; men of the fifteenth century, not the sixteenth. And so we have to leave them, with only a little allusion. The giants and the monsters of Hawes had, there can be little doubt, a real influence on Spenser, and though of his two allegorical hounds, Grace and Governaunce, the former was not always with him, and the latter, in the sense of Criticism, a most truant and unmindful companion, yet he keeps a certain intrinsic charm. Barclay, the least charming of the three, is the most modern in tone: his *Eclogues*, if not his *Ship of Fools*, savour of the Renaissance not a little. Skelton, as is the wont of those whose genius inclines to the satiric, is, though intensely interested in his time, half outside of it. As with Aristophanes, as with Lucian, as with Butler, as with Swift, his occasions are temporary, but his quality is extra-temporal. So we must deny ourselves recurrence to his graceful celebrations of Isabels and Margarets, to the vigorous foulness of the *Tunning*, and the grotesque strength of *Why Come ye not to Court?* And the same must be the case with Fisher and with Berners. But Fisher's younger companion in misfortune, More, and one or two others, may receive some notice here before we turn to the really representative figures of the School of Elizabethan Literature.

More.

Sufficient reasons—at least reasons which seem sufficient to the writer—have been given in the notice of More included in the chapter on Humanism (*supra*, p. 86) for refusing to consider the *Utopia* among English books. But the Chancellor's actual work in English is not inconsiderable, though both in subject and in style it is quite inaccurate to estate him as "Father of English Prose." Indeed there are strong doubts how far one of its most remarkable constituents, the *History of Edward V. and Richard III.*, is really his: and how far it may be the production, perhaps in Latin, of his patron Cardinal Morton. It is very well written, but by no means so much in advance of other work of the time as has sometimes been said. Another division of More's prose consists of tracts against the Protestants—not quite so free from the rough-and-tumble argumentation or objurgation of the time as those who regard More as a pattern of sweet reasonableness would wish, and not always attaining the level of force at which partisan virulence may be almost or quite forgiven. He was a writer of verse as well as of prose, but the most notable thing in his verses is an attempt to extend the seventh line of the rhyme-royal into an Alexandrine, in which some have seen a possible—and the only possible — original of the great Spenserian stanza.[1] It is perhaps enough to say, first, that More's extension is not uniform, and may be a mere accident; secondly, that the rhyme-royal is not a stanza of substance quite sufficient to bear the Alexandrine at its end. It is the extraordinary homogeneity, the proportion as of pre-established harmony, in the Spenserian itself, which shows that it must have been a stroke of genius on the part of its inventor.

The chroniclers, Graftons and Halls and what not, of the time need no detailed notice, nor does Leland, an invaluable friend to literature, but himself only a journeyman of letters. Sir Thomas Elyot (1490-1546) may perhaps have a little more

Elyot.

[1] The poem is on the death of Elizabeth of York, and the final lines are lengthened, that each may end with the words, "for lo, now here I lie!" It may be found quoted in Warton (ed. Hazlitt, iv. 90).

room, if but by patent or precedent. He has indeed been rather accidentally fortunate in having had the honour and advantage of reprint, bestowed, not merely once but twice during the nineteenth century, on his chief work, the *Governour*.[1] This book displays the positive mania for pædagogy, which is a main note of the time all over Europe, and which, only a little altered and conditioned, shows itself also in his other works, especially the medical *Castle of Health*. That Elyot meant to be a man of letters, and to some extent was so, there can be no doubt. The *Governour*, a most well-intentioned work on the old Plutarchian lines, but much developed, quite observes its own precepts in speaking English, which is "clean, polite, and articulate-pronounced." But it has no particular distinction, and for once its matter is of more purely literary importance than its style. We have better examples of the same drift elsewhere, but not in English: and though the commendation of Homer, Virgil, Lucan, and Silius Italicus to some extent continues the haphazard confusion of the Middle Ages, yet Elyot, like the rest of the Humanists, perfectly well knows what he is doing in commending the classics generally.

Logically, as well as for reasons of convenience, we are fully entitled here to take the entire theological and religious-controversial work of the period in England together. It will divide itself very well into three heads, the first and third mainly grouped, the second including one remarkable individual name.

[1] The latest, most accessible, and best edition is by H. H. S. Croft. 2 vols. 4to. (London, 1883).

That is to say, (1), the Controversialists, in verse and prose, of the Reformation battle on both sides; (2), Latimer; (3), the translators of the Bible and the compilers of the Anglican Liturgy.[1]

Theological polemic.

Of the first we may make short work, voluminous as the division is, and distinguished as are, in some few cases, the names of the persons who contributed to it. Religious controversy has sometimes produced good, and even sometimes also great, literature, but not at this time. Even style could not at the moment hope to find any such exponents as were furnished later by Parsons[2] to some extent on one side, and by Hooker still later, and to a far greater extent, on the other.

In few countries did railing take the place of reason, the bludgeon of the rapier, more uniformly than in England. As for the pamphlets and lampoons in verse and prose, the examples of the Wyclifites, and even of such non-Wyclifites as Langland (who came again into much notice now) earlier, and of Skelton at the very cock-crow of the day itself, were not wholesome. And such half-famous things as Roye and Barlow's *Read me and be not Wroth*, with Fish's *Supplication of*

[1] There is an excellent *thesaurus* of these divisions in the publications of the Parker Society about the middle of the nineteenth century. The larger part of the 55 vols. no doubt only concerns history or controversy; but literature claims Latimer, Cranmer, Coverdale, and others.

[2] I must confess that I think Parsons has earned his reputation in this respect rather lightly; but his partisans, from Swift to Swift's biographer, Sir Henry Craik, are neither to be spoken of without respect nor provoked without temerity.

the Beggars, and the rather ingenious, though of course wholly one-sided, *John Bon and Mast Parson*, are, whether verse or prose, rather curious than admirable, and very much more aggressive than convincing. Of men like Bale and Foxe, the former of whom will have his deserts in our dramatic chapter, while the latter, in respect of his most famous work, comes after our time, it can only be said that, while neither shows much literary gift in form, both must, with impartial judges, choose between the status of impudent lying, and that of sadly unscrupulous, if not utterly blind, partisanship. With such a wise historian we need not and will not deal, in such a book as this: especially as both they and the whole class have but the vaguest and most general connection with our matters. Controversy, however ill-written on subjects of great general interest, necessarily exercises the powers of writers and whets the appetite of readers: and this is, as a rule, except in such rare cases as that of the *Provinciales*, about its only literary merit.

Latimer.

One, however, who can hardly be acquitted entirely of being a partisan—though if he that way sinned, the fire in front of Balliol should surely have served as his sufficient purgatory—nevertheless, partly by his moral, and still more by his literary qualities, rises far above this welter of men and serpents, who from time to time change each into the other form. That Hugh Latimer[1]

[1] The standard edition of his not extensive work is that of Corrie (Parker Society, as above, 2 vols., London, 1843-45). Two vols. of Mr Arber's invaluable reprints contain some of his best sermons.

(1490?-1555) had any intellectual or philosophical quarrel with Roman theology may be doubted; though his valiant soul and healthy conscience made him throw up his mitre, and put the head that bore it in considerable danger, by refusing the Six Articles. It is not so much probable as certain that his adherence to the doctrines of the Reformation arose mainly, as similar adherence did in so many other cases, from the association of the contrary doctrines of the Church of Rome with corruptions in practice, wherein less heated times have seen no necessary consequence of these doctrines at all. It is exceedingly difficult, for instance, to believe that to a man like Latimer Transubstantiation itself can ever have been either acceptable or incredible on strictly philosophical grounds; while outside of philosophy his natural piety would have made him admit that with God nothing was impossible. But Transubstantiation, like the confessional, the private mass, and the denial of the cup, was a most powerful support to that inordinate position and power of the clergy which revolted the conscience of men like himself, priests as they were, only less than the shameless immorality which these doctrines indirectly shielded. Therefore Latimer, a shrewd, clean-living, affectionate Englishman, not too refined, not in the least subtle, with an enthusiasm for the wellbeing of the people at large, a hatred of tyranny and vice, and an almost fanatical love of justice and fair-play, was a Reformer, and could not but have been one unless he had had the reach and grasp necessary to foresee the dangers of Reform.

We may dwell unwontedly on points of this kind, because for once the personal nature of the man is so directly reflected in the literary nature of his work that the latter cannot be understood without the former. Here, if anywhere, the true version of the saying "le style c'est *l'homme même*" applies; and it is as impossible to understand Latimer's work without understanding him as it is to understand that of his great, but morally inferior, modern analogue, Cobbett, without understanding Cobbett himself and his views. Like Skelton, but much more so, Latimer stands outside his time, except in so far as that time gave him his immediate subjects. And he is even more "disengaged" than Cobbett, because he had, unlike Cobbett, no Bunyan and no Swift to "play the sedulous ape" to in his youth. At all times he would have been himself—applying the common English of his day, whatever it was, in a concentrated, inspirited, but not in any case sublimated or quintessenced form, to such questions as enlisted, on one side or the other, his sound and shrewd if rather limited sense, his ready sympathy, his disgust at vice, and, most of all, his furious, though not in the least insane, denunciation of injustice and tyranny.

As it is, these qualities, clothed in the clearest, most vigorous, even within certain limits most picturesque, English, that had yet been applied to strictly prosaic purposes, apply themselves to subjects varied enough. There is the famous description of his yeoman-father's life and livelihood; the grim repetition of the story of Cambyses flaying the unjust judge, and covering the judgment-seat with his skin "to encourage the others"; the consummate speech of "that diligent prelate and preacher the Devil,"—that "busy ploughman" who has no time for "lording and loitering," but must be at his own business day and night. There are the constant references (in the same vein as More's on the other side, and natural enough) to the alarming economic changes of the time. "I think we shall be constrained, if this continues, to pay for a pig a pound," says Latimer—which point had indeed been reached before 1900, and for a sucking-pig, too. There is the somewhat ominous attitude to kings—they are not to be stinted of money or power or honour, but they are to do what Latimer thinks just—the bitter denunciation of flatterers and bribers; the vivid anecdotage; the amusing (though indeed it was then no laughing matter) intolerance of heresy when it is not his own heresy; the quaint scraps and tags of Latin, that point the raciness of the English. There is no affectation; but there is everywhere a restless glancing personality.

The translators and liturgists.

Latimer, however, though a most interesting and satisfactory individual, and to history a member of an always interesting and sometimes satisfactory class, is, as has been said, something of an exception, and an exception of a kind not always historically of good omen. The danger of writing like Latimer's is seen to some extent in his own contemporaries; but to see it at its full we must go to the end of the seventeenth century.

The "good plain" style, out of the hands of masters, is in constant danger of becoming a bad plain style—of being unkempt, colloquial, vulgar, if not of reaching positive slang—the "pozz," and the "upon rep," against which Swift protested in his famous *Tatler* article. At this precise moment, however, the danger, except in the necessarily ephemeral literature of controversy, was rather less than at another. Firstly, because the mere scholars had their classical point of honour before them, and, though they might be un-English or jejune, were not very likely to be slipshod. Secondly, because—by one of those half-mysterious *bonnes fortunes* of literature, those "windfalls of the Muses," which do now and then occur—very exquisite models of style were being furnished, of a kind the most opposite to mere vernacularity, mere idiom, and yet thoroughly idiomatic and vernacular. And these models were made familiar, from youth to age, in the ears of even the most unliterary for mere hearing, and in those of the literary for imitation. They were provided to some extent (though to a less than by their consummate followers, the compilers of the Authorised Version, at the beginning of the next century) by the translators of the Bible—to a far greater extent, to an extent never yet surpassed, or even rivalled, by the editors of the English Prayer-book.

Puzzles of their work.

It is curious and provoking, though not really important, that in the former case to some extent, in the latter almost wholly, we are unable to identify the benefactors to whom we are so much indebted. The authorship of the unequalled collects of the Prayer-book is pure guess-work, and the guess that attributes them mainly to Cranmer (1489-1556[1]) derives very faint corroboration from the Archbishop's certain work. Much Bible translation was avowedly done by joint-work; and even where there was a single author—as in the cases of Tyndale (1484-1536[1]) and Coverdale (1487-1568)—a peculiar difficulty remains. It is in the circumstances practically impossible that any translation of the Scriptures, unless it were made by the result of one of the fantastic experiments we read of—a man being educated to know Greek and Hebrew, but never to have heard of the Christian religion—could be first-hand. The most unbounded genius and the most unbounded conceit combined could not in the conditions sit down to "do" the Bible "out of its own head," and with no regard to predecessors. Even if prudence, reverence, and the desire to get the best version possible did not dictate study of these predecessors, importunate memory would insist on thrusting itself in, on recalling the Vulgate, and the partial and imperfect but widely spread vernacular translations of the fourteenth and fifteenth centuries. As a matter of fact, all our Biblical translators seem to have availed themselves as far as possible of *all* their predecessors—an ever-lengthening train,—and it is pretty certain that Tyndale, in his New Testament, consulted not merely the Greek in the recension of

[1] After reading the work of these and other Reformers carefully and consecutively, I have come to the conclusion that Coverdale has most "magic of style," Cranmer much less, Tyndale hardly any.

Erasmus, not merely the Vulgate, not merely Wyclif, but Luther's then new German version itself. The results of such a mosaic need not necessarily, but in most cases will, evade or overcome the individuality of the operator altogether.

Its unsurpassed literary quality.

Fortunately the literary quality of the Bible is so remarkable and so pervading that it suffices of itself to colour and shape every version of it that is not made by an utter dunce. The small amount of Hebrew which the present writer did actually learn at school has passed away from him too completely to make it possible for him to give any critical judgment of the merits of that language. But if it have not in itself qualities of greatness, then one may certainly find a Warburtonian argument of the most irresistible kind for its divine authorship, in the faculty which it has in making all the translations of it great literature. Of the Greek, and of that Vulgate which, half against their will, but to the great credit of their intelligence, influenced the Renaissance translators only less than the fourteenth-century versions, one can speak more frankly. The above argument covers the Old Testament proper: whether the literature comes from the Hebrew or was put in by the Seventy, it is there. The more purely Greek books of the Apocrypha are still less open to question, because some of them at least we seem to have in the original. *Wisdom* and *Ecclesiasticus*, if they were as bad philosophy as Mr Tupper and as bad morals as some of Lucian, would remain great literature—literature of all but the very first class, and sometimes of that. As for the New Testament, the purists cannot deprive the Gospels of narrative qualities of the most remarkable kind, or prevent the writings of St Paul from being rhetoric of all but the very best. Furthermore, the genius of St Jerome, and the peculiar charm of his, not indeed pure, but admirably literary, Latin, positively added a grace to the Vulgate itself, while missing very little of the graces of its originals. And in especial, there flowed in upon the modern vernaculars—none of them except Italian, upon which these translations exercised no influence, quite accomplished in their own rhythms and style—a flood of strange exotic harmony, a volume of new vocabulary, and phrase, and idea, which could not fail to enrich, to train, to refine, and to vary them.

The results of these things are in the earlier translations of the Bible less perfectly, as has been said, than in the later and practically final one.[1] But they are there.

In the *Prayer-book* they are complete. Here the hands of the compilers were freer; but lest this should be a doubtful advantage, they were supplied with additional materials and models in the *Breviary* and the various local Uses; in the enormous body (some of it bad literature, and much indifferent, but some exquisitely good) of devotional and concionatory Latin from Tertullian to à Kempis; and not least in the ineffable music of the Latin hymns. The result of it all, in the

[1] The "Revised Version" does not exist for literature; and the laity might surely be spared its frequently controversial alterations of sense and its generally hideous cacophonies of sound.

Collects and Prayers as well as in the composition and arrangement of the different services, is generally acknowledged, and indeed is a standing marvel. We have admirable men of letters among the hierarchy of to-day; but it is much if they manage by sedulous aping to write an occasional example in this kind which is inoffensive. The Prayer-book rhythm, that wonderful echoing accompaniment of pure sound (not mere suiting of sound to sense), is found in the Collects of the Burial Service, the simple but masterly rise and fall of the prayer of St Chrysostom, and of the second Collect at Evensong, the victorious trenchancy of the Athanasian Creed, the varied modulation of the Litany, the sustained and yet alluring stateliness of the Church Militant Prayer, the majesty of the first and general Collect for Advent, the cunning and multiform excellence of those for the Epiphany, for Quinquagesima, for Palm Sunday and Easter Eve, for the Fourth Sunday after Easter, for Trinity Sunday, and for others too many to mention. After these achievements it could hardly be said that anything was impossible in English which required either suggestiveness of expression, or modulation of sound, or exquisiteness of individual phrase. All that was needed—and it was soon done, first by the poets of the end of the sixteenth, and then by the prose-writers as well as the poets of the seventeenth century—was to extend to profane subjects the mere art of language, here so happily taught in reference to sacred ones. What had been done for one order of thought could now be done for all, and all were kept in constant mind of it.

But we have yet to speak of the group of Prose-writers who, towards the end of our period and just beyond it, but appertaining to us by the same rule which abstracted Berners and Fisher, made the centre of the sixteenth century one of the greatest turning-points in English prose. Their work, though in the hands of only one member of the school did it reach positive excellence as a part of English literature, was obviously conceived in common; reflections of it appear outside themselves; and though it is in some respects too limited, and in one or two positively mistaken, it has that characteristic of being "the right thing at the right time" which distinguishes all the favourites of fortune in history, whether it be political or literary, or of any other kind. This is the remarkable Cambridge group, the leaders of which were Cheke, Ascham, and Wilson.

The Cambridge prose-men.

The younger university had been less eager than the elder to receive the New Learning in the first instance; the Vandals—respecting whose planting at Cambridge one of her chief nineteenth-century glories made an unkind gibe—still ruled there when the Greeks, through Grocyn and Linacre, More and Colet, had won Oxford. But amends, owing no doubt to the tradition of Erasmus's residence, though that residence was for the time ineffectual, were soon made. Both Cheke and Ascham "taught Cambridge Greek," and while the former also "taught King Edward," the latter performed the same office to King Edward's much more interesting sister and cousin, in regard to the language which has been directly and indirectly the teacher of literary greatness to all others. But the two, and their friend Thomas Wilson, took various ways of enforcing the doctrine which was common to them all—the doctrine that, great as were the classical languages, hopeless as it might be to try to equal them in the modern, yet it was the duty of every Englishman to make the best of English, and for that purpose to avail himself of the help of Greek and Latin, not as supplanters, but as assistants.

The importance of this, and also the *eukairia*—the "nick of time"—at which it came, require no voluminous indication, though they have not always been appreciated as they deserve. For not much less than two centuries fresh stores of vocabulary had been constantly poured into the treasury of English prose by the custom of translation from Latin, French, and latterly Italian and Spanish. The practice, original as well as in translation, of a wider and ever wider range of subject, had at the same time provided the workman not merely with new material, but with new tools and methods. And latterly, at least in Fisher and Berners and the Biblical translators, definite rhetorical device had been discovered and employed. But all this had been done—as is common enough everywhere, but nowhere quite so common as in England—in a haphazard and generally unmethodical fashion. Nothing like standard English could be said to exist; and between "aureateness" at one point of the circle, archaism at another, mere vernacularity at a third, and, all around, the tendency to regard Latin as the language in which an educated gentleman must write, there were dangers enough about. The men of whom we are now speaking set themselves to guard against these dangers—to put the national house in order in this respect as far as they could. They were not in even one instance men of genius; only in Ascham's case could any one of them claim more than average literary talent. But this was rather fortunate than otherwise. Your genius does not usually do what is wanted on these occasions: he does usually either go off into eccentricities, or corrupt the world with one good but not universally applicable custom. What was wanted was a capable brigade of schoolmasters; and these men—who were actually schoolmasters, or at least teachers, by profession—had the better *ethos* of the schoolmaster as few have had. They saw literary English prose through its rudiments; they brought it about that the revolutionary extravagance of Euphuism in the next generation did good without doing much, if any, real harm; and their lesson directly produced, though at Oxford, not at Cambridge, one of the greatest writers of English in Richard Hooker.

As is always the case in these school-movements when they are good for anything, the leaders did not merely duplicate each other's function. Sir John Cheke (1514-1557), though at least at one time the most prominent in station, was not much of a constructive man of letters, and was a good deal of a crotcheteer. Some of the crotchets he espoused were wandering truths, and gave offspring *pour le bonheur du genre humain:* some did not quite deserve

Cheke.

that description, and were fortunately sterile as regards enduring progeny. It is to him that we owe that English pronunciation of Greek which has made perhaps more scholars appreciate the real beauty of Greek literature than any other nation can boast, whether it be or be not (which is extremely unimportant) near to the unknown original. And he has left us a striking pronouncement[1] of the saving doctrine of the whole school on the importance of cultivating the vernacular. On the other hand, he tried to reform English spelling —a proceeding which, as spelling is a natural growth, is always absurd; and he endeavoured to keep going that curious process of "Saxonising" Greek and Latin words, of which we find the most remarkable example seventy years earlier in Reginald Pecock, and which is based upon a misconception of the real nature of the blended modern language. But nothing came of these things, and good came of the others.

Wilson.

Thomas (later Sir Thomas) Wilson, the second member of the group (——?-1587), was its chief formalist. His *Arte of Rhetorique*, first published in 1553, but evidently written earlier, and reprinted with important additions[2] ten years later, is not indeed actually the first book of the title in English. The honour of having produced this belongs to one Leonard Cox, a Reading schoolmaster, and a friend of Erasmus, who had anticipated Wilson

[1] In a letter to Sir Thomas Hoby, published with Hoby's *Courtier*, and to be found reprinted in the Introduction to Mr Arber's edition of Ascham's *Schoolmaster*.

[2] Both are rare. I possess the latter, which ought to be reprinted.

by twenty-one years. But Cox's book is a mere technical abstract of scholastic-traditional dealings with the Art. Wilson's is a real application of it to English.

His Art of Rhetoric.

The little quarto—first of all English books to deal systematically with the means and methods of English literature—has a dedication to Northumberland (at the time Earl of Warwick only), with the usual flattery (the book is to be put to school to Dudley, he is so great an orator); a prologue to the Reader, with some interesting facts on the book's and the author's history; a preface on the divinity of Eloquence—God-given, lost by man, and recovered by the Giver's help; a couple of copies of Latin Elegiacs—by the prolific Dr Haddon to the author, and by the author to his book; 113 leaves of text, and a very methodical and elaborate Index. At first, though he never confines himself to them very slavishly, Wilson seems to be mainly observing the lines and repeating the system of the Latin *Rhetorics*, which (themselves altered but little from the earlier Greek treatises of Hermagoras, Hermogenes, and others) had for more than a thousand years been chief among school-books. The early direction of the matter to the "persuasion" of the hearer, the later more than half-legal absorption in *status* and similar things, make full appearance. And though Wilson's examples take a wide range, and he is evidently at least endeavouring to be as a rule philosophical rather than merely jurisprudential, it is probable that the expense of time and pains, then almost necessary on these things, has helped to deprive the book of what it ought to have had long ago—a new edition, with proper editorial apparatus. But the efforts to modernise and vitalise are, even in these parts, constant. As instances of a certain kind of Amplification, he contrives to pay compliments to two of his friends, Latimer and the above-mentioned Dr Haddon—representing the one as the father of all Preachers, the other as the best Latin writer in England. Not only Jack Straw, but the recent Norfolk rebel Kett, comes in for mention as an example, with the Siege of Boulogne and the Battle of "Muskel-borowe" (Pinkie). The curious taste of the day for waggery—sometimes, like that of all days, not so waggish to posterity—comes out frequently, with the inevitable tendency of all good Protestants to make the Church of Rome defray the expenses of the jest if possible. In fact, the Division of "Pleasant Behaviour" occupies ten folios, or twenty full pages, towards the end of the Second Book. The Third, according to precedent immemorial, at least from Aristotle downward, is devoted to the really literary part of the matter. And it is in the exordium of this that we find those passages which have always been regarded by good judges as giving Wilson no mean place in the story of English literature. Discussing the arts of Elocution, he strikes at once and repeatedly at Outlandish-English, French-English, English Italianated, pedantic technicalities, Archaism ("The fine courtier will talk nothing but Chaucer"), and, lastly, the extravagant "aureation" or Latinising which had been the curse of the fifteenth century. To exemplify this latter he gives a letter from a Lincolnshire gentleman, which is pretty certainly imitated from the Limousin scholar in Rabelais, or perhaps from the original thereof in Geoffroy Tory; following this up with another example of sheer Malapropism, which he avouches to have been addressed to the Provost of King's during his own Cambridge days ("you are a worshipful Pilate," "keeps an abominable house," &c.) He turns from this jest-earnest to the usual business of Figures and the like, and pursues his task once more on the old lines, descending even to gesture and the like. But he never forgets the vernacular; and close to the end of the book he gives us an example, under the head of Pronunciation, of that glossing and slurring which has always been characteristic of English in England, by telling us that some called "black velvet" "black vellet."

This constant bringing of matters home to the mother-tongue is one of the main *notanda* in Wilson;

"Ink-horn terms."

another is the aversion to "ink-horn terms." This, in its own way and division, almost famous phrase and obvious metaphor—as though the ambitious composers could not be satisfied with the surface of the receptacle, but must dive into its depths for strange dregs and lees of speech—became fashionable, and is pointedly referred to by contemporaries. It is of great importance for our purpose.

To a very small extent, no doubt, it reflects that classical distrust and almost horror of the *inusitatum verbum* which was certain to become fashionable among the Humanists of the Renaissance. But to regard it as reflecting this only would be a very gross error. As has just been said, the great curse of style, especially prose style, in France, and in England (which in literary matters so closely followed France) during the fifteenth century, had been the mania for aureate and rhetorical tricks. But this mania had been rendered still more dangerous by the popularity of the triplet. Whether Wilson in his Lincolnshire squire's letter is glancing at Fisher, who was not popular with the extreme Protestant party, it is difficult to say; but he certainly puts a triplet in the forefront of the composition. And, whether in triplet or in couplet or alone, the "ink-horn term" was certainly then only too much in evidence. It was therefore of real importance to eliminate it, if possible, in any process of arranging and constituting the English tongue for the general purposes of literature—of as much consequence almost as to expel mere solecisms and barbarisms. Nor is the objection to the courtier's Chaucerisms less noteworthy. These excellent scholars were, on the whole, much less sound on English verse than on English prose, and it was in their midst, it would seem, that the most pestilent of all monsters, the English hexameter, was fostered. They could not regard with any affection such a formidable champion of English verse proper as Chaucer. Besides, the somewhat priggish and prudish morality which characterised the Protestant party was no doubt scandalised by him. Yet it is fair to remember that there was at the time something to be said for them. Chaucer's language, delightful as it is, was not fitted, and would not have sufficed, for the general purposes of English, especially of English prose, at this date; and its popularity necessarily served to postpone the settlement of English pronunciation. Now it can do us no harm, and does us an infinite amount of good. Then it would have been rather terrible if England had gone back to the superfluous *e*, with its sixteen[1] different grammatical possibilities of value.

Ascham.

But the third of the group is by far the most important in his influence (an influence working mostly for good, but also a little for ill) upon English literature. Roger Ascham (1515-1568), though by no means a pedant, was a pedagogue born; but he must have had also no small powers of literary creation. Not merely his two substantive works,[2] the earlier *Toxophilus* (1545) and the later *Schoolmaster* (1570), but the not inconsiderable body of his *Letters*, show this beyond all doubt. Some have tried to find in Ascham such a restless and multifold working of the yeasty spirit which often shows itself in men of parts just before a great literary period, that they have even regarded him as a follower of Berners and a predecessor of Lyly in the genesis of Euphuism. But it is quite certain that, by example as well as by precept, Ascham was strenuous in the practice of the literary vernacular, and untiring in his endeavour to

[1] I do not pledge myself to sixteen, which I extract—though the enumeration is not there—from Drs Morris and Skeat's Introduction to the *Prologue*. Fourteen or fifteen—nay, four or five—would do to show that "'twas time for it to *go*."

[2] Both reprinted by Mr Arber. Of the whole works the best edition is that of Giles, 3 vols. in 4 (London, 1864-65).

raise it to higher powers by the imitation and inspiration of the classics. In his almost youthful *Toxophilus* he elects boldly to "write this English matter in the English tongue for English men," though it would have been so much easier for him to have written it in Latin. In the collection of his *Letters* we see him gradually, and no doubt gladly, exchanging the universal language of Humanism — almost of Europe — for the struggling, and to foreigners half-barbarous, vernacular of England. In the posthumous *Schoolmaster*, anxious as he is to perfect the teaching of the learned languages, he is at least equally anxious to perfect it through, and so as in turn to perfect, the vernacular itself.

Even his literary sins—or, if that be too harsh a word, peccadilloes—are only the effect of misguided patriotism. There is no doubt that he favoured the classical metres, and that his doing so is proof among others, to which we shall come soon, of his want of the sense of poetry. But Spenser was scarcely destitute of that sense, and he was saved, only so as by fire, from the composition of trimeters and hexameters, whose harmony is that of the salt-box and the cleaver. And there are other excuses for Ascham. In his young days a man could, even if he hungered and thirsted for poetry, find very little to satisfy him in any contemporary English. Chaucer was archaic, and Ascham's school, as we have said, was bent on the future, not the past. Since Chaucer's time until the new Italianated efforts of the young courtiers—which Ascham doubtless thought frivolous *xenomania*—the range of English verse was simply a desert. Of the poets who existed while he was himself young, Hawes would offend his classical taste from one side as Skelton from another, and Barclay could satisfy him from none. Meanwhile half Europe was going astray on this curious by-path of classical metre, and why not England?

So also Ascham's prudery and Puritanism were only patriotism a little gone wrong. It is very horrible *to us* to read his Philistine judgment of the *Morte d'Arthur*, and we know that Italy and France, especially the former, had at this moment an almost infinite amount to teach England. But they had also, and again especially Italy, a great deal to teach England which Ascham might be justly eager that England should not learn. It is to be feared, from his judgment of Malory, that even if he could have glanced at "that Elvish Queene," of which, not impossibly, a poor scholar of his own university dreamt just after Ascham's own death, he would not have cared for it: it is quite certain that in Ariosto himself many things must have left Ascham unmoved, and some have moved him to nothing but indignant testifying. The latest editor of Painter's *Palace of Pleasure*, Mr Jacobs, thinks that there is direct reference in the *Schoolmaster* to that Collection; but whether this is so or not, Ascham's wide reading and travel must have made the Italian *novella* and the French *nouvelle* perfectly familiar to him. And we know well what he must have thought not merely of the "blasphemy and bawdry," to use the terms which he might as justly have applied here as he applies them unjustly to Malory, but of the detestable cruelty and savagery which is unknown in the romances. As for the *Capitoli* and suchlike things, it needed no Puritan to deprecate *their* introduction. Ascham, a man, like most of the best of his contemporaries, thoroughly penetrated with the Plutarchian ideal of education—in which moral, spiritual, and bodily health is the one thing needful, though learning is a desirable addition—could not, being what he was, have held different ideas on these points.

But all his ideas were harnessed to one single chariot, the determination to make England, and Englishmen, and English things, but especially the English tongue, a little better when he left them than as he found them. He succeeded. His own stamp of prose, short as it comes of universal validity, is admirable in the plainer kind. It needed only a genius like Hooker's to make it more admirable still in its merits, and an eccentric talent like Lyly's to instigate men to work themselves free of its weaknesses. For sureness, vividness, correctness, command of method, no forerunner had equalled him. In the *Toxophilus*, the pleasant whimsical vindication of shooting from the charge of taking up too much time, the admirable argument for the union of Great Britain, the exact but nothing dull description of the implements, and the masterly sketch of the winter ride from Topcliffe to Boroughbridge—in the *Schoolmaster*, passage after passage of shrewd sense and sound learning, could be cited to prove the truth of this encomium in prose. And as for verse, those contemporaries, of whom he may have known (and perhaps thought) not very much, had already, long before his death, set English on a better way even than his own.

Undoubtedly, however, *the* literary work of the period is work which was not printed till the period itself was in strictness over, but which had been composed in its youngest examples at least ten, in its eldest perhaps more than thirty, years before that actual publication in 1557.

The position and work of Wyatt and Surrey.

This is, of course, the work contributed posthumously and unintentionally by Sir Thomas Wyatt (1503-1542) and the Earl of Surrey (1517?-1547) to the famous *Tottel's Miscellany*, or *Songs and Sonnets*,[1] which Nicholas Grimald, of Christ Church, edited on the very eve of Elizabeth's accession. There is known to be work by others of Henry VIII.'s courtiers—Lord Vaux, Lord Rochford, Sir Thomas Bryan—in the book, but their shares are not identified as are those of Wyatt and of Surrey. The general certainty of their contributions, however, with some vaguer indications elsewhere and a corroboration of probability, has caused some to start the hypothesis of a considerable but mainly lost poetical activity about 1525-35, stimulated perhaps on the one hand by the Italian influence, which is now of most importance to us, on the other by the publication for the first time of Chaucer's minor works (as well as of a good deal not his) in 1532. Nay, Professor Skeat has even gone so far as to suggest that the mysterious and much

[1] Reprinted (London, 1870), by Mr Arber.

wrangled-over *Court of Love* may be one of the fruits of this activity. We need not enter into these exceedingly dubious and rather dangerous speculations. That there was such a court activity is by no means improbable, and the mere chance, which seems to be all that has preserved us the work, or some of the work, of Wyatt and Surrey, *may* equally well have doomed that of others to perish. But let us turn to certainties. The interest of the work of the two poets may be taken under three stages or heads. The first, of their intrinsic value; the second, of the influences or models which helped them to express that value; the third, of the special means which these influences prompted them to use. The first is the most obvious and striking; the second takes chief rank among the general historical aspects of the case; the third is the most genuinely interesting to the historical critic of literature.

Their poetic value.

As to the first, there has been but little difference, save among mere paradoxers or persons wholly or partially insensible to poetry. Hasty judgment has indeed acknowledged it by cavalierly ignoring, or still more cavalierly refusing, attention to all strictly English poetry between Chaucer and *Tottel* itself. This is totally uncritical and unhistorical; but it involves an exaggeration of a real fact. Hardly once in this interval of a hundred and fifty years—longer than that which passed from the dropping off of the Caroline poets to the issue of *Lyrical Ballads*—do we find in any strictly English poem (outside the shadowy flittings of anonymous ballad-mongers and carol-singers) the peculiar tone, the "cry," the appeal of poetry, which strikes us at once, in spite of some serious drawbacks, in the work of these two. It is idle to urge that they are still to a great extent translators or adapters; the demurrer applies equally to Chaucer and to his followers of the Interval, and there is some difference between *them.* And it is still more idle to urge that in the work of both Wyatt and Surrey there is much more that is feigned and "literary" than that is actual "emotion recollected in tranquillity." These attempts of criticism to limit and black-mark poetry are themselves uncritical. The critical question about poetry is not, "Is it sincere? Is it original? Is it this, that, and the other?" but, "Is it poetical?" To this question, in the case of the writers of the Interval, we can only answer "Yes" on the rarest occasions, with some hesitation even then, and with constant allowances. We can answer, in the case of Wyatt and Surrey, "Yes; *sans phrase.*"

Their models and masters.

The second point also is not exposed to much danger of serious controversy. For these hundred and fifty years the reigning influence over English poetry, direct or through Chaucer at one or two removes, had been French: it is now not French at all. In the very cases where Wyatt adapts French matter (as from Saint-Gelais), it is French matter which had been composed on Italian lines; and in most others his and Surrey's models are Italian direct. From the Italian they borrowed the sonnet, though they had the good taste to recognise that the form of the sonnet which happens to have been most popular in Italian, and which perhaps suits the ways of that language best, need not suit the ways of English best, and need not therefore be exclusively adopted in English. From Italian Surrey borrowed blank verse; Wyatt a kind of half-satirical epistle;[1] both the tricks and ways and atmosphere which, since Petrarch's time, had been characteristic of Italian poetical handling. And although the following up of the Italianising tendency was delayed—partly by the time during which their work remained unpublished, partly by the ecclesiastical-political troubles of the day, but most of all by the fact that neither the man nor the hour had come—yet no other took its place, and it was constantly being supported by fresh onsets of the same power. Gascoigne, not the best, but the most fruitful and active poet of the first half of Elizabeth's reign, went constantly to Italy for the originals of his various innovations in poetical and dramatic kind. The protest of Ascham in the *Schoolmaster* showed how prosaic and Puritan persons dreaded this influence. And when Spenser comes there is no doubt. He is perfectly loyal to Chaucer, and he is, in the true sense, sure of his own poetical originality. But though it is probable that if there had been no Ariosto the *Fairie Queene* would still have been written, yet it would be childish to deny the influence of Ariosto here, while it would be equally childish to question the influence of Petrarch upon the *Amoretti*, and of

[1] There may have been *some* French influence here: but even this was ultimately Italian.

other Italians elsewhere. Generally Italian reigns as French had reigned, and Wyatt and Surrey are its Warwicks.

It is when we come to the details that the difficulties and the differences of opinion naturally begin.

Their means and methods.

There are those who, in order to suit general or particular theories of their own, decline to acknowledge any remarkable prosodic and rhythmical change in the verse of these two poets. And there appear to be even some who think that the oddities which we perceive in their metric were quite natural things representing popular pronunciation. Those who have no theory to serve will probably question very much whether any popular English pronunciation ever called David Davìdd, or laid stress on the *eth* of the third person singular. And some light is thrown on eccentricities of the kind when we find proposals to scan the line

"With his bright brand,"

not as reason has it—

"Wīth | hĭs brīght | brānd,"

the line being made all the more effective by the metrical licences known in Greek as anacrusis and catalexis, but

"With hìs | burrìght | burrànd,"

which is at once vulgar and ineffective.

Let us, again, take the facts and stick to them. For some generations, as has been explained at the opening of this chapter, English versification and English pronunciation, owing mainly to the loss of value of the final *e*, but also to other causes, had been getting completely out of gear with each other, the difficulty being aggravated by the fact that practically every poet endeavoured to keep Chaucer's prosody, while he could not wholly, and perhaps could not at all, keep grip of Chaucer's word-system. Hence the joggling, staggering stuff for which, in Lydgate, people have endeavoured, by processes analogous to the figure-ticketing of the Greek Rhetoricians, to discover invention and accomplishment; hence the other stuff which less anxious charity has set down to the credit of those uncomplaining victims, the printers or copyists of Hawes. Every day the difficulty was getting greater; yet every day (at least about 1530) the attachment to Chaucer was increasing.

Now the adoption of the sonnet, of *versi sciolti*, and even to some extent of the English Alexandrine and fourteener (which about this time forced their way up from ballad and popular use into regular literary employment), freed Wyatt and Surrey, without their own consciousness, from part, though not from the whole, of this difficulty. Not one of these metres was Chaucerian; none carried with it the least jot of that Chaucerian association with which the couplet and the rhyme-royal were loaded. Furthermore, in the case of the sonnet at least, and to some extent of the rigid blank decasyllable, the strict and definite prosody of their Italian models practically kept them from the licence which Chaucer's occasional indulgence in nine-syllabled lines, and his not infrequent admission of trisyllabic feet, had induced in English. They had stays and staves in these minutiæ, and the danger now was stiffness, not slipshodness.

But part of their difficulty remained. There are times and seasons in every language when it is ill-suited to poetry, when it has grown out of one prosody and not grown into another. The stock example of this—so remarkable that it is surprising more notice has not been taken of it—is the difficulty about the word "Heaven" entertained at an interval of from two hundred to two hundred and fifty years by two most intelligent and acute students of English metre, Gascoigne and Mitford. Gascoigne, in mid-sixteenth century, thought that it was at the best a very great poetic licence to pronounce the word as a dissyllable. Mitford, at the end of the eighteenth and beginning of the nineteenth, thought that not to do so was a mere vulgarism. Yet again, the study of the strict syllabic prosodies of the classical languages made our poets adopt a fashion of slur which is not only very ugly, but which long weighed on English verse. They wrote, though it is very improbable that they pronounced, "to embrace" "tembrace," and so forth.[1]

If we now turn to the actual Songs and Sonnets, giving subsequently a few special remarks to Surrey's blank verse in the *Æneid*, and to Wyatt's so-called *Satires*, with some notice of Heywood's *Epigrams*,

[1] I do not wish to ignore the occurrence of similar spellings—"tescape," "tespie"—in Chaucerian MSS. But I believe these to be in the same way the result of a mistake—of the nervous reluctance to admit trisyllabic feet.

we shall have sufficiently covered the period as far as English is concerned, reserving only some space in the critical, and much in the dramatic, chapters for our countrymen.

The English sonnet.

The first thing, and perhaps the greatest thing noticeable, is of course the appearance of the Sonnet itself, and the preference—which long distinguished English sonneteering — of the form ending in a couplet. There has been for some time past a habit of speaking of this form as if it were in some way inferior and even bastard, because it does not follow the usual Italian arrangement of octave and sestet. But this seems to be altogether unreasonable, and to proceed from neglect of the fact that the prosody of one language never can be, and never ought to be, an exact reproduction of the prosody of another. As has been pointed out above, in dealing with Ariosto, the peculiar character of the Italian language, and especially of the Italian hendecasyllable with feminine rhyme, gives a certain character to any Italian stanza which winds up with a couplet. This character is less suitable to the gravity and intensity of the sonnet than the triplet-ending with rhymes disjoined. But nothing similar happens in the slower and more sententious movement of English, with its usual, if not invariable, restriction to decasyllables and masculine rhymes. On the other hand, the couplet-ending to an English ear does very much to clench and impress that single, or at anyrate prominent, meaning which is so much of the essence of the Sonnet. To say, as it is sometimes said, that the great name of Shakespeare, or

—as the more courteous and fairer arguers on that side put it—his magnificent achievement, creates an illegitimate prejudice in favour of the couplet-ending, is quite unjust. The advantages of the form, and its equal or perhaps superior adaptability to the needs of English, as compared with the octave-sestet with entangled final rhyme, show themselves in the early experiments with which we are now dealing. Certainly no one of taste would emulate the proscription of the English form by recommending the proscription, in English, of the Italian; or would be at once ungenerous and inept enough to insinuate that Milton and Wordsworth and Rossetti have given to it an illegitimate or at best accidental charm. But the first and last word on the banner of English poetry is Freedom!—freedom to produce the best effects by any means whatsoever, and without any arbitrary restriction, so long as the poet is able to produce them. And the restriction here is quite arbitrary, while the removal of it has produced the very best effects.

Not of course that these effects are quite at their very best here,—to expect that were unreasonable. Hampered by those drawbacks which have just been detailed, both Wyatt and Surrey have often failed to get quite clear of them in matters of accent and rhythm; while it is open to any one who chooses to say that there is too much conventional "Petrarchism" in their tone and thought, if too little in their form. Yet some of their sonnets are really charming things, for all their lisp and stammer: and it is surprising to find how much of the clangour and resonance of the original form they have managed to transport into a language then of far inferior accomplishment, and always of entirely different cadence. The early English sonnets have in this respect very greatly the advantage of the early French. And we can easily understand how inestimable, though of necessity slow, must have been the influence of these examples of swell, and rise, and dying fall in rhythm, of careful selection of the beautiful and harmonious word, upon men who had recently been accustomed to nothing but the blunted stanzas and hobbling couplets of the late Chaucerians, the doggerel of Skelton, and, to some extent, Heywood, the "lollop" of the fourteener, and the monotonous skip of the octosyllable.

The "Poulter's Measure," &c.

From none of these did the new poets wholly abstain: but they did a good deal towards transforming them. They sometimes at least transformed the fourteener, by itself, or with the Alexandrine, into four-lined stanzas of eights and sixes, or six, six, eight, six respectively, while they evaded the faults which had grown upon the octosyllable since Gower, by shifting it into quatrains of alternate rhyme. Not a little of the "sing-song" and "derry-down" effect still remains; but the alternate rhyme, by at once relieving and "baiting" the ear, leads almost automatically to that splendid soar and moving droop of the shorter quatrain which we find in full perfection during the seventeenth century. To explain the meaning — which though most simple seems often to be mistaken—let us take, not an exceptionally good but, a quite ordinary stanza from Surrey's first poem of the kind :—

> " And now the covert breast I claim,
>   That worshipped Cupid secretly;
> And nourishèd his sacred flame
>   From which no blazing sparks did fly."

This is no wonder; but see how far superior it is to the couplet arrangement, which expresses the same sense, and keeps almost every individual word and letter :—

> " And now the covert breast I claim
> That nourished the sacred flame ;
> It worshipped Cupid secretly,
> And thence no blazing sparks do fly."

In the one case the rhymes come rattling, like money told down on a counter ; in the other they are cast in the air to flutter a while, till each finds its pair and settles down in *l'amorosa pace.*

The division of Alexandrine couplets into continuous sixes, with alternate rhyme, is less happy; but the long poulter's couplets, arranged not as quatrains but as distichs, sometimes have a certain charm. Surrey's decasyllabic quatrains are particularly interesting, because (for what reason it is not very easy to say) that metre, with the ordinary alternated rhyme, is a difficult one in English. Lord Tennyson and Mr Swinburne have both achieved splendid effects with it: the first by shortening some of the lines, as in the *Palace of Art* and *A Dream of Fair Women,* the latter by the device of leaving the third line rhymeless for the moment, till the next stanza supplies the expected echo, as in *Laus Veneris.* But in its simple form even the gigantic strength of Dryden has not invariably made it successful; and though Gray completely escapes failure in the *Elegy,* that is because he has strictly confined himself to expressing contemplative melancholy. There is a forecast of the danger in Surrey himself.

Wyatt, Surrey's master in the sonnet, tried other metres, though, as is natural to the pioneer, he was not always so deft with them. His rhyme-royal of octosyllables is by no means unpromising—it is odd that it has not had more followers; and the quintet *aabab,* in octosyllables also, is good; and the clusters of three monorhymed lines with a fourth, rhyming either differently or not at all. In both, and in the "Uncertain Authors," the not more than occasional attainment of absolute success is more than atoned for by the omnipresent evidence, first, of the introduction of a new style of thought, with its accompaniment of appropriate diction; and, secondly, of the determination to recover something like those varied lyrical forms which had been by no means strange to English in the early fourteenth century, but which had died out, partly from Chaucer's not adopting them, and partly because of the dislocation and disorganisation of the pronounced language in the fifteenth.

Wyatt's three curious "Epistles" to Poins and Bryan have sometimes been thought to deserve, rather than Gascoigne's *Steel Glass,* the title of the first English attempt at regular Satire. It is not very important to decide this, especially as the decision would have to consider Barclay's *Eclogues* and other things. In form they are considerably behind the lyrical pieces and sonnets. Their rough decasyllables, rhymed in awkward alternation, remind one much more of the hobble or stagger of Lydgate or Occleve than of their actual author, though no doubt Wyatt was presuming, as his successors down to Donne afterwards presumed, on the licence of the Satire to be rough.

Blank verse.

Surrey's blank verse is of far greater interest, from the mighty results which have followed on its adoption —one can hardly say by Norton and Sackville—but by Marlowe in drama and by Milton in narrative, with all the marvellous bulk of poetry that in both lines, from Shakespeare to Tennyson, has consequently enriched England. To give Surrey credit for any foreknowledge of the unique suitableness of English for blank verse—to which primacy hardly even German gives a real second, while there is no other language "placed" at all—would be fantastic; to deny him a lucky hand (and perhaps a reasoned instinct) in transplanting this root also from Italy, would be ungenerous and indeed unjust. There is little reasonable doubt that he *did* transplant it from Italian, which had already taught it to Spanish with not much result, and was soon to teach it to French with far less. It is, however, not undesirable or unreasonable to observe that the idea *might* have arisen independently. It has been pointed out, a thousand times, that there is a sort of "underground" blank verse in the opening of Chaucer's *Melibeus;* the unrhymed verses or lines of Langland, among the other forms which—with prophecy like that of the melted lead in the water—they take sometimes, fall into the decasyllable not seldom. And it was certainly not beyond the reach of a comparatively moderate ingenuity, at the time when rhyme was already decried as a barbarous invention, to ask itself, "Why should I not strike the rhyme out of Chaucer, and keep the metre?" But in sober fact the origin probably was Italian.

It could not be expected that the first essay in a thing so difficult should be completely or even immediately successful, especially when the strong delusion of the time about the rigidly decasyllabic character of the English heroic line, and its almost fixed pause, are remembered. Blank verse never attains its highest excellence till, on the one hand, it ceases to be rigidly decasyllabic, and, on the other, it learns the trick of incessant variation of pause, so as to constitute, by dint of this variation, a sort of stanza-paragraph. It is very doubtful if even Milton would have learnt these things—he did not learn the first completely—if it had not been for the partly enforced practice of the stage before him. Surrey, striking into an untrodden path, could not tread it with perfect ease. It is much that in the main, without rhyme or stanza to help him, he keeps clear of the Lydgatian and Occlevian "staggers." The apparent oddity of his occasional accentuation or quantification is exactly the same as in his and Wyatt's sonnets: indeed it existed in Elizabethan poetry far later. It is curious that you may find—

though not perhaps in the same line—in Spenser or in Shakespeare things as abnormally accented as

"By the divine sciènce of Mìnervà,"

where "science," after all, only follows the French accent, and "Minerva" may ask, "Why not? when you say 'ènervàte' without pretending to give the *e* long value?" Surrey's two really main faults are, on the one hand, the staccato inclusion of sense- and sound-clause within the line, which was not completely conquered by anybody before Shakespeare; and on the other, the too frequent adoption of the pause at that fourth syllable where the French use had fixed it. Both faults were almost inevitable, and both, especially the last, were very slowly outgrown. In fact, it is still a kind of heresy to turn the Miltonic practice into a theory, and lay down the truth that the pause may be anywhere, and had better be in as varied places as possible.

Some others.

The shortcomings, however, which we find in these poets, and still more in the "uncertain authors" of *Tottel*, and in all the poets except Sackville of the period between *Tottel* itself and the *Shepherd's Calendar*—Googe and Churchyard, Turberville and Gascoigne, and the contributors, with rare exception, to the miscellanies which followed *Tottel*—are positively interesting when we think of the trifling interval between them and the glories of the later years of Elizabeth. We may even, with some advantage, mention two writers as instances of this curious "darkness before dawn," and discuss one of them briefly. It is, of course, perfectly true that Thomas Tusser (1525 ?-1580) in his *Hundred* (afterwards *Five Hundred*) *Points of Husbandry*[1] wrote directly with the purpose of Instruction, and addressed probably the least literary class in the kingdom. But he himself was a man of education; he had the tongues (as he tells us ruefully) well whipped into him by Udall; and the extreme variety of metre which he attempts shows at least some poetical ambition. John Heywood (1497 ?-1580 ?)[2] also addressed a popular audience; but the pains and ingenuity with which he has woven his "proverbs" into the text of something like a rough novel, or continuous satiric *fabliau*, would have been wasted on the merely illiterate, and his *Epigrams* are at least a flight at classical butts. He was, moreover, a court poet, had (as his Interludes, *v.* chap. vi., show better than his poems) a very shrewd wit, and was not in the least a mere caterer for the sixteenth-century equivalent of Seven Dials. But the doggerel of Tusser is almost proverbial—one may think it a little exaggerated when one comes to read the book through, but still it is doggerel. And in Heywood not merely a certain bluntness and commonness of thought, but a constant inability to give even to that blunt and common thought adequate expression, betrays itself. That there is a vein of utter Philistinism

Tusser and Heywood.

[1] In the shorter form it appeared in the same year as Tottel. Of the whole I use the edition of Mavor, 4to (London, 1814). That of the English Dialect Society (1878) is more heedful of modern requirements and scholarship.

[2] *Proverbs and Epigrams*, ed. Spenser Society (*s.l.*, 1867).

in the Anglo-Saxon temperament the most patriotic and pure-blooded Englishman must admit; but it has never, not even in the late seventeenth and early eighteenth century, betrayed itself so distinctly as at the end of the fifteenth and the beginning of the sixteenth. The blame is usually put on the Devil-take-the-hindmost tendency, the selfishness and the hardness implanted in men by a long and ruthless civil war: and it may rest there or it may not. But the fact is certain. Coarseness of language (Heywood is by no means licentious, but intensely coarse); constant harping on the pravity of women and the miseries of the marriage state, not after the skirmishing mediæval fashion, but with a kind of dogged animosity; the presentation of mankind as practically divided between reckless spendthrifts, impudent beggars, and close-fisted curmudgeons; a morality and theory of conduct not lacking in shrewdness or unbased on experience, but low and hard;—these things give the tone of the *Proverbs* and the *Epigrams* alike. The expression of this tone in the *Proverbs* may escape criticism here because the fantastic and laborious mosaic of popular sayings in their actual words, which forms the bulk of the text, relieves the writer of all but the responsibility of selection; with the *Epigrams* it is different. That the "mad merry wit," which the author represents as generally attributed to him, too often seems to moderns not to get much beyond want of sense in its madness, and to stop woefully short in its attempt at merriment, is not necessarily fatal. It is just

The Proverbs *and* Epigrams.

possible that our most admired humourists at the junction of the nineteenth and twentieth centuries might not have stirred the muscles of Heywood's contemporaries very convulsively. But we are less in danger of mistake in reference to the phrasing. Heywood can sometimes attain to a tolerable antithesis, as in the actual adage which Lady Macbeth has made in a sense immortal—

"The cat would eat fish, but she will not wet her feet:
She thinketh flesh with dry feet more sweet than fish with *weet*."[1]

But this is comparatively rudimentary, and beyond it Heywood has no epigrammatic turn of words except a rather infantine punning. Perhaps the best turned of all his epigrams is the sombre comment on one of the old "Hendyng" proverbs:—

"When bale is hext [highest] boot is next: though boot be nigh,
What helpeth boot where bale is ever most high?"

But, as a rule, he proceeds little beyond the "You're another" method of childhood or the simplest *paronomasia*.

These are the familiar signs of a language that is "not ready"; that has slipped into disorganisation and has not yet reorganised itself. Great passion will now and then restore effective articulation to such a language; elaborate literary forms will give it

[1] The pronunciation was evidently as the spelling: for it would have cost Heywood nothing to write

"Than fish with *wet* more sweet."

a kind of artificial voice. But familiar, and especially facetiously familiar, composition requires much more accomplishment. And of this accomplishment there is little sign in English during our present period. But it was working hard, trying many experiments, and specially betaking itself—as we have seen and shall see later—to the critical study and exercise of the English tongue: and the next generation reaped an ample harvest of these pains.

When it is remembered that Dunbar himself certainly lived during not a little, and Douglas during much more, of our period, although these and Lyndsay have for sufficient reasons been dealt with in the preceding volume, it may seem strange that scarcely a paragraph should be needed for the special literature of Scotland in this chapter. Yet no just comparative view could allow more. The famous *Complaint of Scotland* (1549)[1] is almost the earliest important piece of even partly original Scots prose; and its originality disappears the more it is examined, while its interest is almost limited to the accidental citations of popular literature which it contains. With Lyndsay himself the striking but short-lived succession of Scots poets ceases—to be continued only by the sometimes lively, if virulent and indecorous, Reformation lampoons,[2] the very good and godly but rather dull hymns and spiritual songs which represent the more serious side of the same movement,[3] the work, not unattractive in

[1] Ed. Murray, E.E.T.S. (London, 1872-73).
[2] Ed. Cranstoun, S.T.S. (Edinburgh, 1889-93).
[3] Ed. Mitchell, S.T.S. (Edinburgh, 1897).

quality but very scanty in amount, of Alexander Scott[1] in Queen Mary's time, and that—not quite so attractive, though a little larger—of Alexander Montgomerie,[2] so far on in her son's that it almost belongs to the next volume but one. Of the two protagonists of the Reformation with the pen, Buchanan has been dealt with already, and Knox requires little dealing. His famous *First Blast of the Trumpet against the Monstrous Regiment of Women*[3] is a vigorous and correct piece of writing, in a style not so advanced as Ascham's; with the rest of his work the present writer has no exhaustive acquaintance. *The History of the Reformation* contains both description and narration of merit, but has been overpraised sometimes. Ninian Winzet,[4] the best of the writers on the other side, is Knox's inferior both in style and in force; and we need not stray into consideration of things like Gau's *Richt Vay*,[5] which are only translations.

The main interest, indeed, of this period of Scottish literature lies in two connected symptoms of decay—the continuance of the merely mediæval character, and the failure to find, even for this, any new dress of style, that shall be the style, not of a dialect, but of a language. The English accomplishment itself is not, as we have seen, great; but in most English writers there is stir, search, unrest, preparation, schooling. In

[1] Ed. Cranstoun, S.T.S. (Edinburgh, 1896).

[2] Ed. Cranstoun, S.T.S. (Edinburgh, 1887).

[3] Ed. Arber (London, 1878). The standard for Knox as a whole is the edition of Laing, 6 vols. (Edinburgh, 1846-64).

[4] Ed. Hewison, S.T.S. (Edinburgh, 1887-91).

[5] Ed. Mitchell and Law, S.T.S. (Edinburgh, 1888).

Scots there is very little of this. In prose, a man like John Major (1470?-1550) is content to be a mere Latinist, and not even a Latinist of the Renaissance type; a man like Bellenden (1490?——?) devotes his nervous Scots merely or mainly to translation. And when we have studied the forms, and style, and general *faire* which might suit a poet of the late fourteenth century, and with which a real if not very great poet like Montgomerie contents himself at the end of the sixteenth, we can hardly wonder that immediate successors of his, like Aytoun and Drummond, deserted Scots altogether in their serious work and adopted southern English.[1]

[1] It is hardly a paradox to say that the most important literary work in Scots during the sixteenth century was done by the anthologists of the great verse MS. collections, the Asloan, the Maitland, the Bannatyne, who saved so much for us from better times than their own.

CHAPTER V.

THE GERMAN VERNACULAR.

POVERTY OF GERMAN NOT QUITE INTELLIGIBLE BUT CERTAIN — THE EXPLOIT OF LUTHER—GENERAL CHARACTERISTICS OF HIS WRITINGS —HIS PROSE — HIS VERSE — ULRICH VON HUTTEN — HANS SACHS — HIS LITERARY CHARACTER — THE 'FABELN UND SCHWÄNKE' — THE 'FASTNACHTSPIELE'—MISCELLANEOUS LIGHT LITERATURE—"VOLKS-LIEDER" — 'BERGREIHEN' — GOEDEKE AND TITTMANN'S 'LIEDER-BUCH.'

Poverty of German

In no country does the separate consideration of the results of Humanist composition in Latin, both in and out of drama, impoverish the tale of vernacular literature to such an extent as in Germany; and it is hardly necessary to add that the result is unavoidable. The Germans wrote in Latin because their vernacular was not ready for them; and their writing in Latin kept their vernacular back. But for one man, it may almost be said, German might have gone the way which, at the same time, Scots was going;[1] and though there are very

[1] The parallel, of course, must not be forced, either politically or linguistically.

profound and very unbridgeable differences of opinion as to Luther's position as a benefactor or malefactor, both to the human race and to Germany on the whole, there can be practically none—between instructed persons—on his office and relation towards the German tongue.

not quite intelligible,

It is indeed by no means very easy to give account of the reasons of this parlous state of the Higher Dutch. Middle High German had been in its palmy days, which were not so very short, a very delightful language, most fortunate in its exponents. If it had been rather dependent upon French for subjects, so had the whole of Europe; and the whole of Europe had not produced a more exquisite poet than Walther von der Vogelweide, though Italy had produced an infinitely greater, and England one stronger, more varied, less occasional. It does not appear (though on points linguistic rather than literary the present writer speaks with diffidence) that the splits between German dialects were at all wider than those between Tuscan and Venetian, between Neapolitan and Ferrarese; and one can say less hesitatingly that mere politics could have nothing fatal or final to do with the matter. Indeed, the ease with which Luther succeeded in imposing a literary dialect on Germany, as Chaucer had imposed one on England, shows that there can have been nothing insuperable to overcome. One can only, therefore, fall back on the old hypothesis that the man was not there to overcome it.

But the facts are certain enough, and their nakedness is confessed in, for instance, Scherer's *History of German Literature*, where great part of the fifteenth century, the whole of the sixteenth, and a stretch beyond it up to Opitz, have to club to furnish a beggarly sixty pages, which do duty also for all the rich Latin literature of the period. A chapter, therefore, much shorter than that given to the other great European countries must here suffice us. The backbone of it must be the great figure of Luther—the sole figure of the period, possessing not merely solid present substance, but high future promise for literature. We shall find a not unpleasant contrast to this in the homelier personage of Hans Sachs, almost mediæval, and still quite Transition, in his forms, in his thought, in his language. An interesting enough addition may be made (though one not concerning any of the nobler departments of literature) by dealing with the satirists from Murner downwards through the unsavoury but characteristic *Grobianus*. But there we shall have to stop, save for a fringe of Folk-song and the like, seldom or never to be attributed to distinguished individuals, and constantly marring its occasional "cry" and nature by its absolute want of art and accomplishment. The accomplished lyric of the early, if not of the whole, sixteenth century in Germany is Latin; the drama, outside mere *Fastnachtspiele* and the like, is Latin; most of the epistolary correspondence is Latin; most of the set orations and treatises are Latin. As for the vast bulk of Reformation polemists and pamphleteers, they must speak by their prior Luther and a few others, such as

but certain.

Ulrich von Hutten, whose best work was done in Latin too. To no country in Europe was "regular" writing at this time so much of an incubus, or a supplanter, or a horseleech, as to Germany; for it not only drained the literature of the best spirits and juices that should have supported it, but gave none of those examples of literary life and instructions of literary manners which other countries received from it. Germany has neither the vernacular Ciceronianism of Italy; nor the fine confused results of mediæval and classic influences which France exhibits in Rabelais and Calvin, in Ronsard and Montaigne; nor the far finer blend of the same kind which constantly raises English, from Ascham to Browne, and from Sackville to Milton. And when at length she does reacquire something like a general literary manner, it is once more an imitation of France, and a France far worse to imitate than the France of the *chansons* and the romances, the *fabliaux* and the *pastourelles.*

The exploit of Luther.

But of all this Luther at least is utterly guiltless; he might, with even better reason, have anticipated the noble and in its degree just boast of Ascham, and have said that he had written "these German matters in the German tongue for German men." And to him, more perhaps than to any man in any language except Dante and Chaucer, may another famous complimentary metaphor be applied. Not indeed that Luther exactly left the German language marble. It is not that yet; probably no Teutonic language ever has been or will be marble; one does not even know whether to wish that the transformation should happen. One of Mr Ruskin's most famous and noblest purple patches, the contrast of an English cathedral and St Mark's, comes in here: and we are more than satisfied, more satisfied, perhaps, than Mr Ruskin intended us to be, with our portion. But Luther found the German of his day for the most part a very common and unlovely brick indeed, the brick of a London back-street, mouldering, but not picturesquely, discoloured, but merely to ugliness. He left it at worst the brick of Hurstmonceaux or of Queen's College, Cambridge; and he opened quarries of divers kinds, from freestone to granite, capable of expressing all the fantastic, and at the same time durable, caprices and imaginations that the Teutonic mind could dream of. Walther, Luther, Heine—these are the three that abide in mastery of German language. A more oddly assorted trio in many ways perhaps no man shall find anywhere; hardly anywhere a greater in power of shaping the national instrument to the national voice.

General characteristics of his writings.

The fact is, that it is difficult to see how anybody who has a sense of literature, and a power of reading the German language, can help falling in love with Luther for his gift of expression, however little he may like the thing expressed. In an altogether admirable phrase of his prologue to the *Fables*, "if you look at Use, Art, and Wisdom, and not at high-elaborated clap-trap,"[1] there is hardly anybody of his time except Rabelais who can be evened with him. The oddities and ugli-

[1] *Hochbedechtig Geschrey—Fabeln*, ed. Thiele (Halle, 1888), p. 1.

nesses of contemporary German literation or pronunciation—the confusion of *b*'s and *p*'s, *t*'s and *d*'s, which began to defray the laughter of the French then, and has continued to defray it to the present day; the hideous *b* after *m* (*umb*, *Wormbs*, and so forth) reminding one of the English vulgarisms "Win*d*" and "Gown*d*," at which Fielding was never tired of laughing two centuries later; the quaint doubling of consonants, which reminds one still more strikingly of our own Orm three centuries earlier[1]—these and other things disappear altogether, or even add a certain zest and race, amidst the crisp humourous phrasing, the hand-grenade force of the attacking clauses, the easy and yet strenuous mastery of the whole system of composition. That Luther was no facile writer we know; there are fac-similes of MS., accessible to every one, in which his hesitation between word and word, sentence and sentence, is patent for all the world to see. But it always—or in so vast a work let us say almost always—came out right. My own knowledge of the minor literature of the particular time and country is not sufficient to tell whether any one of his numerous and quite justly inveterate foes tackled his German as such—nobody except Murner could have done so without the certainty of a very damaging retort. But if any did I daresay they said that his sentences were broken, that he used neologisms, that he was arrogant and self-willed. Possibly: but

[1] Luther goes further than Brother Orm; he puts 3 *n*'s sometimes to the infinitive.

he wrote like a man, and like a great man of letters.

He himself said, with his usual humorous violence, that "as he was born to fight and bivouac against devils and rascal-routs, there was naturally a good deal of storm and battle in his books."[1] There certainly is: while at the same time the nature of his subjects necessarily keeps much or most of his writing on the border between literature and "books that are no books." But all fair-minded critics have long acknowledged that his humour almost equals his violence, and that his command of the more harmonious side of prose is, for his state of language and habit of life, quite astonishing. That the not infrequent beauty of the rhythm of his German Bible owes much to the Vulgate is true, as also, that there were numerous German versions before his, and that he used them freely. But I think there is very little

[1] From the "Preface" to *Colossians*, given at p. 1, vol. iii. of *Martin Luther als Deutscher Klassiker* (3 vols., Hamburg, 1883). I make no apology for confining my citations to this really admirable selection, and to the works republished in Niemeyer's *Neudrucke*. A monographer on Luther, or a theologian, must, of course, attack the entire *Works*, but it cannot be necessary, even for a pretty thorough student of literature, to explore mountains of sermon and deserts of commentary. Without going back to mere "Beauties" or snippet-books, one cannot help wishing that, in the case of such writers, intelligent and copious selection, for the most part of whole works or substantive parts of works, were more common. Two or three moderate-sized volumes, for instance, would give most things of Erasmus that are necessary to the student of literature who has neither twenty guineas of money, nor several cubic feet of shelf-room, nor weeks or months of time to spare for the ten volumes of the folio.

doubt that the superior charm of our own Authorised Version owes something to his, which, from Tyndale and Coverdale downwards, our translators pretty certainly knew and used. His very considerable skill of verse, of which more presently, also reflected itself, as it usually does, in his prose; and the study of Aristotle and Quintilian, which he had diligently pursued, could not be without good effect in principle. While no man of literary gift, drenched, steeped, saturated as he was in St Augustine, could fail to catch in practice something of the marvellous music of the great rhetorician of Tagaste.

His prose.

But, be the causes what they may, the effect is certain. No one who is susceptible to the music of prose, and has exercised his ear to it, can possibly miss it in Luther. It is not of the richest or most sustained character—that was in the circumstances impossible: but it is singularly pervading, or rather, to speak with stricter exactness, it may break out at any moment—in the most scholastic divisions and distinctions of his treatises and sermons, in his hottest heat of controversy, in the coolest audacity or most earnest wrestling of his addresses to popes and princes and peers, in the simplicity of his fables, in his letters, in his criticisms, in his commentaries. It gives him sometimes that strange touch of modernness, or rather of disengagement from any given age and time and country, which the greatest writers of the world almost always though not quite invariably possess. This is all the more noticeable in him, because his contemporaries and compatriots, even at their best, are nothing so little as modern or disengaged from the Time-Spirit; and because Luther himself was in all interests and characteristics, excepting his literary gift, eminently and pre-eminently a man of his time. And—which is distinctly curious—he smacks of that time much more in verse than in prose. This, of course, comes from the fact that, though an admirable verse-writer and songster, he was not exactly a poet, while he *was* a prose-writer born, bred and fulfilled of almost every degree open to him. The only marvel to us is that, with such a clear and accomplished pattern before them at so early a time, the Germans should ever have slipped into the seventyfold coils of involution, should have succumbed to the bald and naked ugliness of form, from which their prose style has not freed itself even yet.[1]

[1] Besides fables, "table-talk," letters, commentaries, and sermons, Luther's chief prose work in German consists of the following: (1) the vernacular versions of his three famous challenge-manifestoes at the opening of the Reformation campaign, the *Epistle to Leo X.*, the *Freedom of a Christian Man*, and the explanation *Why Dr Martin Luther burnt the Pope's books and those of his Disciples*; (2) the famous letter of the same year (1520) *To the Nobility of the German Nation*; and (3) the *Treatise of Good Works* (same year still). All these three have appeared, from MS. or first editions, in Niemeyer's *Neudrucke*, which also contain the *Fables* from his autograph copy, and two or three other small treatises. Besides these there are articles on History and Drama, some important political tractates, chiefly connected with the Peasants' War, and a certain number of treatises or discourses on questions of public interest, such as the importance of Christian schools, Commerce and Usury, the religious aspect of the soldier's profession, the duties of parents and children to each other in respect of the children's marriage. These, together with some of those previously enumerated, and a good selec-

Luther as a verse-writer is almost as interesting, though very much less accomplished and important. His wisest panegyrists have taken good care not to claim for him the name or fame of an original poet. His verse[1] is limited in amount; except mere scraps, it is more limited in kind; and while in that kind he had the priceless matter of the Psalms and the Latin hymns of the Church to guide him, the teaching of the hymns in form was supplemented by the equally priceless floating echoes of folk-song, which were just being caught and crystallised by the press. Almost all the additional stimulus that could have been needed by a genial song-loving nature was supplied by the excitement of the great strife. He never surpassed—he never equalled—the immortal *Ein feste Burg*, the very irregularities of which have the throb and spurt of life-blood. But he has come near it in the *Lobgesang* of Simeon, the "songwise" Paternoster, the various versions of the *De Profundis*, the beautiful "Song of Holy Church"—

His verse.

"Sie ist mir lieb, die werde Magt,"

and the more beautiful version of Notker's Antiphon of Death—

"Mitten wir in leben sind."

---

tion of sermon and commentary, numerous letters, and most of the verse, will be found in the above-mentioned *Martin Luther als Deutscher Klassiker*. Of complete editions, German and Latin, there are several, from the first, which appeared at Wittemberg in the last seven years of his life and after his death, to the latest, which was begun at Weimar in 1883 to celebrate the fourth centenary of his birth.

[1] *Dichtungen vom D. Martin Luther*. Ed. Goedeke. Leipzic, 1883.

The scraps, the *Sprüche und Lieder* (some of these come very close to the great "Wein, Weib, und Gesang" couplet, which cruel editors will not include[1]), show, rough and ready and unpretentious as they are, the same dæmonic power over the material and the form of folk-song and proverb in verse. This power may not be identical with the power of the poet, but it is certainly not included in that of the proseman pure and simple. Perhaps indeed it is seldom found in the same person.[2]

Ulrich von Hutten.

Ulrich von Hutten (1488-1523)[3] has been already more than once mentioned, and it is doubtful whether his connection with the *Epistolæ Obscurorum Virorum* is not his chief real title to literary fame. His eventful and romantic life, his connection with historical figures like Maximilian, Franz von Sickingen, Erasmus, Zwingli, and others have, perhaps, given him a rather higher position than anything he wrote really merits. It was only during the last three years of his short life — which just reached "the middle of the road" and no more—that he wrote in German: up till then his work, prose and verse, had been in Latin. The *Aufwecker der Teutschen Nation* (1520) was the first of a series of verse and

[1] My colleague, Dr Schlapp, informs me that the attribution of the actual couplet cannot be traced farther back than Herder. Its real author is sometimes said to be J. H. Voss.

[2] For a discussion of the relation of German work of this kind to Coverdale's *Ghostly Songs* in England, and Wedderburn's *Godly and Spiritual Songs* (otherwise *Good and Godly Ballads*) in Scotland, see Professor Herford's above-cited book (chap. i. and Appendix).

[3] The standard edition is that of Böcking, 7 vols., Leipzic, 1859-70, a book very valuable on the *Obscuri.*

prose diatribes, polemical literature of almost every kind, some of it translated from his Latin work. It is all remarkable for energy, conviction, and the presence of a certain not unattractive youthfulness of spirit which has been commended by the author's fate. At the same time there is in Hutten, when he drops Latin, little sense of form. And there is a constant exaggeration which, when we once leave Erasmus, and Hutten's earlier companions of the *Epistolæ*, makes most of the writing of this time connected with the Reformation inexpressibly tiresome, except to those whom the history and the literature of the period still leave under the impression that it was a contest between pure angelic light and unrelieved demoniacal darkness. Hutten's constant ill-health (the curse of the Renaissance was upon him almost throughout his life), and the persecutions, not by any means unprovoked, which he endured, may no doubt have exasperated this characteristic in him. But he displays altogether too much of the *Sturm und Drang*, which from time to time characterises German literature, to enable him to challenge a very high place as a writer. A voice constantly at screaming pitch is not a good instrument, either for the words of Mercury or the songs of Apollo.

Hans Sachs.

Hans Sachs, shoemaker in Nuremberg, who seems to have taken an affectionate pride in indorsing his trade, or his birthplace, or both, wherever he possibly could on the signature of his poems, was born in 1494, died in 1576, and spent by far the greater part of his long life in writing almost every possible description of verse. With characteristic minuteness he claimed the authorship of exactly 7362 separate compositions, including about two hundred plays, and the completest edition of him fills five volumes folio. Whether anybody has ever read the whole of this enormous mass without nodding at least, or slipping over pages in a semi-comatose state, may, perhaps, be doubted. But it is remarkable, that since the inevitable and unimportant contempt of the Gallicising period at the end of the seventeenth and the beginning of the eighteenth century, few people who have actually read any considerable part of him fail to speak both with affection and respect, though, of course, making provisoes and allowances. The present writer admits having postponed this reading for many years, and having looked forward to it with some apprehension. But he found much relief and not a little positive satisfaction in the actual process.

His literary character.

The fact is, that the good shoemaker not merely kept the form of the Middle Ages, but continued to be endowed and imbued with their spirit. He might be not improperly described as a *bourgeois* Gower, with less learning and less elegance. His octosyllables skip or slide with the same inexhaustible facility and the same rather wonderful, not to say incomprehensible, faculty of acting as solvent and menstruum to any and every subject that they meet in their unpretentious but irresistible course. Nothing is too old, too new, too common. A fantastic-grotesque legend of Eve and her children, and a faithful report of a Billingsgate match between any shrew of a housewife and any trollop of a housemaid, seem to interest Hans equally, and to leave his hands in the same literary condition. What that condition is one cannot easily describe with critical exactness. It never has the vividness of the great realists or the greater idealists, who transcend the real in the act of giving it. But it is also never quite trivial or merely common. One sees everywhere in Hans (at least, so far as the present writer knows him) the novelist before novels, the observer and imitator of life, from whom the greatest triumphs of literary creation are not to be expected, but who, on the other hand, is always close enough to life itself to make him worth reading. Take, for instance, that situation of mistress and maid, arms akimbo and tongues on fire, slanging each other till the neighbours, or the unlucky master of the house, or sheer weariness, do them part. It is not a beautiful situation; it is not an interesting one; it is certainly not an uncommon. Hans is rather unaccountably fond of it; tries it in *Schwänk* and *Spiel*—tries it over and over again. He never exactly makes it live for us as Shakespeare would have done, even as Erasmus could. But he also never merely repeats himself, and never abides in the abstract, which is all the odder that he generally contents himself with general headings, *eine Frau eine Magd*, instead of Gretchen or Lisabette.

The great majority of his pieces, whether narrated or acted, are, in fact, as has been said, scenes of novels in the rough, and not put together. They are commended neither by expression nor phrase, though not particularly discommended by either. They sum up no situation for ever and ever, in the manner of Cleopatra's death in one kind, or Esmond's renunciation of allegiance in another. But they always hold up the mirror to nature sufficiently if not supremely. One would not care to read Hans Sachs very often; perhaps there are few things of his that, unless for some particular purpose, one would care to read twice. But then that is the case with the average, as opposed to the more than average, novel; and in his time even the average novel (except as a short tale) did not exist. Indeed, he is sometimes even more of a journalist than of a novelist: one can imagine his subjects thumbnailed from the actual streets and lanes of Nuremberg.

The Fabeln und Schwänke.[1]

But he is very far from confining himself to things seen; though he never omits to flavour his work with some spice from them. The mediæval element is especially prominent, and especially serves as an efficient cause of his enormous volume. It is not merely that, with an indiscriminate relish, that savours more of the twelfth than of the sixteenth century, the characters, abstract or concrete, in his interludes and tales cite Scripture and the classics, history and mediæval legend, pell-mell and at a venture, just as any of the four (or of a dozen other heads of matter) comes in their way. Hans Sachs himself indulges in exactly the same promiscuity in the selection of his own subjects, and extends it (in a fashion already alluded to, but so uniquely remarkable in him that it has to be referred

[1] Three vols. of some 1700 pp. in Niemeyer's *Neudrucke*. Ed. Goetze (Halle, 1893-1900).

to again) to multiplication of handlings of the same subject. A tale of Boccaccio (who had just been translated into German), a fable of Æsop, a wise saw or then modern instance, an incident beheld—anything will do for him to fasten on. And, when he has fastened on it, it is odds but he will make it serve for poetical uses as various and as apparently incongruous as if it were a very Snark. He will make a Meistersong of it in *ton* or *weise* of rose or rosemary, a fable, a dialogue, a full interlude or Shrovetide-play. This kaleidoscopic or dissolving-view treatment of literature is eminently mediæval, and no doubt may be connected in a more plausible way than is often possible with the professional exigencies of the travelling poet. And it may be further observed, again without hazard, that the peculiar facility of the octosyllable, and the ease with which it lends, or to old taste lent, itself to almost every conceivable literary form, from song through tale to drama, has a great deal to do with its general adoption. But Hans Sachs is the last, as he is certainly the most fertile, example of this complicated and yet simple practice.

The Fastnacht-spiele.

The great collection of *Shrovetide Plays*[1] (there are eighty-five of them) comes next to that of the *Fables and Pranks* in bulk, and can hardly be said to differ very much in substance. Omit the speech-headings and stage directions, and insert a very few extra couplets to give the information conveyed by them in narrative form, and they would often, if not always,

[1] Reprinted in 7 parts by E. Goetze (Halle, 1880-87).

be practically indistinguishable. This is as much as to say that there is extremely little about them that is in any real sense dramatic. But they are sometimes quite lively *fabliaux* in the form *par personnages.* Seldom can one find anywhere two nicer examples of the story, which German has always told so admirably in looser folk-tale fashion, than, for instance, that of the rash young peasant who wanted to have two wives, and that of the "Wooing of Sophronia."[1] The former misguided young man at first covets, and insists on espousing, *both* his neighbour's daughters, Grede and her sister. With great difficulty he is persuaded to try Grede only for a year by his father and "Fritz Oheim" (this putting of the "Uncle" last, like "Toby Coachman," "Ralph Tapster," &c., is delightfully Teutonic). The year has not passed when the youngster, in the most deplorable condition of body and mind, soliloquises on the joys of matrimony. He is interrupted by his father, his father-in-law, and Fritz Oheim. They have tracked and trapped a wolf which has been devastating the village stockyards; and they are devising the most horrible torture for the poor beast —blinding, flaying, roasting alive, and so forth—when the bridegroom breaks in. *He* knows something much worse—"Let him be married!" The conclusion, the offer of the good-natured father-in-law to relieve him of Grede, would be rather an anti-climax—if it were not for its extreme unexpectedness.

[1] These are Nos. 36 and 35 of the collection, and will be found at Part III., pp. 99-123.

The other piece is in quite a different vein, and the difference is all the more striking because the two come together. We are now in the best of company, and instead of one shocking young peasant wanting to commit bigamy, two young gentlemen of the highest birth and accomplishments, Conrad von Adelstein and Franz von Sternberg, are suitors "in all good and honour," for the hand of Sophronia, niece of the noble lady Plangina von Plankenstein or Plangina Plankensteinerin, as the quaint fashion of the Dramatis Personæ puts it. Conrad is respectful, earnest, but a little retiring and shy. Sophronia tells her dear aunty, "Mumb," frankly, that she thinks Franz handsomer, a better figure, a nicer partner for dancing, and therefore of course for life. The noble and experienced Plangina begs her niece to let her test the lovers, and Sophronia, like a good girl, consents. In the first place, the "Mumb" imposes on them both pilgrimages over sea or by sea, to which Conrad consents joyfully, Franz, though he has the easier task, with a grumble. Frau Plangina, however, is not satisfied with this trial, and, when the suitors return, subjects them to another. Sophronia is told to feign sickness and "make up" to suit the part: the young men are informed that her beauty is lost, and that all her portion has been spent on physicians. The reader anticipates the result—Franz is very sorry, but declines even to see the altered beauty who has "got through her good." He has "shot a Cuckoo," and says good-bye. The noble Conrad, on the contrary, begs to be introduced where the dearest of all girls lies ill, though the most alarming pictures of her state are drawn for him, insisting on marrying her at once, and taking care of her. He has not merely, unlike Kings Easter and Wester, courted her neither for land nor fee; but not even, like King Honour, for her comely face and for her fair bodiè. He will have her and no other, fair or foul, sick or sound, poor or rich, for life and for death. Sophronia has overheard them both; and of course the marriage-bells are set a-ringing without delay.

One might easily enough thus sketch the simple plot of very many of these good-humoured and good-natured playlets, or rather storykins; but the cruel mistress Space forbids. Hans always looks steadily to his moral, and yet is seldom tedious; the pieces are too short, the good temper and good feeling too unfeigned, the cheerful homely wit too sufficient for its modest ends, to allow of tedium.

The *Fastnachtspiele* and the *Fabeln und Schwänke* have seemed for this reason, and not merely for their somewhat greater accessibility, to deserve more attention here than the Meistersongs, the "tragedies," falsely so-called, and all the other vast and various baggage of the good Nuremberger. Here, so far as I have made acquaintance with it, tedium *does* exist and flourish. The songs in all the "tones" and "wises," of which a portentous register (partly from Hans' own hand) exists, and has been reprinted,[1] rarely possess the

[1] *Das Gemerkbüchleim des H. S.* Ed. Drescher (Halle, 1898).

interest and charm of the anonymous folk-song, and have lost all that of the elaborate mediæval "court" lyric.

Indeed these Meistersongs[1] are mainly interesting to the historian as showing the defects of this class of literature. The "tone" or "wise" may be "long" or "high," "silver" or "gold," of "rose," of "fire," of "Frau Exe," or of "Bruder Veit." But it very seldom has the smallest lyrical charm, and the

> "Cold *flat* recurrence of accepted rhyme,"

as, altering a phrase of Mr Swinburne's in one word, we may justly call it, the long-spaced punctilio of returning sounds, which have lost all echo for the ear, makes one understand what Johnson meant, though he was unlucky in his selected example, by complaining of the harshness, unpleasingness, and uncertainty of the suspended rhymes in *Lycidas*. Milton keeps the ear pleasingly eager, and rewards it. Hans Sachs sends it to sleep, and wakes it with an unpleasing thud or jar, suggesting something else that one has forgotten and does not want to remember. Nor are the deficiencies made up from the side of "the subject." One does not in the least care to be told, in "Frau Exe's" or any other "tone"—

> "Ein buch cento novella heist,
> Hat ein poet geschriben";

---

[1] They, or some of them, may be found in vol. i. of the *Dichtungen*, published by Goedeke and Tittmann, 3 vols., Leipzic, 1883-85.

while the wildest debauch of imagination can hit upon nothing less in "fire-wise" than—

> "Her Titus Livius der tut uns sagen
> Als Furius Camillus het geschlagen";

and even such a tolerable beginning as—

> "Wach auf in Gottes namen
> Du werde Christenheit"

dribbles off into a tame abstract of Bible-history about Pharaoh, and the Amalekites, and Jehoshaphat, and so forth. In fact, that serene readiness to treat any subject in any manner, which has been already commented on and praised elsewhere, is here usually annoying and often fatal.[1]

On the other hand, such a tragedy as *Der hürnen Seufried*,[2] where the story is told in seven acts, or rather tableaux, in a succession-procession of speeches, partly by the characters, partly by the herald-

[1] It is perhaps desirable to add, for fear of misunderstanding, that not a few of the Meistersongs are of the class of "Fables and Jests," or (if the other way be preferred) that not a few "Fables and Jests" take Meistersong form. The whole third volume, extending to more than four hundred pages, of Goetze and Drescher's above-cited *Fabeln und Schwänke*, is composed of pieces of this kind. But the fact is in reality only an additional illustration of what has been more than once noticed in the text, the absolute promiscuity of kind, the bald want of sense of appropriate form, which characterises Hans Sachs. Any form is good for any subject, and *vice versa*. Those who are curious about the Meistersong in itself will find a contemporary *Poetic* of it, written while it was still alive, though at the point of death, in the *Gründlicher Bericht* of Adam Puschmann, which appeared in 1571, and has been recently edited by R. Jonas (Halle, 1888).

[2] Ed. Goetze (Halle, 1880).

chorus, with elaborate stage directions, which would do just as well for dumb-show, has all the defects of the Shrovetide plays as drama, without much, if any, of their merits as shrewd and lively presentations of life. It is once more a romance, told, and badly told, "by personages." The method is far more attractively shown in the two other divisions, and if one cannot obtain an idea of a man's power by studying two or three thousand pages of his best, that idea will not probably be achieved by studying any quantity of his less good work. The mote-like crowd of subjects does not, for all its welter and flit, fail to leave some distinct memories, such as the two pieces sketched above; the striking picture of the Venusberg, with the calm triumph of its unrelenting goddess-queen; the parable of Frau Wahrheit, to whom no man will give harbourage; the "Peasant in Purgatory"; the famous piece of God's blessing to Eve's children; St Peter's unsatisfactory experiences on revisiting earth. While as for the non-dramatic tales, it is almost needless to make selection. Very seldom will the reader draw a complete blank; and if he does, he has but a few pages to turn, with all but the certainty of mending his hand.

The work of Hans Sachs touches constantly, in its vast and wandering course, on a subject, or rather a somewhat undefined group of subjects, which—mainly on the principle of "the want of a better"—has usually occupied a very large place in all treatments of the literary history of Germany during the Sixteenth century. We have already seen in the preceding volume[1] of this History, the starting of this irregular cycle, or rather the turning-point whence a new and more important system of epicycles grafted itself on an older system, in the *Narrenschiff* of Sebastian Brant. But prominent as the *Narr* is in all the latest literature of the Fifteenth century, he is yet more prominent in the earlier, and not merely the earlier, literature of the Sixteenth. Indeed, the Ship, Eulenspiegel, The Pastor of Kalendberg, and their company form a kind of Cabbala, if not an unholy collection of Scripture, to all the non-serious, and not a few of the serious, writers of the time. One does not entirely know how to account, on any principles that shall be at once logical and literary, for the curious obsession of the German mind at this time, and not at this time only, by the desire, the struggle, to be lively *quand même*. One of the few celebrated books of the very early part of the century is Pauli's *Schimpf und Ernst* (1519), an overgrown *Joe Miller*, derived from the *Gesta Romanorum*, from the singular monkish collections of stories in *usum predicatorum*, which anticipated the *Gesta* itself, from half the jest-books and story-books of literary Europe, and from indigenous German sources as well. A great German critic once showed his critical shortcomings by comparing Dr Johnson to Gottsched, and boasting that the Germans had had the sense to drop their Gottsched when they had outgrown him. No repartee is in the least necessary; but if one were required, it would be amply furnished by the fact that

[1] *The Transition Period*, p. 175 *sq.*

Joe Miller itself has never ranked in England as literature.[1]

The most remarkable, however—or at least the most remarked in consequence of its extreme oddity—of all these epicycles or episodes of satirical buffoonery is that which centres in the *Grobianus* [2] of Frederick Dedekind. The original beatifier [3] of personified *Grobheit*, or bad manners, appears to have been Sebastian Brant himself, and the idea was taken up by Murner and many others. We have apparently sufficient testimony to the fact that these topsy-turvifications of the mediæval books of "puerile civility" were not a mere debauch of literary whim, but were only too faithfully provoked by the average manners of Germany. The nation had always had—not merely with the Latin races, but in England, which might have looked at home—an ill repute for "heavy-

[1] The *Facetiæ* noticed in chap. i. (p. 100), with much else, come in here. One of the most celebrated humorists of Germany, though a little after our special time, was the poet Johann Fischart, the "German Rabelais," who, besides more original work, imitated the *Prognostication* in *Aller Praktik Grossmutter* (1572) and *Gargantua* itself in *Geschichtklitterung* (1575). Both these curious books will be found among Niemeyer's *Neudrucke*, the latter laboriously edited in mosaic from its different early editions.

[2] My texts for this are the *editio tertia* (that is to say, the third issued by the printer Maire) of *Grobianus et Grobiana*, Leyden, 1642, for the Latin; and the reprint of the first (1551) edition of Kaspar Scheidt's *Grobianus* (Halle, 1882) for the German. This latter contains an elaborate bibliography, but should be supplemented by Professor Herford's treatment in the book so often cited, which is almost a monograph of the subject.

[3] As *Saint* Grobianus.

headed revel"; and its standard of chivalry, if sometimes more ideal than that of almost any other nation in literature, had apparently always been coarser in manners. Chivalry had died with Maximilian—if it was very much alive in him; and unless literary representation lies beyond its wont, German society now consisted of robber barons not improved by a turn towards condottierism; clergy and universities steeped in ignorance and vulgar debauchery; specially *bourgeois* citizens; a brutalised peasantry; and a floating body of *lanzknechts,* in or out of work, who had learned the vices of every country in Europe, getting rid of all home virtues to make room for them. Just in the middle of the century (1549), Frederick Dedekind, a young student of Wittenberg, who did much serious work later, hit off the notion of bad-manners-reduced-to-a-code in an extremely popular book of readable elegiacs, and Kaspar Scheidt, a schoolmaster, two years later, turned this freely into German to the applause of everybody. The author himself seems to have welcomed his coadjutor as no "Grobian" could possibly have done, and took many hints from him in the later editions of his own work, especially in the addition of *Grobiana.* The thing caught the public fancy, not merely in Germany but in England. For Dekker in the next generation produced the famous *Gull's Hornbook,* in direct imitation and part translation of it, and other translations and imitations appeared with us up to 1739, when Roger Bull committed his Englishing to the care of Swift, who was probably not loath to give it.

To tell the truth, this atmosphere of history and tradition is rather necessary to make *Grobianus* go down nowadays. It is often very nasty, and it is not often very amusing. Both versions are, however, worth a glance by the student of literature, not merely for the sake of their transmitted fame. The attraction of the Latin lies in a sort of unacknowledged and probably unintended satire on Humanism itself—the neat and sometimes almost elegant versification serving as a sort of parody of the Ovidian emptiness of more serious poets: while this same neatness, from another point of view, gives edge to the satire. On the other hand, as indeed might be expected, one appreciates the gist of that satire itself better from the German. The blunt thud-thud of the octosyllabic couplets, anticipating something of *Hudibras*, and, perhaps, not impossibly lending something thereto,[1] suits the subject as well by likeness as the elegiacs do by contrast. The comparison of the two is an interesting lesson how in literature, as elsewhere, *par divers moyens on arrive à pareille fin.* But the historical and comparative student of literature has the best of it, not merely with Dedekind, but with all his fellows in this branch of composition.

It is difficult to know what further to single out from the extensive but rarely distinguished mass of German vernacular writing which belongs to this period. Nearly all of it displays that want of ac-

[1] I forget whether any one among the numerous commentators of *Hudibras* has noticed the likeness. But somebody surely must have done so.

complishment, and specially that confusion of kinds, which drew down the contempt of the Humanists on vernacular literature generally. Probably the ablest man of the time, next to Luther and Hutten, though, being on the opposite side, he had less of a "free elbow" than they had, was Thomas Murner (1445?-1536), who has already been mentioned in the preceding volume, and the greater part of whose life belongs to the fifteenth century, but whose best work appertains to our time. To our period belong the *Narrenbeschwörung* (1506?-12)[1] and the *Schelmenzunft* (1512),[2] the most "spiritual" documents perhaps of the whole "fool"-literature: while the tractate *Von dem Grossen Lutherischen Narren* (1522) dates itself by its reference to the controversy, of which it is one of the earliest pieces, and one of the sharpest on the Roman side. It is, however, a great injustice to Murner to translate his title, as I have seen it translated in French, "Ce Grand Fou de Luther." Murner was a man of far too much intellect to make the matter a mere personal quarrel, and, indeed, he expressly disdains this: he seizes, in a fashion which unfortunately the defenders of orthodoxy followed too little, on the *general* weaknesses of the Protestant position, attacking them in the savagest style. His literary work, both in German and Latin, was very large, and extended to quite uncontroversial things, either as regards religion or morals or manners—

[1] Ed. Spanier (Halle, 1894) with a glossary, not a little needed in these sixteenth-century works, but seldom given.

[2] Ed. Matthias (Halle, 1890).

things such as translations of Justinian and of the *Æneid*, while his name has been plausibly coupled with at least the redaction of *Eulenspiegel.*

A good example of Murner's serious work is his reply [1] to Luther's *Epistle to the German Nobles,* which is in effect (with a head- and tail-piece corresponding to the title) an epistle to Luther himself. The Reformer is stigmatised in the opening as the Catiline of Christian Rome; but the writer nowhere descends to mere abuse, and the tractate is in fact a dignified and forcible apologia, weak only in the point (of which Murner was beyond all doubt as well aware as any Protestant) that the defence is a defence of the Catholic Church and of Catholic doctrine as they ought to have been and theoretically were, while the attack was on the Church, and the practice, and great part of the doctrine, as they actually were. It does not seem necessary to discuss in detail other documents of the strife; it may be sufficient to refer readers who are interested to some characteristic specimens,[2] which have recently been made accessible in the excellent series of reprints so often quoted.

The lampoons from the Roman side on the marriages of Luther and his brethren are naturally a little beyond the pale sometimes. But at least one other champion of the Pope besides Murner, John Cochlæus (or, as his

[1] Ed. Voss (Halle, 1899).

[2] *Ein Schöner Dialogus von Martino Luther und den geschickten Potschaft aus Der Hölle.* Ed. Enders (Halle, 1886). *Ein Urteil der Theologen zu Paris über die Lehre D. Luther's,* &c. Ed. Müller, (Halle, 1892). *Drei Flugschriften aus dem Kampf der Schwärmer gegen Luther.* Ed. Enders (Halle, 1893).

nom de guerre went, Vogelgesang), managed to keep his temper and observe limits. The very curious *Heimlich Gespräch von der Tragedia des Johannis Hussen*,[1] a semi-dramatic, semi-colloquial account of an alleged excommunication by Doctor Martin of his friend Johannes Agricola for printing things disagreeable to the Protestant Pope, and his begging-off by Luther's wife—is a composition in parts very dull. But it redeems these by unconventional but racy particulars of the different ministers' wives, with their elaborate courtesies to each other, of Agricola's rather attractive daughter Ortha (whom Katharine Bora disinterestedly fixes upon as her doctor's second wife should she die before him), and, above all, of the ex-nun herself. It is rather difficult to know whether Cochlæus meant to invoke the horror or the ridicule of readers on these vow-breakers by representing the force and fire of their passion for one another; but there is no doubt that he does represent this remarkably. Katharine is quite as guiltless of any shame as Eve herself can have been before the apple; but she is as frankly and sincerely enamoured as a very Fiordispina, and Luther is a much more serious and constant Ricciardetto. On the other side one may notice the furious invectives[2] against Henry of Brunswick by Burkard Waldis, the author also of what has been rashly styled the first German play—a version, earlier than Volder's Latin *Acolastus*, of the story of the Prodigal Son.[3] It is a Shrovetide play, couched

[1] Ed. Holstein (Halle, 1900). [2] Ed. Koldeway (Halle, 1883).

[3] Ed. Milchsack (Halle, 1881). Waldis is also responsible for an *Esopus*. Ed. Tittmann (Leipzic, 1882).

in a particularly hideous dialect, and showing no advance whatever on what we should in English call the Interlude-Mystery form. The list might be indefinitely increased, but this seems hardly necessary.

Miscellaneous light literature.

The dramas and dialogues of the Swiss Manuel will be noticed later, and the literature of the latter form appears to be very extensive, though not much of it is easily accessible, and by no means all of this is of literary value. Zwinglius himself was,[1] as he was bound to be, a man of letters, but he cannot rank anywhere near Luther or Calvin as a master of vernacular, or near Melanchthon and Hutten (to whose sad last days he gave protection in those of his own theocratic dictatorship at Zurich) in Latin. The Germans proudly claim the invention of the newspaper (*Zeitung*) for themselves at this period; and many other kinds of "flying" literature were produced, couched sometimes in prose, sometimes in the facile and rather pedestrian verse which the revived popularity of the iambic octosyllable—most natural of metres to a large part of the human race it would appear—had made possible to almost everybody. The burst of what may be called snippet-literature, "Carriage-books," "Night-books," "Garden-party books," has often been noticed; and both translated and original tales became common. The title of "Father of the German Novel" has been granted with the usual doubtful wisdom to Jorg Wickram, who wrote adventure-stories—prosaisings in more senses than one—of the various common romance motives, between

[1] Cf. his *Von Freiheit der Speisen*, ed. Walther (Halle, 1900).

1550 and 1560: while the epoch-making *Faust* book appeared in 1587.

Volkslieder.

But probably the most important popular literary productions of Germany during the whole century were the redactions of folk-song to something like form, which correspond to our own still more uncertainly dated Ballads, but have a far wider range and an earlier and a more constantly advantageous influence upon German poetry. Collections of *Volkslieder* began to be printed as early as 1512: a really important one was issued by Georg Forster in 1539, and the successive treasuries, with their MSS. sources, have not only been laboriously edited in what is called a "critical" manner during the present century by Uhland, Liliencron, Tittmann, &c., but form the basis of that "uncritical" but ever delightful book—the "Percy" of Germany—Arnim and Brentano's *Wunder-horn.*

The actual prefatory matter of Arnim's work [1] contains references to and quotations from Forster's just-mentioned collection, as well as to Wickram's "Roll-waggon-booklet" (*Rollwagenbüchlein,* 1555), one of the earliest of the curious examples of traveller's-companion literature noted above. And there can be no doubt that a much larger part of the matter than is directly derived from sixteenth-century-printed books or even MSS. goes back to this time or to an earlier in actual origin. It is not necessary to dwell

[1] *Des Knaben Wunder-horn* was itself further sophisticated in some impressions. The reprint by Wendt (2 vols., Berlin, 1873) claims to give the original of 1806-8 faithfully.

at any great length, pleasant as it would be to do so, on the well-known charms of the German folk-song, which kept alive, from Walther von der Vogelweide to Heine, a spirit of poetic "cry" quite astoundingly absent from formal printed poetry in most of the intervening centuries. The ripple of the rhythm and the ring of the rhymes, the wild-flower grace of the language—wherein some magic seems to have changed the homely Cinderella of the tongue of Hans Sachs into a fairy princess—the delightful diminutives, the quaint humour, the pathos, the unfailing yet unpretentious sense of mystery—all these things are out of controversy, and, except by persons congenitally deprived of the sense of literary taste, are recognised as soon as seen. Uncritical though it be, it is perhaps better for all but stern and conscientious students to read the songs in the *Wunder-horn* than in the sixteenth-century books, simply because of the ugliness which, as has been already noted, came upon the personal appearance of the German language as printed at that time. The *diction* is never so vulgarised and depraved as that of our seventeenth-century *Garlands* and the like: but the *form* is still uglier. So the intelligent epicure, regardless of objections as to *rococo, pastiche*, and the like, will still go to the husband and the brother of Bettina, as to those who, if they have something frothed and limed this good sherris-sack, yet have done so with the art of right skilful tapsters.

Those, however, who are not happy unless they have originals before them will find convenient examples in the collection called *Bergreihen*[1] and in the *Liederbuch aus dem 16ten Jahrhundert*,[2] which was edited some twenty years ago by Herren Goedeke and Tittmann. The "Mountain-songs" (which were so popular as to be reprinted four times between 1531 and 1537) are not numerous—fifty-eight in the fullest edition. But they show the universality of the kind by the variety of their subjects, and they include at least one example of the odd fashion of the time for adapting a popular song to "ghostly" purposes. This example is *Ich stund an einem morgen Heimlich an einem Ort*, where, after an identical first quatrain, the song diverges in the "worldly" case to a pitiful parting scene between girl and lover, in the ghostly one to the catching of a sinful youth by Death. Of the rest, the ghostly songs are pretty much of the usual character, not achieving much distinction. The profane pieces, though rarely of consummate accomplishment, have much of the old half-inarticulate music, and not a little of that enchanting variety of rhythm which comes from substitution of equivalent syllabic values and interchange of feet, and which the Teutonic ear misses so terribly in most Romance poetry.

Bergreihen.

> "Der Somer fert uns von hinnen,
> Die lüfftlein sind wirden kalt,
> Mir liebt fur alle mein sinne
> Ein röslein ist wol gestalt.
> . . . . .
> O wie wee mir scheyden thut
> Von meinem Röslein rodt!"

[1] Ed. Meier (Halle, 1892).

[2] Second edition, Leipsic, 1881.

Some of them are pure love-songs of this pattern; some, such as No. 25, *Was wöllen wir aber heben an*, are real ballads with a story in them; some are curious devil-may-care pieces, like 27, where the singer says—

> "Het ich das Keiserthumb,
> Dazu den zol am Rein,
> Und wer Venedig mein,
> So wer es alles verloren,"

subsequently assumes as his arms "three dice and a card," and profanely wishes for six pretty girls, three on each side, as supporters. Here is a very pretty though late *Alba* (30), *Er ist der morgen sterne;* there a joval *Kirmes*-piece with a rollicking rhythm and an echo-refrain to each stanza. In fact, hardly one of the profane songs is without interest, and some of the divine ones have it.

Goedeke and Tittmann's Liederbuch.

If there is so much attraction in this single small and early collection, it is not unreasonable to expect more from the selected *Liederbuch* of Goedeke and Tittmann, which draws not merely on the *Bergreihen* themselves, but on some fifty other song-books, music-books, and miscellaneous collections of the sixteenth century. Nor will the expectation be disappointed. The four divisions of this really charming volume—Folk and Social Songs; Ghostly Songs; Historical Songs (we should call them Ballads); and Meistersongs—are indeed by no means of equal interest as wholes. The last may be, perhaps, recommended as giving the poor-spirited reader a taste tolerable in quality, and not intolerable in quantity, of this too commonly vapid class of composition. The "Ballads" will probably be found most disappointing. They cannot for one moment compare with the "Battle of Otterburn" or the "Heir of Lynne," much less with the gems of the *Minstrelsy* or those of the *Kempeviser*. The "Battle of Pavia" is not quite so good as the "Brave Lord Willoughby." Perhaps the most interesting things are two pieces not strictly in the key of the others, but by, or attributed to, two famous historical personages—Ulrich von Hutten and George Frundsberg. The first—the rather famous *Ich habs gewagt mit sinnen*—is a stout "declaration of independence," but may easily be, and I think has been, overpraised as poetry. The grumble of the great *lanzknecht* about the gratitude of princes is characteristic of an "old soldier," with a quaint rhythm and a touch of humour in it which is rather agreeable. As for the *Geistliche Lieder*, what has been said of Luther's—which, of course, figure largely among them — applies pretty generally. Nothing, perhaps, quite comes up to *Ein feste Burg;* but then no language can be expected to duplicate a triumph in its particular kind, such as that is. The "Song of Christ" of Elizabeth Creutziger, who is generally ranked second to Dr Martin, certainly possesses both sweetness and vigour, though the poetess (like most poetesses, except Miss Christina Rossetti) seems to think that rhyme-rules were not made for ladies. The "Riders' Hymn" of Baron Philip zu Winnenberg would have suited Captain Dalgetty in his more pious moods, and may actually have been sung by him; and there is a curious carolling music about the ghostly *Alba* (a form which needed a good deal of "ghostlifying") by Philip Nicolai.

But when we turn from these to the profaner ditties, which fill nearly half the book, we are unfortunately bound to confess that the Devil, or (not to be harsh), let us say, the World and the Flesh, make by far the best use of the best tunes, if they do not keep them to themselves. Here are dozens of "May" and "cuckoo" songs, hardly one of them without charm. Here is the unapproachable

> "Ich weiss ein meidlein hübsch und fein—
> hüt du dich!"

the mocking music of which is so ingrained in its very words that it has not escaped even in the well-known English translation. Here is the cry, instinct with all our own Elizabethan passion—

> "Ach, herzigs herz, lass dich doch eins erweichen;"

here dozens of other things as charming, sometimes surging off into freaks of half-inarticulate refrain, sometimes pressed into quaintly contorted metrical shapes, sometimes simply enough formed.

Nor, as we may well think, does Bacchus lack his "makers." As one bad man sings—

> "Den liebsten bulen, den ich han,
> der leit beim wirt im keller;
> er hat ein hölzens röcklein an,
> er heist der muscateller."

And all the usual subjects of folk-song and formal lyric muster here, to be treated in a fashion which certainly makes us take leave of this vernacular literature of sixteenth-century Germany, to which we have not been able to be very kind on the whole, "with a sweet mouth."

CHAPTER VI.

THE CHANGES OF EUROPEAN DRAMA.

THE TWO INFLUENCES — THEIR LIMITED WORKING IN ITALY — EARLY ITALIAN TRAGEDY — EARLY COMEDY: ITS DISTINGUISHED PRACTITIONERS — BIBBIENA — ARETINO — ARIOSTO — MACHIAVELLI — GENERAL STYLE OF THEIR PLAYS — GRAZZINI, CECCHI, ETC. — THE ARTIFICIAL LATIN PLAY — IN FRANCE — BUCHANAN'S TRAGEDIES — IN HIGH AND LOW GERMANY — VOLDER'S 'ACOLASTUS' — BIRCK'S 'SUSANNA' — THE 'ALUTA' AND 'REBELLES' OF MACROPEDIUS — KIRCHMAYER'S 'PAMMACHIUS' — VERNACULAR DRAMA IN FRANCE — GRINGORE — OTHER DRAMA — THE FARCES — MYSTERIES AND MORALITIES — DRAMA IN ENGLAND — THE INTERLUDE — JOHN HEYWOOD — HIS PIECES — SOME OTHER INTERLUDES — JOHN BALE — 'KYNG JOHAN' — ITS POSITION AS FIRST OF CHRONICLE PLAYS — AND IN ITSELF.

THE most remarkable achievements of modern literature as compared with ancient, in whole kinds or departments, are, beyond all reasonable question, the immense extension given to Prose Fiction and the changes effected in the Drama. The first was during our present period still far in the future, except as regards the multiplication and popularity of the Short Story. This last, however, whether in the polished Italian Novella or in the rough German folk-tale, in the imitations of the former everywhere and of the latter chiefly in England, is, though interesting and important, scarcely of importance enough to demand or deserve separation from the rest of the literatures. It is otherwise with Drama—indeed, one of the attractions of the short story itself at this time is the impetus and the materials it supplies to this very kind.

In all European countries more or less, though with slight differences in time and important ones in character for the different nations, the sixteenth century generally, and its earlier half in particular, was the turning-point of dramatic history. And here we shall find Italy giving up to the ruder nations that position of leader and schoolmaster, which she has hitherto held almost everywhere and almost in everything. Her dramatic work during the period is indeed interesting, but at least as much for what it is not as for what it is. It exercises, as far as the vernacular is concerned, extremely slight influence over the pupil-nations, even in cases where their general docility induces them—as in that of Gascoigne—to translate Italian work. And that "absence of future," that threatened sterility, which is even in other branches of Italian literature rather ominous, is nowhere so remarkable as here. For once even the influence of Humanism, great as it is, is exerted rather on other countries than on Italy.

That there were at the opening of the sixteenth century two very powerful influences which, in a manner not to be paralleled in any other branch of literature, were likely to work on the Drama, is the plainest matter of history; and, so far as just stated, it can be denied by no sane and instructed person. These influences were, first, those of the great body of mediæval drama in its various forms, and, secondly, that of the classical tragedy and comedy, as just revived and set afresh before scholars and educated men. Further, that these influences worked very unequally in different countries is again matter of history. But that one of them, the mediæval drama, had in some cases—at least in the case which is to us by far the most interesting—no influence, or next to no influence at all, has actually been held by some persons whose knowledge at least cannot be disputed. In such cases the one safe way is always to give the history; to see what, without hypothesis or guessing, the actual facts and the examination of the actual documents tell us.

The two influences.

To begin, as of right, with Italy: it is generally acknowledged by the most ardent devotees of Italian literature that among her great literary achievements the drama by no means holds the highest or even a very high place. That Italians are in a certain way born histrionic—that a typical Italian can hardly accomplish any ordinary act of living without turning it into a little comedy or tragedy, as the case may be—is not contested; that from our earliest knowledge of anything that can be called Italy, pageants, processions, and other half, or more than half, dramatic shows seem to arrange themselves spontaneously under Italian skies, is a well-

Their limited working in Italy.

known fact; that very important applied kinds of drama, with the masque and the opera at their head, have originated in Italy is perfectly true. But it is also true that, despite the notable work of the kind in Italian from Bibbiena to Alfieri, absolute dramatic masterpieces hardly exist in Italian; and that no strictly modern dramatic variety arose in Italy, with the very doubtful exception of the kind of comedy of manners identified with the names of Gozzi and Goldoni, which is later than similar things in England and France, and probably derived from the French.

That some have seen a not very remote or recondite explanation of this fact in the at first sight contradictory facts mentioned earlier, and have argued that a nation which has drama so ready at hand in the home does not want it in the theatre, is a thing proper to be mentioned here, not necessary to be argued out. The facts are sufficient for us. And one of those facts is both significant in itself and pregnant of things significant in the future. This is, that the mediæval drama itself is more meagre and of less importance in Italy than anywhere else. There is, as usual in such cases, a certain amount of otiosity in the attempts to distinguish "Divozioni" and "Sacre Rappresentazioni" from Mysteries. But there is very little difficulty in granting that, in these Italian things, the "show" and the liturgic purpose both had much greater prominence than that strictly dramatic interest and character which emerges so early in the French mystery, and which is seen with us from the very first; that the earliest Italian examples are relatively late; and, lastly, that such purely secular dramatic work as, for instance, Adam de La Halle's, is practically unknown in Italy during the fourteenth and even the fifteenth century, while even such episodic indulgences in pure drama as are constant in the more northern mysteries are very rare and very late in Italian. Pageant and poetry are plentiful: strict drama very rare.[1]

The consequence of this naturally was, that when the other—the classical—influence came into play it met with nothing native or vernacular sufficiently vigorous to offer either any real resistance or any important reinforcement. Some adaptation to the form of the "representation" has indeed been discovered in the *Timone* of Bardo and the *Orfeo* of Politian. But it is admitted that there are strong classical elements in the handling of both, as there are naturally far more in the earlier Latin plays of Alberti and others. And it is most especially to be observed that the *subjects* are in both cases classical. It is not for nothing that England should (whether with strict correctness or not really does not matter) have dated her mediæval drama from a *Ralph Roister Doister* and a *Gammer Gurton's Needle* and a *Gorboduc*, Italy hers from an *Orpheus* and a *Timon*.

And *qualis ab incepto* was here also the catchword. It was not that men invariably, even in our period,

[1] When Mr Symonds said that the Italian anonymous *Mary Magdalene* "rises to a higher level of dramatic art than any sacred play in English," he had not, I think, read the "Digby" *Magdalene*, which is inferior in nothing but the state of the language, and even superior in other things.

abstained from contemporary or from mediæval subjects. There is said to have been a *Fall of Granada* acted at Rome soon after the event itself; and that national tragedy of the Dark Ages, which has been so tempting to playwrights[1] of the most different capacities and genius, was first dealt with in Rucellai's *Rosmunda* as early as 1515.

But both tragedy and comedy were cast, with a strictness which anticipated and even exceeded that of the French, on the model of Euripides or at least of Seneca, of Terence or at least of Plautus. The contemporary critics (see next chapter), who were in more than one case dramatists themselves, helped this tendency by the eagerness with which they insisted on a sort of redistilled blend, with not a few imported elements, of Aristotle and Horace, as the code of drama; the whole force of Humanism was on the same side, and—little edifying as the Italian comedies often are—so was to some extent the mania of the time for education. Already in the first few decades of the century the stock subjects, classical or scriptural—Dido, Cleopatra, Sophonisba, Mariamne, Orestes, by their constant rehandling of which classical dramatists in all countries have made a rather touching confession of the barrenness of their style—make their appearance. And while the Italians, furnished with a better language, were not so tempted as other nations were to write this kind of play in Latin, they seldom or never travelled beyond its limits.

Yet in neither language did they achieve great

[1] Rucellai himself, Middleton, Alfieri, Mr Swinburne.

success. The strange influence of the tragedian Seneca over the whole Renaissance, after being long ignored, has of late been even overestimated in certain points of direction and result, but can hardly be exaggerated, so far as concerns general intensity, volume, and universality of working. The ostensible regularity of these plays, with their huge *tirades* and their rattling *stichomythia*, their choruses, their simplicity of character, and their artfully arranged dialogue, fell in with the assumed literary creed of the time. The stateliness and the not unfrequent fire of the *senarii*, the beauty of the lyrical passages, the gloom, the ghosts, the horrors, pleased its genuine taste. In England the latter group of attractions most fortunately overpowered and swept away the former. In France and Italy, but especially in Italy, the former kept the latter in check. Not that the Italians denied themselves horrors *ad lib.* The excellent Trissino, whose *Sophonisba* (often followed) ranks as the first popular Italian tragedy, did indeed strive to follow the Greeks rather than Seneca. But the *Rosmunda* of Rucellai, which came close on the heels of the other, shows the Senecan influence completely, not merely in its abundance of horrors (decently "messengered," of course), but in the messengering itself and the confidant business. And the same characteristics are to be found in the only other Italian tragedies, which (if but with the "feeble voice" of ghosts) claim part in historic mention—the *Marianna* (*Mariamne*) of Dolce, the *Canace* of Speron Speroni, and the *Orbecche* of the novelist Cinthio

Early Italian tragedy.

Giraldi. The stories of the two former belong to the world's literature; the *Orbecche* is a very choice Italian *pot-pourri* of incest and parricide, well spiced with other varieties of adultery and murder. In all these "the height of Seneca his style," which is actually visible in some of the northern Latin plays, not absent in French, and abundantly present in the vernacular tragedies of the first Elizabethan period in English, is very rarely reached, while really dramatic incident and motive are almost as rare as messengers, confidantes, and choruses are abundant.

Early comedy: its distinguished practitioners.

When we turn to comedy the failure of Italy to produce great modern drama is made at first sight all the more remarkable by the fact that in no country, at this particular time, did so many men of anything like the same ability attempt dramatic composition. The best names to be mentioned later in this chapter — Kirchmayer, Buchanan, Gringore, Heywood, Bale — range from the second class downwards. But Bibbiena or Dovizio was at the least a singularly witty and accomplished scholar and writer; Aretino, though a vulgar scoundrel, had unquestionably a keen eye for fact and no small amount of bestial force in expression; while Ariosto and Machiavelli are among the greater gods, not merely of Italian but of European literature. And all these betook themselves, if in no single case with their main activity, to dramatic production, followed by Grazzini, Cecchi, and others of no mean repute. That they should have adopted not buskin but sock is not so very surprising. Plautus and

Terence provided models abundant, in the former case at least, long popular, not by any means difficult of adaptation, and thoroughly germane to the Italian taste.

And the quartette, so remarkable in ability, shows, in the very act of adapting itself to comedy, the unsuitableness of the national genius, even to that kind of drama which in France was to triumph, if tragedy did not. It has been confessed, and justly confessed, that the whole of this comedy "holds up the mirror not to Nature but to Plautus or Terence." Aretino, who is least liable to the charge, escapes it chiefly because his brutal realism had necessarily to take actual life for its subject, and because his unscholarly disregard of form found no need of the pattern to which the others resorted, for want of will or wit to devise a new one. The other three lay on their Plautine or Terentian skeletons some modern touches, a great deal of lively wit, in some cases at least admirable style; but their framework is always old and often obsolete. The novelist, Il Lasca, shows himself as one of the best critics of his century, and even of his age and some ages to come, in the memorable prologue to his *Gelosia.*[1] The old "discovery" is ridiculous, he says; and people do not live in Florence as they lived in Rome. The institutions of slavery and of adoption, on which so much turns, are simply not modern institutions at all. This, it may be feared, would have shocked, and possibly did shock (for he very likely knew it) Sir Philip Sidney, as much as it would have

[1] P. 6, *ed. cit. infra.*

shocked Vida and no doubt did shock Scaliger. The English dramatists acted on it; but hardly any others out of Spain, and most certainly not the Italian.

Bibbiena.

For all its drawbacks this batch of plays is justly celebrated in the literary history of Europe: and though fortunately, in England at least, the style of them met with little continued favour, yet in England as elsewhere they were received with the respectful and almost humble deference which was bestowed upon all Italian products of literature. More than one of them is familiar to all English readers of a tolerably studious kind, as matter for Shakespeare. For instance, Bibbiena's *Calandra*[1] has some resemblances in the main incident of its plot (the resemblance of a brother and sister) to *Twelfth Night*, with something also to the *Comedy of Errors.* All of them possess brilliancy or force, or both, of one kind and another; most of them, Aretino's excepted, are literature; most of them, Aretino's perhaps most of all, draw upon genuine life.

Aretino.

But the fault of them, from the general and impartial view of literary dramatic criticism, is, that they do not possess life enough, and do not possess it in the right way or of the right kind. Very likely Aretino has given us quite a faithful portrait-gallery of those associates of his, in tavern or brothel, whose society Berni branded on him in a famous

[1] This, with the *Clizia* and *Mandragola* of Machiavelli, Aretino's *Ipocrita*, and Lorenzino de' Medici's *Aridosio*, will be found in vol. i. of Lemonnier's *Teatro Ital. Antico*, Florence, 1888. All Machiavelli's plays are in the collected edition above cited: all Ariosto's in the *Opere Minori* as above.

capitolo: but then they are people about whom we do not want to know, and the author can tell us of no others. Even in the London of 1901 it is doubtful whether Machiavelli's *Mandragola* could be acted. The much and justly rebuked prologues and epilogues of Dryden are decent beside those of Ariosto to the *Lena* and the *Suppositi*. And this ugly feature is made uglier by the fact that though we cannot say that it was exactly false to the time, it was certainly intensified by mere corrupt following of the ancients. So that this following did harm in two ways—by supplying a vicious model, and by suggesting more vicious details and decorations.

Ariosto—Machiavelli.

It is not fair to judge plays by titles; indeed, it may be said to have been part of the dramatic genius of our Elizabethan playwrights to give their plays titles from which as a rule nothing could be guessed. The Italians, still true to their classical models, were more downright. "Calandra" is simply a proper name. The *Cassaria*, the *Suppositi*, the *Lena*, the *Negromante*, the *Scolastica* of Ariosto, for the most part tell their own story as much as *L'Etourdi* or *Le Grondeur*. Two of Machiavelli's comedies, or of the comedies attributed to him, have no titles at all, but are simply "A Comedy in Verse," "A Comedy in Prose." Of the others *Clizia* is the name of the heroine, *Mandragola* the name of the drug to which is assigned the peculiar virtue which is necessary to the action of the play. Of Aretino[1] the

[1] All these, with the tragedy *Orazia*, are in 1 vol. of Sanzogno's cheap collection (Milan, 1882).

Cortegiana, the *Ipocrita*, the *Filosofo* are outspoken, if the *Marescalco* and the *Tallanta* are not.

General style of their plays.

In all appears that curious notion of comedy which seems to have come in with the New Attic variety, which accounts to some extent for the scorn of Aristotle (though in his time it had not yet triumphed), and which has cropped up again so repeatedly that it must be allowed a certain genuineness of character. It is absolutely necessary that somebody must be made a fool of: and the selection of the somebody is not determined by any considerations of poetical justice, nor the treatment of him governed by any scruples of decency and good feeling. Even Restoration Comedy is not unfrequently a good deal above the *Mandragola* and the unnamed *Commedia in Prosa*, while in this whole class of play we are at such a distance from *As You Like It* or the *Merchant of Venice* that it may seem almost profanation to mention them in connection. Types, and as a rule degraded types, of character; a few stock plots, in which the revolutions and discoveries are awkwardly provided by the substitution of Turk for Greek pirates; and the maintenance with little change of that impossible servant, whom Aristophanes would have regarded with as much scorn as Shakespeare, supply the plots. Expressed or suggested indecency gives the jokes. It is a style of drama to which the praise of cleverness may be generally granted, that of goodness seldom or never. Even the dialogue, which is not seldom witty, almost loses that quality when it is contrasted with Molière and Congreve; of the higher humour there is hardly a trace.

Grazzini, Cecchi, &c.

This being so, it does not seem necessary to devote any great space even to the major examples, to the greater writers—still less to the minor, Gelli and Cecchi, Firenzuola, Ambra, Il Lasca[1]—to see whether the phrases bestowed on their occasional scenes by historians can be sometimes approved, or the strictures allotted by the same historians to their art and their morals can ever be toned down. It is sufficient to be certain that here, as not unfrequently occurs in literature, the talent and the genius, not merely of an individual but of a considerable group of writers, were simply travelling on a road which led nowhither. Even if Ariosto with his own genius had had the ideas of Il Lasca, and had completely (he has in one or two plays more or less) shaken off the mere false imitation of the ancients, in order to take to the true *mimesis* of nature, it is not likely that much would have followed from it. Of the two springs of genuine modern drama, as has been shown above, Italy possessed the one in a scantily flowing rill, while the other was suited not to correct but to intensify the faults to which she was naturally inclined. England to a great extent, Spain to a less, France to some, Germany, when unkind fate

[1] Of these, Cecchi's six comedies, *La Dote*, *La Moglie*, *Gl' Incantesimi*, *La Stiava*, *I Dissimili*, and *L'Assiuolo*, are in one volume of the Sanzogno collection (Milan, 1883); Gelli's *La Sporta* and *Lo Errore*, with his dialogues, in another (Milan, 1887); and Grazzini's comedies in one of Lemonnier's (Florence, 1897).

would let her, were enabled to correct what was bad and develop what was good in the mediæval drama by the influence of the classics and their Humanist imitators. But Italy had next to no mediæval drama to be corrected by the classics, or to correct them, and so a copy of these classics themselves, with the faults exaggerated, as in all copies, and the virtues weakened, as in most, was all she could achieve.

The artificial Latin play.

In the countries where drama was to be a literary kind with a real future—a condition which, as has been seen above, excludes Italy—something besides Plautus, Terence, and Seneca on the one hand, and the mediæval drama on the other, has to be taken into consideration. This is the artificial Humanist Latin play, both tragic, comic, and mixed, which was formed on the models of Plautus, of Terence, and of Seneca themselves. To most of us the tragedies of Buchanan and Muret, the comedies, or mystery-comedies, of Volder and Kirchmayer, are mainly, if not merely, curiosities in themselves, deserving higher rank than this only because of the light they throw on certain periods of the history of literature, and the influence which they had upon certain stages of literary development. These considerations will indeed, in the eyes of the catholic student of things literary, always save them from ignorant and one-sided contempt. But they can scarcely secure for them, from such students, much more than a respect of esteem.

The value of the *Jephthes* and the *Acolastus* and the *Pammachius* in literature (the last named at least has an additional claim from the point of view of history, ecclesiastical and general, as well as literary) is mainly this, that they carried the less advanced countries over a period in which good vernacular drama was still impossible, and meanwhile practised Germans, Englishmen, Netherlanders, and, to some extent, Frenchmen, in those habits of "regularity" which were necessary, not indeed to supplement but, to correct the mediæval luxuriance and to supply the mediæval lacks. In the first archæolatry of the Renaissance, and before the vernaculars had been brought further into shape, it was better that vernacular plays of any ambitious kind should be kept back; and this was especially the case in English. The Humanist drama not merely was a famous exercising-ground for the modern dramatist, but enabled him to work off the extravagance, as well as to train the vigour, of childhood in a form which, while it secured all the profit of practice, gave few of the dangers of example.

The amount of this drama composed north of the Alps must have been very large, and the amount of it in actual existence is probably not small; but it is not necessary to pay individual attention to very many instances. Some general remarks on it, with more detailed consideration of noteworthy examples in the text, will probably suffice before we pass on to the drama, which, scanty and rudimentary as it mostly was, was not mere school-work, but, being vernacular, had life in it.

The phrase school-work is capable of a double application. For these Latin dramas, in all the northern countries, were closely and almost inextricably connected with the education-mania which, as has been already often observed, is one of the main notes of the period. It is not easy to decide what principle, except that general and no doubt very wise one of "not letting the devil have all the best tunes," determined the very early and very general adoption of carefully adapted school-plays as a combined engine of instruction and amusement in schools and universities. The Church had more or less the control of education; the Church was, not merely on old scores, but for some solid perennial reasons, deeply suspicious of the stage; and yet the Church knew very well that the tendency of man was histrionic and the tendency of youthful mankind rather particularly so. Therefore the same considerations which had dictated the permission and patronage of the Miracles dictated also the permission and patronage of the school-play. Nor did the earlier and wiser Reformers, those over whom Humanism retained a considerable influence, hesitate to go and do likewise. Reuchlin wrote plays; Buchanan wrote plays; the fiery Kirchmayer wrote the most remarkable play of the whole group we are now considering. In the English grammar-schools and colleges, which arose after the dissolution of the monasteries, plays were constantly performed until, and to some extent after, the definite rise of the baleful star of Puritanism.

As we should expect, the tragedy of this group is even less important, in comparison with the comedy or nondescript play, than is the case in the vernaculars.

The Latin tragedy generally had been, so far as we can make out, a copy of the Greek even paler than in other cases of corresponding Latin and Greek literature; and Seneca's own work is chiefly remarkable for isolated beauties of poetry, and for the strange, strongly projected, and yet practically impersonal individuality which looms behind them. The paleness was bound to get dimmer and more blurred in modern imitations of the Senecan *pastiches*. Indeed, though the number of such plays is undoubtedly large, few have retained even a precarious hold on memory. They seem, in the light of subsequent events rather interestingly, to have had most influence in France, where, as elsewhere, they were frequent school exercises. No less than three of Montaigne's masters at Bordeaux in the middle of the century wrote them for their boys to act. One of these, Guérente, is chiefly a name; another, Muretus, ranks high among the French scholars of the Renaissance; the third was that learned Scotsman who was the acknowledged master of Latin verse in his time.

In France.

Of the four Latin tragedies[1] which we possess from the hand of George Buchanan, two, the *Medea* and the *Alcestis*, are, and pretend to nothing more than being, translations from Euripides. The other two, *Jephthes* and *Baptistes*, are original, and the latter is even a drama with a purpose, to attack tyranny and justify principles approaching much nearer to republicanism than Buchanan's pupil, to whom late in life he dedicated it, at all approved.

Buchanan's tragedies.

[1] To be found in either of the editions cited, *supra*, pp. 49, 51.

But this, as well as the earlier *Jephthes*, which had been, it would seem, actually performed by the students or schoolboys under Buchanan's rule at Bordeaux, are tragedies rather on the Senecan model than that of strict Greek tragedy, even in Euripides. They display, moreover, to the very fullest extent, that adherence to the Senecan form which was so general, if not universal, on the Continent, but which England, equally to her honour and to her good fortune, dropped almost entirely after *Gorboduc* and a few other pale experiments, though she retained a strong if crude affection for the ghosts and horrors of Seneca as well as for the somewhat "ampullated" style of that singular and mysterious dramatist. Both *Jephthes* and *Baptistes* are written in stately *senarii* and choric metres, often displaying to the full that elegance which no one can refuse to Buchanan's Latin verse; but here their attraction ends. The *Nuntius* rules supreme; through his agency passes the whole meagre action of the play; when he appears we may expect something livelier, or more interestingly deadly, than the interminable periods of the *tirades* and the snip-snap rattle of the *stychomythia* or line-for-line dialogue. When he disappears we must resign ourselves to these, or to the elegant, but distinctly casual and negligible, descants of the chorus.

In High and Low Germany.

Buchanan was not a comic writer; and it would really seem as if the exceptional strength of indigenous comedy and farce in France, and the fairly early introduction of the new Italian manner by Larivey and others, had kept the Latin comedy and mixed play under in that country, though no doubt examples might be found. In Germany, High and Low, the conditions of the vernacular were very different, and the development of the Latin play there was much more important and characteristic.

Volder's Acolastus.

The *Acolastus* of Willem Volder, or Fullonius, or Gnapheus,[1] was one of the most successful, and is one of the most notable of these. It appeared in 1529, and in little more than ten years' time was translated into English by the useful Palsgrave. Volder, himself a pupil of the Brethren of the Common Life and a Reformer, had troubles as the latter, but surmounted them, though he had to lead rather a wandering life in consequence. He was always more or less of a schoolmaster or tutor; and it was for his schoolboys at the Hague that he wrote *Acolastus.* It is said to have been printed forty times in its author's lifetime, which (to be sure) lasted as many years after its first appearance, and it was widely imitated, the Latin being much admired. But the really dramatic character of the piece probably contributed more to its success. In fact, though not so elegant in Latinity as Buchanan's pieces, and not so full of something not unlike genius as the *Pammachius*, it is probably the best of all these Humanist plays as a play.

The story is simply that of the Prodigal Son—a very favourite motive at the time—and the scheme is that of the Terentian or Plautine comedy. The alterations of this comedy *in usum scholarum* were supposed to

[1] All of course equivalents in the different languages for "Fuller." The *Acolastus* has been edited by Joh. Borte (Berlin, 1891).

adjust the morals of the originals to their purpose. But the Renaissance was seldom very pudibund, and the slight indications of the Biblical story are generously filled out, on the principle, we must suppose, of *salus adolescentulis.* Still, no more than tolerable liberties are taken with the story itself. The elder son makes slight appearance; but both the father, Pelargus, and Acolastus himself are duly equipped with confidants, who are not so otiose as usual. The son's friend, Philautus, or Self-will, is soon dismissed, to make room for other stock characters, a pair of greedy parasites, who in their turn are handled with considerable freedom and success, as are also the rascally innkeeper and pandar Sannio, and the courtesan Lais. Lais indeed is presented with a force and gusto which we should rather have expected from an Italian poet than from a Dutch schoolmaster; and though as heartless and greedy as the worst of her class, she has something of the fire of an Imperia about her, and feigns passion with surprising vigour while her lover's money lasts. When it has come to an end, parasite, host, and mistress of course all turn upon their pigeon, and he is driven literally to his last shift in the story itself, the feeding of actual swine. The father's confidant, Eubulus, justifies his existence in the last act by ascertaining for Pelargus the destitute condition of his son; but the repentance of Acolastus is genuine and self-wrought, and the "happy ending" comes all the more fitly for the stage by reason of the omission of the elder brother. That the piece is really good is sufficiently shown by the fact that it can be read now with a great deal of interest, though the story is as well known as the multiplication table, and though the machinery is as hackneyed as it can possibly be. And it is worth observing that this worthy Dutchman really to a great extent does achieve the great triumph of the modern drama, the transformation of stock types into individual characters. The average ancient slave, parasite, and so forth, might as well be called by a number as a name; and this is too much the case with all but the best of his representatives in some modern drama. Gnapheus, on the contrary, if he has not given to Pantolabus and Lais the character of Doll Tearsheet, much less of Falstaff, has at least carried them a long way from being merely Servus X. and Meretrix Omega.

Birck's Susanna.

Some other celebrated plays of this class deserve individual mention. The *Susanna*[1] of Sixt Birck or Xystus Betulius is chiefly remarkable for the extreme elaboration of its picture of the trial of the heroine, in which the respectable members of the court, who are extremely numerous, distinguish themselves by giving their judgment dead against Susanna, in great individual detail, on the unsupported testimony of the Elders, and dead in favour of her when Daniel's ingenious and fortunate, but after all not entirely conclusive, cross-examination has been allowed. The *Rebelles* and the *Aluta*,[2] especially the former, of Georgius Macropedius or George Von Langveldt, are much better things. The *Aluta* is a not very long and rather coarse dramatis-

[1] Ed. Borte (Berlin, 1893). [2] Ed. Borte (Berlin, 1897).

ing of the story—fairly widespread under more than one variant in ballad and folk-tale—of the silly and drunken peasant's wife, who goes to market with a cargo of poultry, is cheated into selling it for nothing, who celebrates the transaction by getting disgustingly drunk at the village inn, and in that condition not only loses her one remaining fowl (kept by the innkeeper in payment of food and drink), but in her drunken sleep is stripped almost to the skin by her previous defrauders, and reaches home in a half-insane condition, believing that she is somebody else, frightening her child out of its wits in the supposition that she is either mad or a ghost, and bitterly distressing her very forgiving husband. The actual state of the case is only discovered by the man-of-the-world parson who is fetched in to exorcise. The thing is a farce of a decidedly Teutonic kind, but (to strong stomachs) not unamusing.

The Aluta *and* Rebelles *of Macropedius.*

The *Rebelles* flies far higher. It is a professional piece; for Langveldt was, like Volder, a schoolmaster, and his main moral is the efficacy of the rod, and the folly of mothers who would have the child both spared and spoiled. But it is almost free from mere nastiness (which the *Aluta* is not), and it is, in part at least, full of amusement. The opening soliloquy of the more amiable of the two mothers, Philotecnium, with her rueful reflection on the wrinkles and the grey hair, which remind her that she has "eaten not a few Easter eggs," has much piquancy. She is in trouble about her eldest boy, Dyscolus, who would, of course, be a fine scholar if it were not for the ignorant brutality of the schoolmasters. In this point her neighbour and relation, Cacolalia (a virulent scold and shrew, who "combs her husband with a joint-stool," while the amiable Philotecnium is cruelly beaten by hers), quite agrees with her, for she has a hopeful, Clopicus by name, whose tender flesh and skin are equally troubled by the brutal birch. They have heard of one Aristippus, a teacher of high renown, who is said (like Marryat's Mr Bonnycastle) to abstain from the use of the rod, and they determine to intrust their treasures to him. They do so: Aristippus declines to do more than promise to suit the treatment to the cases, and the matrons—Cacolalia with grumbling and threats, Philotecnium with mild entreaties—are forced to be content. After the intervention of a pair of devils (who are charged with the task of bringing the two boys to evil, and who play the part of twin "Vices" throughout, more, let it be hoped, to the amusement of contemporaries than to ours), the two boys appear in school, bent on nothing so little as on learning. Clopicus, who, as his name imports, is a young sharper, persuades the stupider Dyscolus to play an ingenious game, with coins hidden in their books, Clopicus reserving for himself two chances to one. Dyscolus does not discover the cheat till he has lost all his money, and then, of course, there is a battle-royal. Aristippus discovers his hopeful pupils at it, and they are "introduced" (the technical term) to receive their deserts, but not *coram populo*, for this would shock Horace. The mothers are in agonies, Cacolalia of rage and grief,

Philotecnium of grief purely, and they both rush to Aristippus, Cacolalia threatening personal reprisals. But the intrepid schoolmaster blandly says to his staff, "*Introducite!*" adding "*Sternite!*" and a fearful vindication of his majesty is only prevented by abject submission of the matrons, who, however, of course take away their darlings and decide to equip them for trade at once. The young rascals promptly go the same path as Acolastus, and, being swindled at dice, try to procure fresh money by theft. They are arrested, sentenced to death, and only saved by Aristippus, who, at the despairing request of the mothers, claims them as his schoolboys or students, subject only to scholastic correction, has his claim allowed by the obliging Judex, and so vindicates the birch as an instrument of direct, as well as indirect, redemption from the gallows.

The piece is very well written, mainly in *senarii* of a strict type, not in the looser Terentian forms, and has a really capital blend of humour, which seems constantly turning to grimness, but which is really kindly enough. Of the lighter drama of the class, I should incline to put it as distinctly at the head of those I know as the *Pammachius* at the head of the more serious, while it is superior to that play in the adumbration (no doubt here far easier) of character. The shrew Cacolalia is a stock personage; but the kind, silly, lachrymose Philotecnium is a person; the two boys are good types, and, what is more, almost individuals, of the two main kinds of ne'er-do-weel youngsters, the sneak and the bully; while Aristippus is on a level with Philotecnium.

Kirchmayer's Pammachius.

The *Pammachius*[1] may have been rather over-praised; but it is impossible to read it carefully without being considerably impressed by the power of the author, though hardly with his skill. The versification is rough and heavy; the *senarii* constantly beginning with single tetrasyllables of dispondaic value—*applausurum*, *irascatur*, and the like. The action is not only impeded by immense didactic tirades, but not credibly arranged; for why should Pope Pammachius, at the very moment when he has achieved a great Christian triumph by converting the Emperor Julian and freeing Christianity from persecution, use that persecution as an excuse for deserting to Satan? Although there is a certain amount of grim humour, it is oddly combined with a deficient sense of the ludicrous, as where Our Lord reminds the Apostles of their own observations in the Epistles, and they dutifully say "*Memini*"; or where the honest scold Parrhesia—a sort of ancestress or antitype of Jenny Geddes—interrupts the Pope and his wily spokesman Porphyry with fish-fag railings. Nor can the extravagant and almost personal hatred of the papacy fail to be very wearisome and a little disgusting. But the intense and wholly disinterested earnestness of the man carries a certain amount of contagion with it; the Satanic scenes are particularly good; the parts of Planus (Heresy), Stasiades (Party Spirit), and Chremius ("Mede," as Langland would—nay, had—put it, altering the sex), are cleverly distri-

[1] Ed. Bolte and Schmidt (Berlin, 1891).

buted, and once or twice (as where Satan crowns Pammachius with these words of investiture—

> "Hanc coronam suscipe
> Tenebrarum et cæcitatis ! Regibus impera,
> Dominare populis, inferorum maximis
> Præsis portis ! Omnes tuorum pulverem
> Pedum lingant : secundus in regno sies !")

we are nearly in presence of a great dramatic utterance, and should be fully so here if it were not for the metrical cacophony of the last two lines.

But the piece undoubtedly grows upon one; even a High Churchman of the old rock may admit that the Protestant position is nowhere[1] put with quite such energising intensity as in *Pammachius*. There is real dramatic power—for all the drawback of the morality-personages—in the scene between Veritas and Parrhesia which opens the Fourth Act, and in which martyred Truth finds no other place to go to but the very feet of Christ. There is more in the Satanic orgie of the second scene, and in the fiendish but festive resolve of the Powers of Evil that they have won all along the line, and that *nunc est bibendum*, with nothing more to do. The *crescendo* is not lost in the third, the council of war between Our Lord, St Peter, St Paul, and Veritas, which results in the mission of the two last personages to Germany to start a return campaign. And that savage but real humour which has been

[1] Certainly not in the author's *Regnum Papisticum*, a huge and tedious verse-invective, translated, with full justice to the tedium, by our Barnabe Googe, and re-presented in this form, much more handsomely than it deserves, by Mr R. C. Hope (London, 1880).

noted appears capitally in the remonstrance of shivering Truth on hearing their destination—

> "Heu! num me etiam vis macerare frigore?"

and the answer of Our Lord (to be commented at many a stake)—

> "Confide, calesces plus satis."

The disorderly *réveillé* of the Evil Ones at the news of this in the fifth scene, and the plan of campaign against Truth and St Paul and "Theophilus" (Luther) in the sixth show no falling off; while the audacious refusal to attempt a Fifth Act at all, because the struggle is still going on, is about the most effective finale that can be conceived. It is no wonder that the thing rang through all Europe on the Protestant side; what is wonderful, and shows the weakness of the Papacy, is that, so far as I know, no answer of the slightest power or validity appeared on the Catholic side. It certainly could have been made; but it was not.

To separate the dramatic from the other work of Hans Sachs would be difficult, and it is itself of an older stamp: so we have taken it in the vernacular chapter. There was of course no absence of vernacular drama in Germany outside the Shrovetide Plays and the other work of Hans, of Waldis, and the rest of the writers mentioned in the last chapter. The work of the Swiss Nicolas Manuel includes not merely dramatic dialogues (the most famous of which, *Die Krankheit der Messe*, sent wide circles of Reformation influence throughout Europe), but irregular and almost regular plays in the same interest for popular consumption. But no such work has attained, or apparently deserved, anything like the repute of the *Acolastus* or the *Pammachius* or the *Rebelles;* indeed, it is not till we come to Jacob Ayrer, at the extreme end of the century and the beginning of the next, that the vernacular German drama supplies a name of some importance to dramatic history. And even then the work ranks pretty low as literature.

Two useful volumes of Burckhart's *Deutsche Dichter der* 16*ten Jahrhunderts,*[1] enable any one who cares to trace the work from Manuel to Ayrer through Paul Rebhun, Lienhart Kolman, Jacob Fünkelin, Sebastian Wild, Petrus Meckel, and Bartholomæus Kruger—names with which fame has rarely meddled since in Germany, and hardly ever out of it. Kruger and Ayrer lie beyond our beat, though the latter has special interest for English readers because of the connection of his name with Shakespeare's in certain lucubrations. Of the whole the wise frankness of their editor, Herr Tittmann, admits that "the [German] drama of the sixteenth century is *ein Schauspiel ohne Schauspielkunst.*" The specimen which he gives of Manuel, who has been completely edited by Swiss patriotism, is a very short Shrovetide play, and hardly even that, being merely a dialogue of comment by two spectators at a carnival procession, contrasting Christ crowned with thorns, His disciples, and the poor, with the Pope in "effeir of war," and followed by a mighty train. Its extreme earliness (1525) is its chief attrac-

[1] Ed. Tittmann (Leipsic, 1868).

tion. Paul Rebhun, a Wittemberg student and schoolmaster of whom little is known, gives a pretty long *Susanna*, ten years later in date, and chiefly interesting to compare with Birck's Latin version (*v. supra*, p. 341). It has an attempt, however, at a vernacular lyrical chorus which deserves note. Kolman's *Widow*, written after the middle of the century, is a dramatisation of the story of Elisha and the Widow's son. Some years later Jacob Fünkelin gives us a profane subject—a sort of morality-interlude—in the *Strife between Venus and Pallas;* and Sebastian Wild a somewhat similar piece, *The Doctor and the Ass* ("The Old Man, his Son, and their Donkey") which he is good enough to call a "tragedy," an expression perhaps known to the Philostrate of *A Midsummer Night's Dream*. And then, as late as 1571, we are back in pure Mystery-matter, with Petrus Meckel's *Satan the Accuser*, in which that personage, God the Father, Christ, some archangels, and a sort of chorus of sinners play all the parts, and the piece terminates with an address by the poet. It is not ill written, but quite archaic in form, taking us indeed back to the Latin liturgic dramas of the twelfth century. The collection is of real value as showing, from a fresh side, the literary backwardness of Germany. It may be well to add to it a work of Hans Rudolf Manuel, son of Nicolas. This is an enormous and curious *Fastnachtspiel*,[1] in the Swiss dialect, satirising drunkenness, which has been lately reprinted, and has received as

[1] *Das Weinspiel* (the original title is less direct and far longer), ed. Odinga, Halle, 1892.

much praise as it deserves. It is not without merit, but is chiefly remarkable for its extraordinary length (over 4000 lines) and the number of its personages (some fifty). Its date is 1548.

Vernacular drama in France.

What has been said in a former chapter about the general character of the literature of this period in France will apply with only a little change to the special department of drama. It is in general a period of the closing of the mediæval rather than of the beginning of the modern play, but it has characteristics which deserve less summary and more immediate treatment than the German. It was not till the rise of the Pléiade, which is treated in the next volume of this work (*v. The Later Renaissance*) that this latter really arose. In most respects France is a little in front of England in showing Renaissance influences, but not in all; and in this particular department, although when the change came, France again showed it somewhat earlier than England, yet the sway of the purely mediæval theatre endured longer in the more southern country. This was no doubt partly due to the influence of the Confraternities, which was so strong that, as is well known, the great "Confraternity of the Passion" actually became a company of comedians, forbidden to play their old mysteries, but licensed to play farce and secular drama, thus continuing the tradition of the French theatre unbroken, from the heart of the Middle Ages to the time of Corneille and Molière. The other theatrical clubs, too, as we may call them, the Clerks of the Basoche, the *Enfants sans Souci*, and the rest, were as a rule more influential and less local than the honest guilds which still continued to act the old miracle-play in England. And, lastly, we have, as usual, to reckon with the familiar and not unwelcome phenomenon of the casual person of genius, or at least of talent, who quite as often buoys up a sinking as he floats a rising style.

Gringore.

The person in this case was Pierre Gringore or Gringoire, whose lifetime covered about the same period (1478-1544) as that of most of the remarkable men of our time, and who—in France and in drama—was the only important individual of the day. We know very little about his life, but it must have been rather an interesting one, for its accidents in date and circumstances were distinctly favourable. Louis XII. may have had justification, or he may have had none, for his Italian policy. But he had the wit to recognise the importance of taking the people into his confidence, or at least of working upon theirs in carrying out the task of centralising monarchical government; and if not a man of letters himself, he must have inherited some literary sympathies from his father, Charles of Orleans, and reinforced them by the influence of his second wife, Anne of Brittany. At any rate, he either encouraged or suffered Gringore, both in his poems and in his plays,[1] to meddle with politics in a very daring and very unusual way; and this royal patronage or toleration enabled the dramatist to practise—with

[1] Ed. MM. d'Héricault, de Montaiglon, and de Rothschild. Bibliothèque Elzévirienne, 2 vols., Paris (1858-77).

back unlashed and neck in proper continuity of joint—the most audacious, the most short-lived, and for both reasons the rarest of the mediæval or fifteenth-century play-kinds, the *sotie*. This was so called, because it was performed by the *soi-disant* courtiers of the "Prince des Sots"; but it was in reality a political comedy of almost the purest kind. It is to Gringore, too, that we owe the most noteworthy example of the complete mediæval tetralogy, the resemblance of which, to the similar but more prevailingly serious tetralogy of the Greeks, is so curious, because so certainly undesigned. The full mediæval arrangement included a "cry" or summons to the audience as All Fools; the *sotie* itself; a morality (which in this case is again more than half political); and a farce of the broadest kind, which, however, has also here a certain relevance to the subjects of the first three parts.

In the *Cry* the change is rung with a Rabelaisian iteration (which is not at all "damnable") on all the kinds of Fools, who are invited at the end of each stanza (the piece is in Ballade form) to listen to and profit by the announcement that—

"Le Mardi Gras jouera le Prince aux Halles."

In the Sotie itself the Fools ask such dangerous questions as—

"Mais que font Anglois à Calais?"

"Général d'Enfance" is appeased with a toy, the "Seigneur de la Lune" arrives in state to take his seat in the Prince's Parliament, the "Abbé de Plate Bourse" and the "Sotte Commune" join the party, while the Mère Sotte, one of the most important personages of this stock company, audaciously personates Mother Church herself. The Morality is more sober but equally bold: Peuple Français, Peuple Italique, and L'Homme Obstiné have to do with the more shadowy personages of Ypocris and Symonie, and at the end "Divine Pugnicion." While the Farce, which is as audacious in another manner as the interludes of Lyndsay's *Three Estates,* teaches in a very unblushing parable that the national vineyard must be cultivated, and the national business done.

Other drama.

Not much less worthy of notice is Gringore's mystery, *Saint Louis,* which had also a present purpose, if not in the king's character, in his name and his foreign expeditions, while the extremely remarkable *Les Folles Enterprises,* though not ostensibly dramatic, is in fact a series of monologues or *parabases* on burning questions of Church and State. Gringore's adaptation of the mediæval forms was, however, mainly, if not wholly, the spirt or "sport" of an individual brain. Moreover, the political and occasional play is of its nature a kind which can only live with frequent and considerable intermissions of trance, not seldom brought about by violent means. When the ruler is favourable, the writer deft, and the audience sympathetic, much may be done: but when the last condition is wanting, the writer's occupation is gone; when the second fails, the work is intolerable; and when the first is lacking, neither work nor writer is tolerated. It may be almost impossible (not quite) to suppress a book; but it is perfectly possible and easy to close the theatre to an obnoxious play, and it has been done, in the case of political satire, not merely by absolute monarchs, but by the governments of happy constitutional lands within the not distant memory of man.

The Farces.

The bulk of the dramatic production of 1500-1550 in France—and it is a very large bulk indeed—consists of mysteries, moralities, and farces, more or less guiltless of any modern touches, but guilty in the first two cases of enormous length and dulness, and in the last of the old fault of the farce, undisguised obscenity. It must be admitted, however, that these farces are by no means seldom amusing, though a pudibund person might wish for the "vizard-mask" of Restoration playhouses to enable her, or even him, to laugh unabashedly. Their light octosyllabic verse, diversified, after the curious fashion which still kept its ground, with triolets, &c., worked into the dialogue, is far less unsuited than might be thought to be the medium of brief dramatic work: and (as to do its graceless personality justice the farce always has done) they kept alive the true spirit of drama against the extension of the pulpit over the stage on the one hand, and the predominance of alien and unsuitable "rules" on the other. It is probable that many if not most of our chief *répertoire* of farces, the precious early printed collection discovered in Germany, preserved in the British Museum, and reprinted in the *Ancien Théâtre Français*, vols. i.-iii.,[1] date from this time.

Mysteries and moralities.

The mysteries and the moralities are, of course, more respectable. But not only will the frivolous find them much less amusing, the serious student also must pronounce them of much less importance. Almost all that they can be said to have done is this—that they kept up the habit of dramatic writing after a fashion, and that they proved, beyond doubt or controversy, the innate and genuine attraction of the dramatic form for the general. If human beings would sit through a morality of six-and-thirty thousand lines (for this terrible thing does actually exist in *L'Homme Juste et L'Homme Mondain*, and was presumably acted), it must have been the form, the form alone, that was eloquent to them. It is, I believe, a fair calculation that five hundred lines an hour is about the utmost that actors can manage. The French dramatic line of this time is literally shorter than the English decasyllable, and is still more speedily pronounced in comparison to its length; but six or seven hundred must be a liberal allowance in this case. It would follow that an audience must have sat for some sixty mortal hours while the Just and the Worldly Men performed; and as these sixty hours could not well, in the conditions of human endurance, have been continuous, the play must (as we know that some of the mysteries *did* last) have lasted for at least a week of more than eight hours days. *Vixere fortes!*

[1] *Bibliothèque Elzévirienne* (Paris, 1854). See *The Transition Period*, pp. 271, 272 *note*.

But the serious plays, save for this assertion of the taste for drama, and even the farces, save in that point which has been above noted, could do little for the modern drama in France. It is as true in France as it is false in England that the serious modern play, at least for the best part of three centuries, owes nothing to mystery or morality, owes everything to imitation of the ancients. The farce had more power of resistance, and held out till Molière turned it into *la bonne comédie:* but even here Terence had almost too strong a predominance, for a time at least, over the author of *Pathelin.*

Drama in England.

The English Drama during our period has indeed no single person of talent equal to Gringore's except Sir David Lyndsay (who lies outside the general procession of the kind, and has, moreover, for reasons, been dealt with in the preceding volume), and, by a good deal of allowance, John Heywood. On the other hand, it has the great advantage over French — an advantage hidden, perhaps, when we look at itself only, but clear when we take it with the next age—of being much more germinal and experimental. And in particular it is, beyond all doubt, though on constructive rather than direct evidence, the period of the remarkable kind of Interlude. And this kind, though we cannot call it wholly English, inasmuch as there are somewhat similar things in the drama of other countries, is yet, as an eminent and separate kind, English more than it is of any other nationality, and had much to do with the great real drama to come.

The Interlude has been partly treated in the preceding volume (*The Transition Period*, p. 288), but its importance is too considerable not to justify a little repetition and more addition.

The Interlude.

The origin and meaning of the word have been the subjects of the usual well-intentioned investigation and discussion. It is one of the mistakes common in such things to endeavour to identify it with the Italian *farsa* or the French *sotie;* for though there were of course points of contact, the first is too general, and the second too special a thing. But the similarity of title and the close parallelism at this time between Spain and England in matters dramatic make the Spanish *entremese* much more legitimate matter of comparison, and it is not trivial that both are heard of first at very nearly the same time, the Entremese in the sixth, the Interlude in the seventh (1464), decade of the fifteenth century. It is not quite certain what is the exact bearing of the preposition in the word "interlude," whether, as would seem most likely, it indicates something placed "between" other plays, or a dramatic or semi-dramatic performance introduced among other forms of entertainment. The first explanation has the very considerable merit of connection with the history of the thing, which is at least probably an extension, in the direction of the pure drama, of the comic interpolations—themselves miniature Interludes—of the Mystery-play. But it does not really matter. Looked at from another point of view, the Interlude may be regarded as a child of the Farce crossed with the Morality—the special popularity of which (to us) rather terrible thing in the fifteenth century would help to account for the Interlude's appearance. It not only appeared, it not only proved itself a most valuable and suggestive schoolmaster to the drama proper, but it held its ground against, or at least with, that drama in popular estimation after a very remarkable fashion. Although we have lost so much of the Elizabethan drama, and although our losses are sure to have been largest in the more popular and less literary kinds of the theatre, yet not only have we fairly numerous Interludes from our present period and the earlier part of the next, but we have others—whether so called or not—scattered over the whole of the great age. And we actually possess from the hand of its very last master, Shirley, a precious pair of pieces[1]—*A Contention for Honour and Riches*, and *Honoria and Mammon*—which are identical in substance, but in the first of which the Interlude form is present simple of itself, while in the other it is worked up and dressed out into an ordinary play with an allegorical bearing. Drop the too nakedly suggestive names, throw in a little by-plot and by-play into this latter, and you would have an ordinary play pure and simple, to which the reader or spectator might attach a moral or not, just as much and just as little as to nine out of ten dramas. Interludes continued to be popular long after Shirley in certain districts, and George Borrow's *Wild Wales*[2] contains interesting accounts

[1] *Shirley's Works*, ed. Dyce, vol. vi. 1-84 and 287-314.

[2] Chaps. lix. and lx.

of some, written at the end of the eighteenth century, popular within the nineteenth.

With the history of this form during our period, one name is inseparably connected. Had John Heywood[1] been born fifty or sixty years later, he might have been one of all but the most important figures of English dramatic history. In that case he would have escaped the critical part of the Catholic-Protestant dispute in England, he would have fallen upon a period of the highest literary production and excitement in general, and in particular on one in which the rough work of preparation for the new drama had already been achieved. As it was, he was put, though with less fatal consequences, in the same dilemma with his friends, More and Fisher, as regards religion; he had to work in a period which was partly one of decadence of the old and partly one of inchoate struggle for the new; and he had to take his part in the very rough hewing just referred to, with no patterns before him, and with the material of language and the tools of metre and grammar in the crudest and rudest state. That he did as much as he did is proof of his talent; to have done more he must have been a very great genius. He was born in 1497 (?), and seems to have been a Herefordshire man, was, it is said, introduced to Henry VIII. by More, and had various court employments as musician and playwright. Nor, though he was, as he afterwards showed, a staunch Catholic, was he interfered with, either in the bewildering vicissitudes of Henry's later years, when

John Heywood.

[1] For his *Epigrams*, *v. supra*, p. 278 *sq.*

Catholics and Protestants went to execution together, or under Edward VI.; while of course he was at home under Mary. But the accession of Elizabeth was unwelcome to him, and he exiled himself, dying at Mechlin in 1580 (?), when he had nearly or fully attained fourscore years.

His pieces.

Heywood's wit, though polish is not a term applicable with propriety to any writer of the time, was much less unpolished than Skelton's, and the one thing of his that everybody knows, or is supposed to know, from its inclusion in Dodsley's *Old Plays*—the Interlude of *The Four P.'s*, with its sudden and ingenious decision of the contest of lies by the judicious announcement of the Palmer that he never saw a woman out of temper in his life—would probably have been, in Skelton's hands, a piece of ultra-Rabelaisian grotesque. It is rather a Quadrilogue than in strictness a play of any kind, for there is no action; and the interlocutors—Palmer, Pardoner, Pedlar, and 'Pothecary—simply describe themselves in the style of the mediæval *dit*, and then indulge in their lie-combat. Another, *Wit and Folly*,[1] honestly calls itself a dialogue; the characters, John, James, and Jerome, arguing again in mediæval style—that of the *debat*. In the play of *Love*, which, like the other plays of Heywood still to be mentioned, was printed in 1533,

[1] Ed. Fairholt, for the Percy Society, London, July 1846. The long *Introduction* to this contains, according to the invaluable wont of the Percy Society books, a full account, with extracts, of the other interludes of Heywood, and is indeed the most accessible source of information about him. In any other country a full edition of any writer half so interesting would have been given long ago.

the parts are those of an unloved lover, a cruel mistress, a happy wooer, and a neutral personage, who is the "Vice." This important character also figures, as "Merry Report," in *The Play of the Weather*, in which most English piece appear Jupiter, Merry Report, a Gentleman, a Merchant, a Ranger, two Millers, by water and wind respectively, a "Goodly Dame," a Laundress, and a Boy. No one, merely from these plays, could have argued for much devotion on the dramatist's part to the *Regnum Papisticum*. *The Four P.'s* itself, both in the extremely lively and amusing account given by the Pardoner (of his journey to Hell to rescue his erring friend Margery) and elsewhere, is anything but reverent to the Church; and though the "Weather" piece and the *Love* do not give equal scope for free speech, the two not yet mentioned might have proceeded from any Lutheran. *The Wife, the Husband, and the Priest* puts the old view of the relations of this trio (which in Teutonic countries at any rate had as much to do with the progress of the Reformation as all other causes whatsoever) in the crudest and most damaging fashion; while from the strictly ecclesiastical point of view *The Friar, the Pardoner, the Curate, and Neighbour Pratt* is worse still.

Except that it is free from the virulent scurrility which injures rather than helps the satires of the actual Reformers, and that it has more literary talent, this farce (for it is a farce, pure and simple) might be the work of Roy or of Bale. And nothing could show much better how thoroughly convinced nearly all respectable and intelligent Catholics were of the necessity of some Reformation, until the actual Reformation took place in its actual fashion. The whole piece turns on a scandalous brawl in church, between a Friar who has obtained the Curate's leave to preach a charity sermon for his own Order, and a Pardoner, who, with his relics and his indulgences, unceremoniously invades the building and offers his wares. After each has made an elaborate commendation on himself, the two begin a duet, or rather antiphonal duel of single lines, arranged so as to make the *quiproquos* dear to audiences in the infancy of the drama. At last they turn on each other, and engage in a scolding match, in which each, in the most forcible language, tells home-truths about the other's profession, till at last they come to actual fisticuffs. The scandalised Curate enters and remonstrates, but as they are recalcitrant, he summons Neighbour Pratt to his aid, and the pair try to expel the brawlers. The sturdy rogues are, however, too strong for them, and after giving the parson and his assistant a sound drubbing, depart at their own pleasure. There is a good deal of rough vigour about the piece; but, if ever acted, it must have damaged the Church more than twenty Lutheran sermons.

Some other interludes.

Three individual and anonymous interludes of this time are worth mentioning — the *Four Elements*, probably written before 1520, the *Interlude of Women*, which was printed in 1530, and that of *Thersites*, which, though not printed till later, seems, from internal evidence, to have been written before 1537.[1] The *Interlude of Women*, among other instances, connects English Drama, if not for the first time, yet interestingly, with European drama generally, in a kind different from any of those which belong to the Middle Ages, and which, for the most part, come from, or are earliest illustrated in, France. For it is derived from the famous Spanish *Celestina*, important both in the history of the drama and in that of the novel.[2]

The last, *Thersites*, has an opposite kind of interest, because it is, though a very rudimentary and, so to say, infantine, yet an apparently independent, attempt to devise a dramatic situation and work it out. The characters are to some extent borrowed — Thersites himself, and Mulciber, from the classics, quite obviously. But the writer, whoever he was, did not merely borrow—at least his creditor has not yet been identified. Thersites, a braggart coward (the demagogue-lampooner side of the Homeric character does not come out), has himself furnished by Mulciber, in defiance of the tender anxieties of his mother, with arms. He is then going to conquer everybody and everything, and begins with a snail, over which he sings songs of victory, because it literally draws in its horns. But there supervenes a discharged soldier, and Thersites, like Georgy-Porgy in the rhyme, runs away. Very simple, of course: far inferior to not a few

[1] These and others, which may be as early, will be found in Hazlitt's *Dodsley*. They and most of their known fellows are well handled in Dr A. W. Ward's *English Drama*, i. 117-139, 234-250, 2nd edition.

[2] See *The Transition Period*, p. 309, and *The Later Renaissance*.

mediæval or fifteenth-century plays or scenes in *vis comica.* But also possessing something which is the childhood of the greater drama to come.

On the Protestant side of the religious quarrel, but a doubtful ornament to it, there was a dramatic writer, perhaps of less literary power than Heywood, but, partly by accident, of a wider practice in dramatic kinds. This was John Bale, whose merits to literature as a historian thereof and as a dramatist are not inconsiderable, though he might have shown much more accuracy in his compilations and much more talent in his original work. Bale, in the earlier part of his career, wrote mysteries, to which he had himself applied the terms "tragedy" and "comedy," according to the old simple criterion, "Is the end happy or unhappy?" On this principle he seems to have composed a whole series—some half-score—on the Life of Christ, which are all lost but one, but which may be confidently taken to have been very similar in handling to the Miracle Plays on the subject, and adjusted to anti-Romish views. And if we may believe him—an "if" by no means unnecessary—he also wrote nearly as many more on subjects of a kind more definitely political than even the pieces of Gringore and Lyndsay,—plays on the King's Marriages; on the Impostures of Thomas à Becket; on the Treacheries of the Papists, &c. It is, however, improbable that any one of these was ever acted. Only one of them, not yet named, does exist, and is of great importance, being nothing less than the first of the famous series of Chronicle

John Bale.

Plays which provided Shakespeare with some of the best opportunities of his genius, and England with a body of dramatic history which no other country can parallel.

This is *Kyng Johan.*[1] The utter preposterousness of turning a treacherous, lecherous, murderous, cowardly scoundrel like John into a persecuted, popular, patriotic, and almost pious hero, may not, in the circumstances, have been so preposterous as it seems. It was the imitation of this very play by persons with whom Bale, save for his precursorship, is unworthy even to be named, that made some knowledge of English History popular. Most of the auditors Bale proposed to himself probably knew nothing about John at all, or only that he was opposed by the French and the Pope, which is exactly the point Bale cleverly fixes on. And it is even not impossible that this most unepiscopal bishop was himself blinded by his hatred of the Pope to everything else. Nor need the violence of the attack on Stephen Langton, who, instead of being a champion of freedom, is represented as not merely a devil incarnate but a mere tool of the Pope, excite any surprise. The Reformers were not champions of freedom in any sense—even freedom of thought. In some cases, indeed most, kings and princes were against them, and so they were against kings and princes. In

Kyng Johan.

[1] Ed. J. P. Collier, Camden Society, London, 1858. Extracts from it, as well as from *Thersites*, *The Four Elements*, *Mary Magdalene*, and *The Pardoner and the Frere*, appear in Mr Pollard's excellent ***English Miracle Plays***, Oxford, 1890.

others, republics received them, and so they were for republics. But in England the Reformation had been the creature of the Royal Authority, and the Royal Authority was therefore (till it was thrown by Mary into the other scale) all that was good and right.

Its position as first of Chronicle Plays.

Whether, as Professor Herford thinks, Bale was influenced by the *Pammachius*, is a point which, though we cannot entirely neglect it, need not here be discussed. It is enough to say that, though the influence may by no means improbably have been exerted, yet in the first place it is an influence purely of suggestion, and in the second does not bear at all on the side of *Kyng Johan* which is most—we might almost say which alone is—of interest for literary history. The *Pammachius* is in form merely a semi-classical play. It only touches the mediæval drama in the point that its personages are partly Scriptural, partly allegorical. They can hardly be said to be even partly historical, for Julian plays a part absolutely different from and diametrically opposed to that which he played in the actual history. *Kyng Johan*, on the other hand, however audaciously it may travesty the king's character and the motives of his antagonists, is a strictly historical play in its main subject of action. And further, this new historic element in it is, in the most original way, blended with, thrown into, worked out by (or whatever metaphorical phrase may seem best to suit) the machinery and prosopopœia of a regular Morality. Except the King (who may himself after a fashion be said to be no exception, since he practically reappears after his death, born again as "Imperial Majesty") there is no real person who is not the double of an abstraction: and the stock part of the Vice is maintained by the real opposition-hero or wicked personage of the piece—Sedition, who is also Langton. This double presentation almost deserves the name of a stroke of genius, whether we look at its adaptation to the author's actual objects or at its literary results. That the stock abstractions of the Interlude-Morality were expected by the audience and made the piece "go down" is true, but is very far indeed from exhausting the truth. They also helped to enforce Bale's moral, and, as being equally applicable to the two sets of circumstances, to bring out more forcibly than anything else could well have done the persistence and identity of Papal encroachment in the sixteenth century as in the twelfth. But though a double meaning might very frequently attach to Chronicle Plays, as time went on it was the other side which became of importance.

As Morality and Interlude became obsolete or provincial, the morality-interlude turn of history-plays ceased; but by this time the taste for them had been created, and the capabilities of history for dramatic presentment had been shown. Moreover, by accident or necessity, the combination had brought out features which were destined to be accentuated in the English play generally, and, before two generations were over, to give it an almost wholly independent position. The comic underplot, or at least by-play, was indeed certain, given the temper of the nation, to be developed out of that, such as it was, of the mysteries and moralities in any case. But the experimentalising inventor of history-plays was particularly likely to lay stress on it to diversify his serious matter. A wholesome contempt for the Unities of Time and Place, and an exceedingly liberal construction of that of Action, had been equally prominent. But the handling of Chronicle subjects was almost bound to push the two former finally out of doors, while it was equally well suited to establish the Unity of Action, not in its too limited Aristotelian sense, but in a wider and freer transcendence. And, lastly, the enormous scope opened to the dramatist was a matter of the highest importance. True, the ancients had not neglected historical plays; but the *Persæ* and the *Octavia* could hardly have been left to keep each other company as relics, if the kind had been very largely cultivated. And Bale's manner of cultivation was far more promising than such things as the *Rosmundas* and *Sophonisbas*—things, as a rule, with as little real history in them as if they had been *Phædras* or *Antigones*.

And in itself.

Then Bale must receive praise for actual execution as well as for having blundered on a path which led to the summits of English literature. In some respects, no doubt, *Kyng Johan* is not much beyond its fellows. The doggerel lines, now inclining to the Alexandrine, now to the fourteener, and arranged now in couplets, now in rhyme-royal stanza, are not a good dramatic, and are a singularly bad poetic medium; but they are as good as most of their fellows, or rather better. The occasional coarsenesses on the part of the Vice were a stock necessity; they do not exceed those of a much more estimable bishop, Still, much later in *Gammer Gurton's Needle;* and they are much less than we might have expected from the author of *The Acts of English Votaries.* The ludicrous impropriety of the language put in John's mouth is part and parcel of the general conception; and so is the extravagance of the denunciation of Pope and Clergy. But after the reader has made a proper critical adjustment of the compass of his mind on these points, the thing can be read without any disgust and with some admiration. There is much more political insight than may at first appear in the dialogue between the King and his widowed and clergy-ridden Realm of England, with the apparently trivial but really dangerous Sedition intervening. The effective side of the Morality, cumbrous as it seems to us, appears in the obvious consideration that though it would be a patent absurdity for John Nokes to interfere with Mrs Styles's plaint to her sovereign, the interference of Sedition between the King and his subjects is a very sad and sober verity. Bale, too, has hit on the worst part of the mediæval conception of Church government, in making Sedition reply with cool insolence to a remonstrance of the King's that he is an unnatural child to England—

> "I am not her child; I defy her by the messe;"

adding a similar abjuration of Spain and France, and

a declaration of loyalty to none, save the Pope. And the "wobblings," as modern politicians would say, of Nobility between Pope and King are drawn with a good deal of liveliness, and with less deviation from strict truth than one could wish.

The central conspiracy of Sedition, Dissimulation, Private Wealth, and Usurped Power, with the transmogrification of three of them into the Pope, Cardinal Pandulph, and Stephen Langton, is effected with much less outrage to theatrical probability than might be thought; and the outspoken Dissimulation, who remains, performs useful work, in the "Messenger" spirit of the classical drama, by revealing their conceit and purposes with a frankness which makes the Pope justly call him a blab. There is a rather amusing survival of an old quarrel in the part assigned to "Civil Order"—the Civilian or Lawyer, who is as rotten a reed to King as Nobility, and for less creditable reasons—and in the appearance of "Commonalty," too poor and blind, oppressed as he is by the other orders, to do any good, and deserting the King, like the rest, at the ecclesiastical threats of Pandulph and the terror of the French and other threatened invaders. Nor is real dramatic force lacking in the outburst of vulgar triumph with which Sedition greets the King's enforced submission in spite of the protests of England. The middle of the play is in a very confused condition, and the poisoning of the King and himself by Simon of Swynset (Swinestead), introduced by a curious wassail-song,[1] is slightly "promiscuous"; while the

[1] Compare Still again.

conclusion, in which Imperial Majesty restores order, reduces the erring Estates to obedience, and punishes the malefactors, lacks the combination of Morality and History which has hitherto been effective. But on the whole the piece is one of great idiosyncrasy, and, as is not invariably the case with curiosities of literature, deserves rather more praise than it has usually had.

Stress has been laid upon Heywood and Bale, because they show us, rather more definitely than is done by writers of any other country, the transition stages between the mediæval and the modern drama. In Italy and in Germany, as we have seen, the revived ancient forms step more or less simply into the place of the mediæval. In France, this is also the case in the Latin plays; while those in the vernacular show hardly any differences at all from the old mediæval models. But here we have forms of indigenous theatrical performance which, whether influenced by ancient models or not (in Heywood's case probably not, in Bale's probably a good deal, directly or indirectly), indicate an advance upon the mediæval and an approach to the modern. The value in each case lies not so much in the actual productions or the actual form which they present, as in the probabilities, or rather certainties, of improvement which that form possesses. The lively realist action of the Interludes is sure, by degrees, to push the abstractions of the Morality from their seats; the Vice will become the Clown, the Fool, the living comic character generally. So, too, when political or historical action of interest and complexity (the story of which, or some part of it, may be known to the audience) is brought upon the stage, it must, little by little, be intolerable to have Deadly Sins and Theological Virtues elbowing peers of the realm and members of Parliament. The *fatalis machina* has been introduced, full of live combatants, into the city of mediæval drama of the artificial kind, and we know that it will do its work. During the sixty or seventy years which passed from the *Four Elements*, the forty or fifty that passed from *Kyng Johan*, to Marlowe, every year was making audiences more eager for action on the stage, for the comic intermixed with the serious, for bustle and variety and stir. The very admixture of realism with the improbabilities and abstractions of the Morality and Mystery may have inclined them to tolerate those other improbabilities which shocked the classical critics. If a mystery covered the whole life of Christ, why might not a chronicle or a tragedy cover the whole life of some secular hero? And so, in our own and usual way, driving the nail where it would go, caring nothing for anomaly and a great deal for precedent, going never by rule, except of thumb, disdaining "technical education," working *supra grammaticam* in the royal English fashion, we produced—Shakespeare.

CHAPTER VII.

THE REVIVAL OF CRITICISM.

THE MIDDLE AGES NECESSARILY UNCRITICAL—THE RENAISSANCE NECESSARILY CRITICAL, BUT WITH LIMITATIONS—CHARACTER AND REASONS OF THESE—THE ACTUAL RISE AND PROGRESS OF ITALIAN CRITICISM—ITS FAR-REACHING IMPORTANCE, AND CONNECTION WITH THE FORMATION OF MODERN LITERATURE—UPSHOT OF IT—VIDA—LILIUS GIRALDUS—GIRALDI CINTHIO—J. C. SCALIGER—HIS 'POETIC'—CASTELVETRO—HIS IDEAS ON DRAMA AND EPICS.

It has been said that in literary kinds (as distinguished from individual works on the one hand, and from the general tendencies and character of literature on the other) the period with which we here deal, under the head of the Earlier Renaissance, is chiefly remarkable in respect of two—Criticism and the Drama. We have just seen how, during these fifty years (with the decent fringes and margins necessary in the case of individual countries), the powerful influence of the classical drama was brought—for good mainly, if also for ill—to bear upon the existing materials and methods of the European theatre. But we have also seen how, enormous as this influence was, and vital as were the changes which it effected, it did not succeed in obliterating the characteristics of the mediæval stage in any country as regards comedy; while, in respect to tragedy, two great literatures, the Spanish[1] and the English, were very mainly rebel to classicism and faithful to romance, if not exactly to any direct mediæval tradition.

The Middle Ages necessarily uncritical.

The case of criticism is different. For that branch of literature the Middle Ages are almost non-existent. With the single great exception of the *De Vulgari Eloquio*, one of these exceptions which do, in the best and fullest sense, prove the rule, not a single critical text of excellence dates from the thousand years between A.D. 500 and A.D. 1500; while texts, not merely of excellence, but of any kind, are mostly wanting. The Middle Ages were nothing if not uncritical, and, from some points of view, very fortunately so. Criticism was not their business: they had neither the temper nor the opportunity for it; and, if they had tried it, it would have interfered with what was their business—their precious, their inestimable, contribution to the original literature of the world.[2]

On the other hand, the Renaissance was, and could be, nothing if not critical, "*after a sort*"—the qualification being most important. Its dissatisfaction with mediæval, and its enthusiastic quest of

[1] See *The Later Renaissance.*

[2] I hope I may without impropriety refer to vol. i. Book III. of my *History of Criticism* (Edinburgh, 1900) for facts and arguments in support of this paradox.

classical literature and learning, were in a way, and even a very decided way, acts of criticism. Its constant and almost desperate endeavour to revive, to imitate, to establish the classical methods of creation was, in a way, criticism of the most active kind. But there was more than this. In the newly discovered texts, as well as in those which, though not exactly newly discovered, were studied and imitated in quite a new style, there was practically the whole *corpus*, as it still exists, of classical criticism itself. Not one single such text of any real importance has been added since Robortello unearthed Longinus just before the conclusion of our period; while the one great critical text of mediæval times, the *De Vulgari*, had been published a score of years earlier. It would have been astonishing indeed if Humanism, and literary energy generally, had not thrown themselves eagerly on this division, which is as much as any other the *differentia* of classical from mediæval literature, and which would seem to offer the solution of the problem — the understanding of antiquity—at which all were aiming as regards the past, and to give probably complete, certainly indispensable, guidance towards the conduct of creative work in the future. If we are to be surprised at anything, it must be that the actual development of criticism—vigorous as it was when it came—was so late—that the fifteenth century passes without any important effort of the kind.

The Renaissance necessarily critical.

But if we go back to our qualification, we shall find that it throws light both upon this delay and upon the character of Renaissance criticism when it makes its appearance. It was said that the Renaissance was critical "*after a sort*"—that is to say, it had inherited a good deal of the uncriticalness of that mother-age to which it was so undutiful, but of which so much survived without the knowledge and against the will of the rebellious child. To begin with, the decision—the *krisis*—between classical and mediæval was made in a spirit as little judicial as could possibly be, contemptuous pooh-poohing and ignoring being all that the past, and even to some extent the present, of the vernaculars and of mediæval Latin received. But this crime was in a manner revenged by the equally uncritical indiscriminateness with which the classics were swallowed. As we have seen in the chapter on Humanism, the fifteenth century was far advanced before any real discrimination of styles, ages, literary values was attempted; and long afterwards such absurdities prevailed as the adaptation of Pagan mythology and rites to the treatment of Christian subjects, of the machinery and frippery which even in Latin had been mostly borrowed from the Greek property-shop, to modern love-making, modern bereavements, modern country and even town life. The ages which tolerated Sannazar and Vida had very little critical right to object to those which mixed up Arrian and the Pseudo-Callisthenes.

But with limitations.

To some extent, though to a less perhaps than some authorities[1] hold, the Renaissance line in criticism

[1] All English-reading students, whether of Criticism or of the Renaissance, owe to Mr Joel Elias Spingarn the heartiest thanks for his very

was forced, and disadvantageously forced, by mediæval prejudice and the reaction against it. I do not think that it is at all true that Poetry was "disregarded or contemned" during the Middle Ages, or even that it was "valued for virtues that least belong to it." But it *is* true that there had been, from the time of St Augustine downwards, a strong distrust of profane literature on the part of the more earnest ecclesiastical writers and thinkers. And it is still more true that as the Middle Ages began to pass away this distrust was taken up by the various sects and schools which foreran the Reformation, and, as soon as that movement declared itself, by the Reformation itself. Indeed ancient criticism itself had been occupied, and very mainly so, by the discussion of practically the same point. From Plato to Plutarch and later we find it busy with such questions as, "Is the poet a good or a bad citizen?" "Is the study of poetry corrupting or prophylactic to the young?" "Is the poet an enemy of the philosopher, or his friend, working in a slightly different field with slightly different implements?" "Must the orator and the poet be good men?" and all the rest of it. These questions exactly suited, on the one hand, that

Character and reasons of these.

useful *History of Literary Criticism in the Renaissance* (New York, 1899), a book which most courageously and carefully explores and maps out a region of Literature hitherto far more talked of than known. There are, naturally enough, points on which I disagree with Mr Spingarn, and others on which I cannot go with him the whole way. Of these, that touched on in the text is one. But no differences can prevent my acknowledging the help he has given me here, and still more elsewhere.

tendency to moral disquisition which is partly accounted for by the non-moral character of Greek and Roman religion; and, on the other hand, that mania for disputation and declamation which was characteristic both of Athens and of Rome. And they were constantly resorted to by men of letters as a means of escaping from what antiquity generally seems to have regarded as the rather undignified business of pure formal criticism, or even of inquiry into the sources and phenomena of the æsthetic pleasure. Accordingly, no sooner does the very earliest Humanism show itself than we find the vindication of poetry against Plato taken up. It appears in Dante; it appears in Petrarch; and it fills the two last books of Boccaccio's *De Genealogia Deorum*, which, in this venturing to differ with those who count it as a mediæval text-book, I should call the first critical treatise of the Renaissance itself. In reading the *De Genealogia* an Englishman might excusably think that he is reading one of our own Elizabethan critics; and when he comes to investigate the matter, he soon discovers the link between the two in the writings of Boccaccio's countrymen during our present period.

The actual rise and progress of Italian criticism.

For a time, however, even this rudimentary and partly mistaken line of criticism was abandoned in favour of the almost ferocious, though for us very fortunate, eagerness of Italian Humanism, in the late fourteenth and early fifteenth centuries, to seize and swallow whole whatever remains of antiquity could be secured from the sinking ship of the Byzantine Empire or discovered in the motley treasures of Western Europe. Only by degrees, it has been said, did very distinct preferences of authors manifest themselves in regard to those very classics, and it was later still before anything like general theories of literature and literary criticism established themselves. When, however, the time came—

> "Postquam exempta fames et amor compressus edendi"—

the critical mood, which usually succeeds the satisfaction of mere appetite, did not fail to make its appearance. There is nothing surprising in the fact that the best age of Italian Latin writing was past, and that this writing had already sunk into a barren and dilettante Ciceronianism when this critical time came. But the fact is certain. Vida's adaptation of the Horatian *Ars Poetica* to the "heroic poem," which was to serve as a Duessa to Europe for more than two centuries, was a little earlier than the great outburst of Italian prose criticism, mostly in the vernacular, of which the earliest extant monument would seem to be Daniello's book in 1536. But there can be no doubt, though the exact connection is not in all cases very easy to make out, that the publication, at various dates in the first half of the century, of editions of the *Poetics*, of Dante, and of Longinus (the two latter for the first time at all, the former for the first time critically), must have powerfully affected the movement.

Its far-reaching importance.

A quite extraordinary number of such treatises[1] appeared in the second and third quarters of the sixteenth century in Italy, with a fresh burst at the end; their matter was reproduced, first in France, and then in England: and as codified in somewhat different senses by Castelvetro and by the elder Scaliger, they not only decided the critical view of their generation, but actually governed those of more than two centuries to come. Meanwhile the popular interest in them in their own time and country was shown, among other things, by the almost appalling avalanches of criticism of particular work let loose on such an occasion as the appearance of the *Gerusalemme Liberata.* And, two hundred years after Tasso had found rest for his perturbed spirit, the weapons with which the last defenders of neo-classic orthodoxy were resisting the rebels of Romance were those originally forged by the Italians of the sixteenth century.

Hard things have been said[2] of these critics, and to some extent deservedly; but for a long time they have been much more despised than read. Even here[3] it would be improper to spend much of our dwindling space on individuals, with the rarest exceptions. But

[1] See an excellent chronological table in Spingarn, *op. cit.*, App. A. The most important, not formally discussed below, are those of Trissino, 1529-63; Daniello, 1536; Muzio, 1551; Minturno, 1558.

[2] For instance, by De Quincey, who, in his Essay on *Rhetoric*, couples them with the Greek rhetoricians as responsible for "the two most worthless departments of universal literature."

[3] I hope to repair the omission elsewhere in a more suitable place, the second volume of the *History of Criticism* above referred to.

a general account is very particularly necessary, not merely as of an important part of the literary contribution of the actual period, but much more as of an influence on the literature of the time. Throughout the next five volumes of this series, and till the latest of these in increasing measure—that is to say, including the present, throughout half the entire *History*—we shall find the ideas of these critics at first tentative and militant, then in triumph, then fighting for life. Nor can they be said to be dead yet: though for the last century their partisans have been more and more in a minority. And it is very probable indeed that the coming century may see altered forms of them actually triumphant, according to the usual law. That there is something more in this law than the mere swing of the pendulum may be very cheerfully granted; that, even if there had been less real truth in the Italian critics than there was, they deserve infinite thanks for having restarted criticism, may be granted more cheerfully still.

The actuating, if not perhaps always the fully understood, idea at the root of all their inquiries was connected with the one really important question of the day, the question, "How can the vernaculars be made as near as possible equal to the classical tongues for literary purposes?" And this, with an inquiring generation, naturally turned itself into a much larger set of questions affecting a great part of the history of Literature. At first, as was natural, a great deal of scholastic technicality infused itself into the discussion,

And connection with the formation of modern literature.

and we find men arguing that Poetry is a part of philosophy, and what part it is, whether it is not even a form of logic working by example instead of syllogism,[1] and so forth. This way lies nothing but mere logomachy; and though there are not wanting modern equivalents for it, it is a way which never has led, and which (it may be boldly said) never will lead, to any good whatever. A more practical turn was given to the study by the edition of the *Poetics* (not the first, but the first which seems to have drawn attention), published in 1536 by Robortello, the sponsor of Longinus in 1548. This at once started the critics on the theory of *mimesis*, or, as it is most unfortunately translated in Latin and modern languages, "Imitation." This Imitation theory, it is well known, though developed by Aristotle, is to be found in Plato, and very probably was his originally in so far as anything ever is originated by one man. There was therefore a certain excuse for the blend, not to say the muddle, of Platonic and Aristotelian ideas which meets us in the notions of these Italian critics about the nature of poetry.

Upshot of it.

By degrees, however, and especially after the publication and dissemination of Scaliger's *Poetics* (1561), although the Platonic-Aristotelian idea of the high and serious character and destiny of poetry by no means went out, and though the Aristotelian doctrine of Imitation of Nature always survived in theory, Renaissance criticism rearranged

[1] This apparently enormous absurdity is, in fact, nothing more than a variant of the old confusion of Poetry with Rhetoric.

itself on a basis not necessarily connected either with Aristotle or with Plato. On the one hand, the tendency of the Greek Rhetoricians, and still more of their Latin followers, to make strict *a priori* distinctions and limitations of Kinds, made itself perceptible. On the other, partly the insensible swing of taste from the Greek to the Latin classics, and partly the fact that these latter lent themselves better than the former to the process, brought it about that although Homer, the Three Tragedians, and a few other Greeks, were constantly talked about, Virgil, Horace, Cicero, and other Latins were made the real objects of admiration and study. This, which Scaliger did avowedly, and with the arrogant *tapage* of his nature, was done practically by almost all the critics of the later sixteenth, seventeenth, and earlier eighteenth centuries. Hence came the Three Unities—Gorgons unknown to Aristotle himself as a trio, though he knew the Medusa of the group, the beautiful one—with their baleful faculty of turning a large part of European drama to stone or wood. Hence came the grotesque excogitation of the "Heroic Poem," or artificial Epic, with its good hero, its supernatural but carefully discriminated machinery, its voyages and revolutions and journeys to the other world, its poetic justice, and its hopeless *Antiphysis*. Hence by natural, though unwisely guided, reaction, came the Battle of the Ancients and Moderns. All this and much more came from the Italian critics.

With some notice of the more important of these we may conclude a chapter, the shortness of which is dictated by reasons of "architectonic" not less than by the mere length of the volume already, but which is of weight disproportioned to its show. Du Bellay, the first and weightiest critic of the sixteenth century in France, is noticed with the rest of the *Pléiade* in *The Later Renaissance* (chap. x.), and before him there had been nothing of more than antiquarian and scholastic interest. Wilson, the earliest English critic, has been dealt with already (*v. supra*, p. 255), and so have those critical references of Erasmus which are almost all that Germany (construed in a liberal sense) has to produce.[1] Even if Spain did not lie outside our present review, it is acknowledged that early Spanish criticism of this time is little more than an adaptation of Italian, and moreover begins even later than English. So we are driven by converging reasons to confine ourselves to Italy, and even then to take but a few eminent examples. We must merely refer in passing, on the one hand, to critical remarks, such as those of Grazzini (*v. supra*, p. 329), which, though not in the common estimation, are really worth volumes, and almost shelves, of "meanderings" in quest of the nature of Poetry or the relative value of Ancients and Moderns; on the other, to the estimable woodenness of Trissino, wooden in criticism as in drama, in drama as in epic, or the minor *points de repère* of

[1] Had it not been jangled and jarred by the Reformation, the Humanist movement in Germany might have produced much in this way. As it is, there is more than has been generally noticed—for instance, the *Dialogus in Defensionem Poetices* of Augustinus Moravus Olmucensis (Venice, 1493), the use of a copy of which rare book I owe to Mr Gregory Smith.

Daniello and Muzio, of Tolomei[1] and Minturno.[2] We shall find sufficient material for representative illustration here in Vida, in the half-namesakes Lilius Giraldus and Cinthio Giraldi, in the somewhat imposing, if both pedagogic and pedantic, legislation of Scaliger, and in the erratic but strangely vigorous reflections of Castelvetro.

Vida.

The critical-poetical gospel of Vida[3] may almost be summed up in two words, "Follow Virgil." Of course he *says*, "Follow Nature"; but this is obviously a mere obligatory formula. From the beginning of the Second Book (for the First, *v. supra*, p. 26) to the end of the Third the prescriptions for epic or heroic writing, which is all that Vida really touches, are wholly and solely extracted from the practice of the ancients. And though at first Homer and Virgil appear to be drawn upon indifferently, yet very soon cavils are made at the older and greater poet, and a somewhat invidious preference bestowed upon the younger and lesser. In a little further space the odious comparison is almost avowedly extended to Greek and Latin as wholes: Greek prosodic freedom, Greek compounds, other things

[1] The Italian predecessor and probably original of our Drant. He was born at Sienna about 1492, and died 1555, after writing much on Italian linguistics and prosody.

[2] Mr Spingarn throughout his book lays great stress on Minturno both as a centre and an origin of the critical ideas, philosophical and formal, of Renaissance Europe. I have not yet thoroughly satisfied myself that this estimate is not exaggerated.

[3] The *Ars Poetica* is in the Oxford *Poemata Selecta*, cited above, as well as in Pope's. Pitt's English version is in Chalmers, vol. xii.

Greek, come in for reprehension, or at least for black marks, as things not to be imitated by the poet save at his peril. This is even more noticeable in the Third book, which deals with diction, than in the Second, which handles the treatment of the subject. This Third contains elaborate verse-descriptions of the chief Figures of Speech; and the key-note of much, if not all, subsequent orthodox criticism for the best part of three hundred years is struck in the anxious cautions against excess of any kind. Vida is shocked, for instance, at the poet who

"Crines magnæ genetricis gramina dicat."

(Thank Heaven, Elizabethan poetry at any rate caught at his instances and scoffed at his rule!) The anxious distinction between epic and dramatic style reappears. The *verbum insolens* is not absolutely barred, but is to produce the most elaborate certificates of origin and destination, and to be, as it were, kept under strict surveillance. Compounds are subject to severe imitations, and "harsh" names are to be softened, as Sicharbas into Sichæus—a curious instance of the arbitrariness and futility of this kind of rule-making, inasmuch as, to some ears at any rate, the former is far more poetical than the latter, but an interesting ancestor of Boileau's horror at "Childebert."

Of more interest, because positive and not purely negative, is the elaborate inculcation of the "sound-echo-to-sense" principle. This curious degradation of what is essentially a true and all-important doctrine was, it is well known, a particular favourite of the Neo-

Classic times, and Vida, in this as in other instances, deserves the not wholly unmixed glory of being their first teacher in it. That the sound may, and in really great poetry always will, *harmonise* with the sense—that the sound can often be made to add, almost independently of the sense, an accompaniment of music in word and letter superior to anything that inarticulate notes can provide, and furnish the soul with a pleasure even superior to anything that the sense itself can give—this is true enough. But the doctrine that a verse describing swiftness must be crowded with short swiftly flowing syllables, and one describing effort drag in broken lumps of heavily loaded "longs," is at the best a very infantine and rudimentary expression of this truth, at the worst a perversion of it, clumsy in the devising, and teasing, if not positively disgusting, in the effect. Grotesque and burlesque may most properly avail themselves of it, but hardly serious poetry.

The poem (which contains a literal, and in its frankness rather pleasing, exhortation to the poet to steal, steal boldly, steal constantly, if he would be great) ends with a large expansion of the Horatian precept to keep things back and criticise them severely, and a very substantial and circumstantial peroration on the merits of Virgil. Not much comment is necessary on this. Let us give Vida credit, no doubt, that he foresaw so accurately, and expressed so well, the taste of something like seven or eight generations yet unborn. He can less be congratulated on his obvious sharing of that taste, and his inability to understand that, even if the things he liked were good, others were good too, and by no means unlawful. But this inability itself was the principle of Neo-Classicism.[1]

Lilius Giraldus.

The interesting dialogues of Lilius Gregorius Giraldus, *De Poetis Nostrorum Temporum*,[2] belong rather to the History of Criticism than to the History of Literature, yet they can hardly be neglected by the latter. In the first place they form one of the first, and also, until quite recently, one unfortunately of the last, attempts to survey European literature with at least an attempt at impartial range. It may be a surprise to some to find a Humanist at the Court of Renée of Ferrara aware of the existence of Chaucer: the fact certainly presents a remarkable contrast to the absurd and arrogant ignorance of Boileau, a century and a half later, as to all European literature outside of his own (and indeed inside his own to a great extent) and Italian. A grudging reference to Erasmus and a gushing one to More betray, of course, the partisan on the Roman side. But the main interest of the dialogue is different. Vernacular writers are, as will be clear from what has been said, not entirely excluded; not only does Chaucer appear, but Marot (indeed, as a special *protégé* of

[1] There is far more real though undeveloped criticism in the *Sylvæ* of Politian (the *Manto*, &c., noticed *ante*), which are in fact verse-reviews of glowing eulogy on classical poetry.

[2] Ed. K. Wotke, Berlin, 1894. Gyraldus or Giraldus was born at Ferrara in 1478; lived long in Rome, and suffered from the Sack, but found refuge in his birthplace, and died there in 1552. He was a good scholar and a good man.

Renée's he could hardly be missed), Ariosto, and others. But their admission is grudging, very limited in proportion, and almost always accompanied with some sort of scornful fling, such as, "if I must mention writers of this kind," "if anybody chooses to pay attention to such things," and the like. Yet almost every Italian Humanist who had strung an elegiac couplet or a batch of hendecasyllables is mentioned, and foreign versifiers in "the tongues," who have hardly the slightest claim to figure as poets, receive not merely fair critical treatment on their individual merits, but an undoubting welcome as having written real "literature." That posterity, and not unscholarly posterity merely, would be content to give for every new line of Chaucer, or even of Ariosto, many scores of the Humanist verse from Beccadelli to Mantuan, and from Valla to Bembo, was a thought which, if it could have presented itself at all to the excellent Giraldus, would simply have been dismissed by him as an idle paradox or an ignorant blasphemy.

Giraldi Cinthio.

Not thus minded was or could be his namesake, townsman, and no doubt relation, the author of the *Orbecche* and the *Hecatommithi*. Cinthio's *Discorsi*[1] on "Romances" (there is a dispute, not important to us here, except that the other

[1] Venice, 1554. Reprinted (from copies apparently very rare and in parts dilapidated) in two vols. of Daelli's *Biblioteca Rara* (Milan, 1864). It is much to be wished that Daelli had made more of these sixteenth-century critics equally accessible. Giovanbattista Giraldi Cinthio was a member of the same Ferrarese family as Lilius Giraldus, but born much later in 1504. He died in 1573. Besides being a dramatist (he wrote seven or eight other tragedies besides the

party to it was known to and approved by Ascham, between him and his pupil Pigna as to plagiarism), on "Tragedy and Comedy," and on "Satiric drama," are all written in the vulgar tongue, all animated by a hearty appreciation of vernacular literature, but all saturated with classical ideas, and showing not a little critical ability. Although Cinthio does not by any means abandon the quest after the ends of poetry, or the principle that a poet must be a good man and the like, he has perhaps for the first time, and by no means dimly, perceived that not every literary form was known in Athens or even in Rome, and that new forms require new laws. His enthusiasm, personal, patriotic, and, it is fair to believe, critical as well, for Ariosto, may have helped him to see that a poem like the *Orlando* cannot be satisfactorily judged on the rules of a poem like the *Æneid*, and that Romantic Unity may have a *locus standi*, though it is neither Dramatic nor even Epic. His rediscovery of the Unity of Time was not perhaps a good "windfall of the Muses," but he did not make it universally binding. And in his work one may find occasional *aperçus* and remarks of real critical insight. Once, for instance, he goes near to if he does not reach that substitution of the notion of style being the *body* of thought for the older one of style being its *dress*, on which Coleridge complimented Wordsworth;

Orbecche, a pastoral drama or "satira," *Egle*, &c.), a novelist (*vide supra*, p. 161), and a critic, he was a philosopher and a professor of physic. He had known Ariosto, and his critical work seems to represent the decade between 1540 and 1550.

and in the same passage his accompanying comparison of the subject, not to the "soul" but to the "bones," is a distinct improvement.

His great merit, however, is undoubtedly to have hit in a manner—on which two centuries and more did not improve, but rather slid back from it—on the truth above stated, that one literature, however great, can never impose *prohibitive* rules on another. It is, I think, a mistake to lay too much stress on this, as being merely a vindication of the "national" character of Italian letters. Aretino, with his undoubtedly strong, if coarse, sense, long before Cinthio, and Il Lasca at about the same time, had taken the matter from this side, and were right in doing so, because they were dealing with the drama—an avowed copy of real life. It was plain to anybody that the real life of Florence or Venice in the sixteenth century after Christ was not the same as the real life of Athens or Rome many centuries earlier. But a man might have seen this and yet have boggled at the extension of the principle to two compositions like the *Æneid* and the *Orlando*, admittedly feigned, and presenting no definite real life at all. Nationality does not come in here: the defence would have been as valid for any German saga, such as very likely existed in Virgil's day, as for Ariosto's masterpiece. Cinthio had in fact come to one of the "bed-rocks" of criticism, independent of nationality, independent of time—the principle that a work of art is entitled to be judged by its own methods of attaining its own result. Even now there are not a few critics who have not gone so deep.

J. C. Scaliger.

This bed-rock was certainly not reached—indeed, the access to it was fenced off, with all the energy, ingenuity, and learning of a violent character, an able if narrow intellect, and an enormous industry—by Cinthio's famous contemporary, Julius Cæsar Scaliger. As a mere classical scholar, Scaliger was far surpassed by his son, who had an advantage in his teaching, which he himself in his obscure youth cannot possibly have possessed; and for some century past Joseph Justus, and not Julius Cæsar, has been the person thought of when the bare surname is named. This, however, was not quite so formerly; and one may at least venture to doubt whether it will always be so. At anyrate, the father's *Poetic*[1] is a more independent, a more strictly literary, and a more epoch-making book than anything of the son's. The very fact that it has sometimes been over-credited with originality—that doctrines in it, which were accepted by generations, may be traced to obscurer contemporaries and predecessors—is in a way a proof of its eminence. This is what the great books and the great writers always do, like the great rivers and lakes. They gather, they levy, they draw tribute —but they make what they take their own, and they hand it on as such. No one man is really the author of the Neo-Classic system of literary taste which

[1] My copy is the second edition (*s.l.*, 1581). Scaliger, who transmitted to his son more than his own scholarship, more than his own pedantry, perhaps a profounder belief in an exceedingly dubious genealogy from the great Veronese Della Scalas, and rather less than his own arrogance and rusticity, was born in 1484, and died at Agen in 1558. His *Poetices Libri Septem* first appeared at Lyons in 1561.

governed Europe, from Sidney to Johnson, and from Du Bellay to La Harpe; but Scaliger has more of that author in him than any other single person.

We may do him this justice all the more gladly and (to speak as a fool) with all the more authority here, that there can be no question about the disapproval to be expressed of the most distinctive part of his views. The *Poetic*, which in its second edition fills, with contents and index, almost exactly a thousand pages of close small print, is a book as methodical and as exhaustive as it is opinionated and partisan. The First, or "Historic," Book deals, not exactly with the side of the subject to which we should apply that name, but with the origins and kinds of literary composition, the details of the ancient theatres and games, and, lastly, the divisions of poetry—ancient poetry, of course. The Second Book—"Hyle," or Matter—is devoted exclusively to Prosody in all its details. The Third, bearing the name "Idea," is almost purely rhetorical, and is particularly copious on figures. The Fourth—"Parasceve," or Preparation—discusses the kinds and qualities of style, with more figures. The Fifth, or "Critical," Book is an elaborate comparative account of Greek and Latin poetry; followed in the Sixth, or "Hypercriticus," by another of contemporary Latin poets, and then (with a contemptuous flying leap over the Middle Ages) by three divisions of Latin poetry to Virgil, which are dealt with in reverse order—the age of Claudian first; then that of the group *cir.* 100 A.D.; and the later Augustans last. Finally, an *Epinomis*,

His Poetic.

or Seventh Book of after-thoughts and corollaries, deals with a large number of subjects, from wide questions, like those of the parts of Tragedy and the business of the poet with action or with character, to details of Terentian text-criticism.

Such vast gyrations must necessarily elude us here. But we can and must describe their centre or centres. On one very important point Scaliger is at variance with some great authorities among the ancients, and with not a few of the neo-classic critics who partly derive from him, in that he has no doubt about verse being, if not an essential property, an inseparable accident of poetry. But on every other point he is *classique enragé;* and the creed which, if he did not create it, he certainly formulated, may be embodied in three articles which are, as it will be seen, constantly centripetal:—

I. All poetry, not to say all literature, consists of, and should be treated by, definite Kinds.

II. Every Kind has its own central and governing norm or idea, to which alone the would-be poet, in his process of Imitation, has to strive to attain.

III. This norm has in every case been most nearly approached by the ancients, and especially by Virgil, who has indeed reached it so perfectly — has given such an exact reproduction of Nature—that imitating him is following Nature, and you need not trouble yourself about doing anything else.

It will be observed, of course, that these propositions, in the very act of becoming increasingly disputable, become increasingly suitable for popular adoption. The first is a "metaphysical" proposition, incapable of direct demonstration or even of direct confutation, and capable of being scholastically evaded by the admission of troublesome greatness as a "species *per se.*" The second, though an enormous assumption, expressed the candid belief of ninety-nine educated men out of a hundred at the time. The third, which is supported by Scaliger with a great deal of abusive and uncritical belittling of Homer, is of course in itself a critical absurdity, but is scarcely an advance, except in sweeping aggressiveness, on the position of Vida, whom Scaliger pedantically patronises as "an excellent poet but a lame teacher." It must be admitted, however, that his injunction to "echo" the ancients is more diplomatic than Vida's frank advice to "steal from" them. He preached to willing ears, and much more than a hundred years after we shall find men like Boileau and Addison rather dressing afresh and propping up his doctrines than in any way really improving on them. Posterity might sometimes turn blind eyes upon his blasphemies of Homer, and it may be quite true that to speak of the Unities as *Unités Scaligériennes* is a fraud upon the critic to whom we come next. But the principle which governed the selection and erection of these Unities into a law of the Medes and Persians is the principle which lies at the root of Scaliger's whole *Poetic.*[1]

[1] It should be said that Scaliger does not fear or fail to support his views in every case with copious citation and discussion of illustrative passages. The little things of his own, which he sometimes also appends (with the inevitable warning that they were knocked off in a couple of hours or the like), are less legitimate, but more amusing perhaps to some readers.

The critic just referred to, Lodovico Castelvetro (who was born at Modena in 1505, and, having been "delated" by his enemy Annibal Caro to the Inquisition, died in exile in 1571), is not one of the discoveries of modern times. His reputation was great in his own: he was well known to European scholars in the seventeenth century, and to Italians at least in the eighteenth. But it is only of late that he has "come to his own," if indeed he has come to it; for he has been more regarded as a commentator upon Aristotle than as a critic of original views. He invited this by the form which his writings[1] took—a form almost invariably editorial or commentatorial, and not even condescending to the *Discorsi* with which *Italy* was already anticipating or originating the true special form of Criticism, the Essay.

Castelvetro.

This peculiarity of Castelvetro's, aggravated as it is by the great bulk of his writing, makes it rather hazardous to put his views with the same precision as that with which those of a more methodical, if more *borné*, spirit like Scaliger's can be given. From an extremely interesting remark of his younger contemporary, Salviati, which Mr Spingarn has disinterred from MS., it would seem that Castelvetro's sincerity was rather distrusted; men thought he "wrote so as to be

His ideas on drama and epics.

[1] The chief of these are *La Poetica d'Aristotele volgarizzata e sposta*, my copy of which is the second edition (Basle, 1576), said to be fuller and better than the very rare first (Vienna, 1570); and *Opere Varie Critiche*, edited by Muratori (Lyons, 1727), both in quarto. He wrote some other things which I have not yet seen.

different from others." Such a suspicion, though by no means, as some have thought (accordingly provoking it), an infallible proof of originality, is quite consistent with it; and in Castelvetro's case it seems to have been so. His two great titles to position are, that, while fastening the chains of the Three Unities on Drama, avowedly and expressly from the point of view of theatrical representation, he loosened them from the neck of Epic by directly differing with Aristotle. He does not, like Cinthio, base his difference on a corresponding difference of nature between Romance and Epic—indeed by this time the tyranny of Kinds would seem to have been too generally accepted for this to be possible, though a little later Patrizzi[1] nearly re-vindicated the whole liberty of literature as taught by history. But with equal boldness and ingenuity he meets Aristotle on Aristotelian principles, though not in Aristotelian terms. Poetry, according to him,[2] when freed from dramatic restraints, may follow history exactly—observing only the difference of real and invented events. The poet *may* introduce Unity of Action if he likes; but he is perfectly entitled to give the whole life, chronicle-fashion, of one hero, the mixed actions of several, or the *gestes* of a

[1] This great critic (1529-1597) only took up Criticism as part of an anti-Aristotelian crusade. But in the two parts of his *Della Poetica* (Venice, 1586) he has almost founded the historic method, and actually laid down the cardinal truth that a thing is Poetry if it is treated poetically.

[2] In the *Spositione* to the *Particella Sesta* of his *Parte Principale Terza:* in other words, in his commentary on chap. viii. of the *Poetics*, according to our editions.

people. And he proves this by a large comparison of instances and a great deal of very ingenious argument.

It was unfortunate, doubtless—if anything can be deemed unfortunate by that modified fatalism which long study of the history of literature induces—that men turned unequal attention upon Castelvetro's exercises of the Power of the Keys,—that they bound remorselessly what he told them to bind, and neglected to set free what he told them to loose. But the existence of these various tendencies—in neither case directly or wholly borrowed—in his work, together with many other things which there is no room here to mention, shows what a critic he was, and may fitly crown the limited demonstration here possible of the critical importance of Italy in the sixteenth century. Once more, she showed herself—unfortunately it was for the last time hitherto—the mother of European culture, the fountain of intellectual gift. That the gift was of a very mixed nature, the influence not a little questionable, does not matter; and, besides, we have, even in this small space, been able to make it plain that the antidote was supplied as well as the bane.

CHAPTER VIII.

THE MINOR LITERATURES—CONCLUSION.

NORSE—THE DANISH BALLADS—DUTCH "REDERIKERS"—THE SLAVONIC LANGUAGES: HUNGARIAN—THE AGE NOT SPECIALLY AN AGE OF REASON—THE IMPORTATION OF THE OLD AND DEVELOPMENT OF THE NEW—OTHER INFLUENCES, EAST AND WEST—THE REFORMATION—THE GREAT WORK, THE FASHIONING OF THE VERNACULARS: ACHIEVEMENTS AND ILLUSTRATIONS—IN LATIN—IN VERNACULAR—ITS LACK OF THE HIGHEST CHARM—THE COMPENSATIONS—THE CHIEF ACCOMPLISHMENT.

Norse.

NOT much has to be added to the contents of the foregoing chapters before we take a final survey of this great period. The literatures of the Peninsula have received their treatment—for very strong reasons, not merely of convenience—in the following volume. The decadence which had long before set in upon the once great literature of the extreme North had already grown more decrepit. The "blanket of the dark," which dropped suddenly at the beginning of the sixteenth century between the Icelander and his great literary past, is well indicated in the opening pages of Messrs Vigfusson and Powell's

Introduction to the *Corpus Poeticum Boreale;* and such literary energy as he showed was mainly devoted to Reformation gospelling and squabbling. Nor had the younger Scandinavian tongues yet begun to make up for the barrenness that had come upon their mother. Norwegian literature, in the separate sense, is but of yesterday as literatures age — it can count at most but a single full century. Modern Swedish begins at the beginning of the seventeenth, not the sixteenth, and, with one remarkable exception, Danish is very little older. The so-called father of Danish literature, Christian Pedersen (1480 - 1554), one of whose books was the original of Gau's *Richt Vay*, noticed above, does indeed belong strictly to our period, but his work seems to have been mainly theological and popular.

The Danish Ballads.

The exception which has been made is in favour of the Danish Ballads, which, with the English and Spanish, and in a less degree the German *Volkslieder*, make up the quartette of great national collections of this form. The unlucky thing about them is their very late date. The first collection in print dates from 1591, not to be supplemented for another century, and it would not appear that this lateness of print is made good by any earliness of manuscript. The ballads, like a large number (fortunately not all) of our own, seem to have been orally transmitted. And though this transmission often helps to preserve freshness and piquancy, and at anyrate keeps off the ineffable vulgarisation and deadening which the early chap-book versions have inflicted on so many English ballads, yet it is a great stumbling-block to all but those venturous critics who say that they have "proved" a point when they have arranged to their liking a hypothesis which cannot be positively negatived. The well-known characteristics of ballads are exhibited in these Danish specimens (the standard collection of which is Grundtvig's, 5 vols., 1853-1877) in great abundance, both from the literary and from the "folk-lorish" point of view; and for spirit and what used to be called "wildness" the best of them probably have no superiors. Moreover, the comparison of them with the old Norse literature, which so fortunately survives, strengthens more even than in English (where we have but a single surviving example of epic-romance of very old date), and far more than is possible in German and Spanish (where we have none), the theory that Ballads are the detritus of Epic and not Epic the conglomerate of Ballad. But, except for these ballads (the exception being still duly and warningly charged with the indorsement, "Date uncertain,") it does not appear that Scandinavia has anything of importance to give us.

Dutch Rederikers.

Holland may have somewhat more, though nothing so interesting; but sixteenth-century Low Dutch literature is rather of the later than of the earlier part of the century, and will connect itself best with the sketch of the really important Dutch writers of the earlier seventeenth century. The most noticeable thing about its rise is perhaps the fact that here, as hardly anywhere else in Europe, the fifteenth-century indulgence in "Rhetoric" is credited with distinctly good effect. The Dutch *Rhétoriqueurs*—they were actually called *Rederikers*—exhibited, in their fondness for association into Academies or Clubs, that tendency to follow Italy which may have come from a similar discipleship in painting.

The Slavonic languages: Hungarian.

The Russian press began to print Russian books in 1504 according to some—not till fifty years later, according to others; but the literature for some time seems to have been merely of a "business" character, and chiefly ecclesiastical or historical. Poland was somewhat in advance of its future conqueror; but the run of Polish was somewhat hampered by the special attention paid in the country to Latin, an attention shown still later in the already-referred-to work of John Casimir Sarbiewski. A striking—if accurate—gauge of the literary condition of the Poles is afforded by the statement that though the printing-press was set up at Cracow as early as 1474, it did not print a Polish book till some fifty years later. But the most brilliant age of Polish poetry and history (which, indeed, preceded a relapse into Latin) began before our time; and the names of Rej (1505-1569), Kechanowski (1530-1584), Szarzynski, Szymonowitz, and others for the first division, with those of Bielski, Sryisowski, &c., for the second, have a reputation not unknown to Western ears, but somewhat dim and hollow for most of them. Bohemian, like Polish, was just before its Golden Age at this time, though, unlike Polish, it had a very considerable past. Hungarian seems to have been only going to begin.

But these minor literatures may be—not neglected, but passed by with courteous excuse, by the comparative historian, simply because they have for the time either fallen out of, or not entered into, any necessary family of comparison. It may indeed be questioned whether until the present century any of them, save Dutch, effected such entrance or re-entrance at all. The student of them individually may no doubt trace with interest and with profit the influences of the greater literatures upon them, or their spontaneous development on the same lines with the greater literatures. But to the general student they are at most facultative, and the general historian on a limited scale can hardly spare them a faculty of competing.

The age not specially an Age of Reason.

On one distinction, or supposed distinction, of the period, which has become almost a catchword, we shall lay little stress here. It is frequently, indeed constantly, said that this was the period when the Reason began to assert itself, and so forth. A cool and wide study of periods of literature will not perhaps discover much difference between them in this respect. Man has always been as obstinately (if not quite as sanely and without qualms) convinced that he is *animal rationale* as that he is *implume* or *bipes*, and the recent depths of the Nineteenth Century call to the far-off depths of the Twelfth in echo of the assertion. What is probably meant by the common saying is that the Renaissance appealed to a particular form of Reason as against a particular form of authority. But even in this respect it rather appealed to a different form of authority than to Reason ; and it would be very hard to discover more reason in the vast collection of the Erasmian *Adagia* than in any mediæval commonplace-book. "He said it" is the last resort of each. And even if this were not so, the fact would have not very much bearing on literature, especially as regards the greater works of the time. The reviving sense of style, of the propriety and power of language, which is the really great literary feature of the time, in Ariosto as in Rabelais, in Rabelais as in Luther, is very much more a matter of Taste than of Reason. The strong *nisus* towards the story, which is another, is a *nisus* towards the satisfaction of one of those appetites of the soul which have least to do with reason —an appetite which has indeed no objection to accept ing Reason as a joint provider of succulent things, but rejects her at once when she provides things unsucculent. This is even more the case with Drama. The new-found art of Criticism may seem at first to owe more to Reason; but this idea will hardly survive closer acquaintance with the purely irrational Virgil-worship of Vida and Scaliger, or the substitution of the question, "What is the good poet in the abstract?" for "Where is the good poetry in the concrete?" Here, as elsewhere, Reason is fortunately justified of a fair number of children; here, as elsewhere, those who most boldly affiliate themselves on her by no means justify her most.

Certain solid and undoubted facts of the case will supply us with a safer mode of proceeding. Of such facts there are two absolutely beyond controversy, and each of the most imposing magnitude and importance. The first is, the sudden, or almost sudden, increase of the stock of information and of patterns, alike derived from classical literature and history. The second is, the inevitably consequent attempt, not merely to assimilate these stores, but to use them for the improvement, the aggrandisement, the development, of the vernacular languages and literatures. This process, which we saw beginning in the last volume, is now in fullest swing, though with a certain difference of fulness in different countries. In Italy it reaches its very height; no one has surpassed, and very few have even approached, the great writers of this time in the use of Italian as a literary tongue. In Spain it is rapidly approaching a state not far below that of Italy. In England and in Germany, but especially in the latter, it is very much more backward. In France it is in rather an anomalous plight—the language being less advanced by far on its mediæval stage than English, while the men and women who use it are in one instance immensely, and in more than one or two decidedly, above the average English writer in ability. But the process, as has been said, is inevitable: and, faster or slower, it goes on everywhere. The most extravagant "know-nothings" of Italian Humanism, the men who affect to talk of Italian poetry as good for tinkers and grocers, of Italian prose as scarcely worthy the attention of a gentleman and a scholar, cannot prevent the mere process of imitating Virgil, or Ovid, or Cicero, or Livy,

The importation of the old and development of the new.

when they do write Italian, from furnishing weapons to the rebels.

Beside this central fact or factor, all others are comparatively weak: yet some of them are positively strong. It seems to have been some years at any rate before the discovery of America influenced the European imagination very much in the way of literary suggestion. More's famous book of course brings it in, yet one may shrewdly suspect that Plato would have done as source almost without Columbus or Cabot. The peregrinations of Ariosto and Folengo and Rabelais, the adventures and escapes of their heroes, the strange countries they visit, owe much more to Lucian, and even to the despised Romances, than to the quest of the New World, and the discovery of its wonders. And the effect of the decease of the long moribund Eastern Empire had either spent force before our exact period began, or not gathered head again as yet. Mahomet and the fall of Constantinople were far behind: Solyman and Lepanto were some way in front. But no belittling of this kind is desirable or possible in the case of the last great agency usually cited, the influence of the Reformation.

Other influences, East and West.

That this influence was wholly or mainly for good, scarcely the fanatics of Protestantism, if they happen to have any tincture of letters, would think of maintaining: that it was wholly for evil, only those of a similar temper on the opposite side would assert. *Prima facie*, more good than ill might have been augured from it. For the

The Reformation.

purposes of the Reformers it was necessary, as the French say, *faire flêche de tout bois*, and especially to ransack literature and history. Although letters had owed much — almost everything at times — to the Mediæval Church, there had undoubtedly existed, from the time of the Fathers downward, a sort of grudge and suspicion, on one, if not on both sides. In the very early stages of the upheaval, the Reformation and the Muses were by no means bad friends. In almost every country most of the men of literary tendency threw themselves more or less on the Reforming side, from the Liberal Conservatism of Erasmus, and the nondescript attitude of Rabelais, and the mainly "anti-Dulness" crusade of the *Obscuri*, to the irresolute half-Huguenotism of the courts of Marguerite and Renée. Even in Italy, and in such unlikely subjects as Berni and Folengo, the same symptoms show themselves, while, on the other side of the Alps and of temperament, Luther shows no mean knowledge and no mean appreciation of profane literature. But as the struggle waxes hotter, things change. The furious partisanship of the Protestants disgusts men of letters, and Protestantism, in more extreme forms especially, in all more or less, turns to Puritanism, the deadliest foe of literature. Yet not only in the earlier stage of alliance, but in the later of cooled friendship or open war, the Reformation did literature service, both in an open and obvious, and in an indirect and rather paradoxical fashion. The great business of this period, it has been said, in most, if not in all countries, was to get the vernaculars ready: and in more ways than one, which have been already indicated in detail, the Reformation helped in this. Polemic sometimes, though rarely, breeds good literature; it always exercises the literary muscles, trains the eye, gives weight and force and direction to the fist. Carry on elaborate controversy in Latin as they would, men *had* to appeal to the people in the last resort: they could not help using the vernacular, and the prose vernacular too. But this rough-and-tumble practice was disciplined and refined by the coincident necessity of translating into the vernacular the Bible, and the hymns of the Church, and (in the happier countries) her matchless liturgies likewise. Here what was wanted was not rude force but delicate beauty—not merely something that might amuse, or excite, or carry away, but something that could satisfy at once the simplest and the most erudite. This, thanks to the quality of the material worked upon, was effected with marvellous success in England, with less but still with much in Germany, with least permanent profit in France, because the Reformed cause was never long triumphant there, but still with some, as was shown by the great Huguenot writers of the later century. It may also be questioned whether the Reformation excitements did not do at least as much good by "keeping back" the vernaculars during this process of preparation, by preventing them from applying themselves to absolutely untrammelled and original work on general subjects till they were really ready.

Let us, then, be content with the explanation, as far

as influences and such things go, that the purpose of this age—conscious, unconscious, and sometimes even recalcitrant to the forces which shaped it—was that fashioning of the vernaculars which has already been indicated.

The great work, the fashioning of the vernaculars: achievements and illustrations.

It is not necessary to repeat the demonstration, which has been given in the different chapters, of the way in which this was done in the different countries which constitute the Upper House of the Literature of Europe; but we may with advantage endeavour to point out the general effects and results which were actually achieved, and the position in which the period left literature generally and particularly. The period, 1500-1550, eked and fringed in the manner decent and necessary with all periods, is beyond all question one of the most important of all the periods of European literature. But it will hardly, and only by a great deal of allowance and connivance, rank among the very greatest. It is true that in great single works it is by no means poor. It has in Ariosto and in Rabelais two writers who must rank in the most jealously guarded First Class of any rationally constructed canon—if any such canon be rationally constructed—of European literature. It has in Erasmus and in Luther two curiously contrasted but most interesting examples of writers who are very near that first class, and a crowd of attractive seconds and thirds in Italy, a few in France, and one or two in England and Germany. In figures interesting on the historic and comparative estimate it is singularly rich—the quaint, homely, old-fashioned idiosyncrasy of Hans Sachs, the harlequin vivacity of Folengo, the pioneer efforts, crowned with some immediate success, and destined to reap deferred reward, of Wyatt and Surrey, the race and grace of Marot. And it did for Europe certain great things, by its failures and its tentatives as well as by its successes.

In Latin.

To begin with, though, as we have seen, the doctrine that Latin was the eldest child and heir of literature, the vernaculars mere dogs beneath the table, was loudly announced, was largely accepted, and continued to prevail long afterwards, not merely with the vulgar, but in worthy minds, yet the verdict of the period on this doctrine was in fact *Mene, Tekel.* Never again could modern Latin writing have such a chance as it had here. It had the undivided allegiance of no less a man than Erasmus, and of some others not far inferior; it divided the allegiance of almost all the great men of letters in Italy, of the majority in Germany and elsewhere, of no few in France and England. But the result was fatal to it. In no form of literature except dialogue and drama, for which the vernaculars were not yet ready, can the Latin literature of the time hold its own with the vernacular in the estimation even of those who read Latin just as easily as they read their own tongue, and who are fervent partisans of classical learning and education. In no single case where a writer—as in Italy constantly happened—had an equal mastery of Latin and of a tolerably accomplished vernacular does he fail to produce better literature in the modern tongue than in the ancient. This had not always, if it had often, been the case earlier; but it is the case now, and the meaning of it cannot be mistaken.

In vernacular.

But though, in order to accomplish this kind of Helotry, the age had devoted so much of its available talent to showing how that talent could be wasted, it contrived to demonstrate excellently well what could be done in the other line and range of composition. It "laid the keel" of almost every kind of modern literature (including even the essay, in fact if not in name) except the regular prose novel, and made the advent of that practically certain. It very nearly finished the stage of apprenticeship to the drama, quite finished that to the higher kind of history. It saw the beginnings of the reorganisation of poetry in all countries—even Germany—except Italy, and completed that reorganisation in Italy. It began criticism for modern times.

Its lack of the highest charm.

The chief defect or drawback to the period, looked at as a whole, is a certain absence of the highest and rarest *charm*[1] which it shares with other periods of *Aufklärung*, even in its greatest men and books. The amount of this quality in Rabelais is very small indeed, great as are his powers. Erasmus is rather extremely amusing and satisfying to the "sense of sense" and of cleverness than charming: and even Ariosto is just a little too complacent and unruffled to give the peculiar touch which Spenser, a poet not otherwise much greater than himself, gives constantly.

[1] An exception must be made for the strange compound of voluptuousness and melancholy which appears in Marguerite and a few others. But this is more rife in Art than in Literature.

and which Tasso, a poet distinctly inferior to him, gives now and then, in the next generation. The first part of the Sixteenth Century was in Italy too polished and too well satisfied with its own polish (save here and there in isolated cases, so different, yet so akin in their difference, as those of La Casa and Folengo) to achieve this touch. The other countries were too eager, too hopeful, too much bent on "improving themselves" for the future, and in regard to the past too full of a Jack-Horner-like sense of their own "good boyishness," and thorough desert of all possible plums, to develop this supreme quality as the Middle Ages had developed it under the sense of mystery and ignorance, as the late sixteenth and earlier seventeenth centuries were to develop it under that of disillusion. The rage for education[1] and the attitude of the superior person were both very rife in 1500-1550; and the educationist and the superior person are very seldom charming. Ariosto, it is true, does not deserve insertion in either of these black lists; but Ariosto, as has been already remarked more than once, was a

[1] It is almost unnecessary to say that if this were a *History of European Education* instead of a *History of European Literature* no period would yield to ours in importance. From Vittorino da Feltre, through Colet to Erasmus, Ascham, Melanchthon, and Sturm, the time was one of constant application to the reform of practice and the development of theory in the subject. In England more particularly an unbroken chain of distinguished literary persons, from Colet himself and Ascham, hands down, through Lyly and Jonson and Milton, to Locke, far in advance, the tradition of this interest, just as abroad Sturm in the sixteenth century is succeeded by Comenius in the seventeenth, though neither of them is equal in literary importance to the Englishmen. But to dwell on the matter here would be a scarcely permissible excursion.

little too free from divine discontent. It may be doubted whether he ever "ate his bread"—or his turnips—"with tears"; even that supper, which, wet and disappointed, he partook of in a tavern instead of in the Vatican, is not at all likely to have been mingled with such sauce. And the doom which the German poet has pronounced on his fellows in this case, that they do not "ken the Heavenly Powers," is all too frequently apparent in this period accordingly.

The compensations.

But it knew the powers of the Earth very well indeed: it was taking the most extreme pains to know them, and it had its reward. There are few periods, if indeed there is a single one, more remarkable for the application of what we may call in no invidious sense "business principles" to literature. The vague, aimless, promiscuous, happy-go-lucky mediæval mixing of styles, and the indiscriminate application of them to subjects was, except in the case of such survivals as Hans Sachs, got rid of. Directly or indirectly we have had constant occasion to notice the efforts made, and the success to no small extent achieved, in the delimitation and organisation of styles, departments, and kinds in Literature. Some of the main errors in the Criticism of the time were but exaggerations of sound principles in this respect. The disproportionate amount of energy that it spent on composition in the dead languages was, in the main if not wholly, due to the fact that it seemed—owing to the existence of models in most, if not in all kinds—easier and better to keep to the particular kind here.

But for its main justification we must still go back to that specially literary application of its educational predilections, which has been so often glanced at. It was everywhere save in Italy the main school-time, and in Italy it was the finishing school-time, of the Vernacular languages and literatures. The tendency, which for so many a year made men regard it as more than the school-time—as the actual nursery of these—was mistaken, and did a great deal of harm; but there was a certain excuse for it in the actual facts. Nowhere, with the same perpetual exception, did the sixteenth century see actual "modernity" reached in expression or even in thought. In that sense France itself has not left school till the time of Descartes or even Pascal; England not till that of Dryden; Germany hardly during the whole course of the seventeenth century. But all are busily at their rudiments, all have left off merely playing, some are close upon the achievement of almost completely accomplished faculties and attitudes of work. This *status pupillaris*, this benefit of the indulgence given by Goethe to the scholar, that "he need not accomplish, it is sufficient if he exercises himself," excuses that appearance of roughness and immaturity which we have noticed in so much of the work of the period itself—and more than excuses it. In particular it accounts to a very great extent for the pervading absence of charm. The schoolboy is interesting; he is sometimes ingenuous; he rejoices the charitable and indulgent mind of humanity, looking before and after—but he is very rarely charming. When he is clever he

The chief accomplishment.

is apt to be a prig, and there is not a little priggishness in the early sixteenth century; when he is stupid he is apt to be a lump; when humorous somewhat horseplayful; when unamiable a bully and a brute. Neither will these well-known characteristics be wanting in a not too forced carrying out of the parallel.

But if we look at the actual production of the time, there is not much room for grumbling. We have almost got rid of the dead-weight of pedantry which oppressed the fifteenth century, of the cumbrous trappings and creaking wheels of its overloaded style. The nightmare of its allegory is being transformed into a Queen Mab, sometimes positively, and always comparatively, beneficent. Its satire, with Saint Lucian (not the saint whose day is the 8th of January) to help, is in the same way being transformed from the tone of the Jeremiad to the tone of the Polite Conversation. Moralities thirty thousand lines long have given place to farce, and are giving way to comedy and tragedy and history and *drame.* The *nouvelle* is ubiquitous, and the novel is almost in sight. Above all, people are beginning to take a national interest in their own language and their own literature—to determine to write "English matters in the English tongue for English men," *mutatis mutandis;* to think of adorning the Sparta that has fallen to their lot. No doubt there are dangers in this as there are in everything; no doubt it leads in time to a most undesirable cutting of literary communications between nation and nation, which becomes worse as the cultivation of the common tongue of Latin for literary purposes becomes more and more unusual. But its advantages far outweigh its defects, and the vernaculars are, in consequence of it, put in a fair way to develop, after a fashion which would have been simply impossible if the mediæval solidarity had continued, and which, in the case of some languages, though probably not of English, is likely to be rather hampered than helped by any restoration of general international literary comity. In other words, the great literatures are now fairly launched, or on the point of having the dog-shores knocked away, that they may sail the ocean—irremeable certainly, perhaps illimitable—*qua cursum ventus.*

Nor do they sail under any mean or evil auspices, or without cheering circumstance, but, on the contrary—

> "With sound of pleasant music, and dancing on the deck."

If we have just denied the highest and rarest charm to Ariosto, only that can be denied him. For varied grace, for infinite faculty of pastime, for curious and yet never over-laboured art, for the provision of a standard of a certain order of poetical narration, which none has ever excelled and few have even for moments reached, he has no fellow in literature. There is nobody before him, save Chaucer, of anything like his peculiar quality; after him hundreds try to attain it, and most fail. The "width and wisdom" of Rabelais—at least as wise as he is "broad," though nearly as broad as he is wise—give an equally unique combination: we know that here, also, the period may be secure; no after-age is likely to surpass it in this special blending. It is the glory of Erasmus, independently of the actual merit and attraction of his performance, to show us, almost as uniquely, that scholarship may free itself from almost every touch of the pedantry, the one-sidedness, the churlish arrogance and rusticity, by which it is too commonly accompanied, and which were then its almost inseparable companions—to show that a Reformer may be considerate, a critic genial, an enemy of credulity not destitute of sincere belief. Luther, the inferior of his great forerunner in some points, but his superior in strength, in courage, and masculine character, vindicates Protestantism from the charge of necessarily leading to the Puritan Avernus, and contrives to infuse, into a rough polemic, humour, learning, and a certain kindliness. Even Calvin, of whom as a man the less said the better, is as a man of letters, from the formal, and not merely the formal, side, worthy to rank among all but the greatest. And among his fellows of this second rank there are not only crowds of Italians in almost every style, from Bembo and La Casa and Castiglione to Folengo and Berni, but Marot and Marguerite, Wyatt and Surrey and Ascham, the wicked wits of the *Obscuri* and the homely wisdom, not quite untuneful withal, of Hans Sachs, the sugared exquisiteness of Johannes Secundus, the admired and really admirable imitative faculty of Buchanan. Of such jewels no Cornelia need be ashamed: yet once more, and for the last time, let it be said, the greatest pride of the age should rather lie perhaps in the all but universal diffusion of love for literature, and effort in it, of determination to leave the estate of the world in matters literary better at the end than at the beginning.

INDEX.

Saintsbury, George Edward Bateman, 1845–1933

The earlier renaissance, by George Saintsbury ... Edinburgh and London, W. Blackwood and sons, 1901.

xvi, 423 p. 19½cm. (*Half-title:* Periods of European literature, ed. by Professor Saintsbury. v)

1. Renaissance. 2. Humanism. I. Title

Library of Congress PN731.S3 1—27253 u R

2 10/91